THE FUTURE WE NEED

THE FUTURE WE NEED

Organizing for a Better Democracy in the Twenty-First Century

Erica Smiley and Sarita Gupta

Foreword by DeMaurice F. Smith

ILR PRESS

AN IMPRINT OF CORNELL UNIVERSITY PRESS   ITHACA AND LONDON

First published 2022 by Cornell University Press

ISBN 978-1-5017-6481-3 (hardcover)
ISBN 978-1-5017-6482-0 (paperback)
ISBN 978-1-5017-6483-7 (epub)
ISBN 978-1-5017-6484-4 (pdf)

Library of Congress Control Number: 2022931382

Cover and interior portraits by Gwenn Seemel, https://GwennSeemel.com

Contents

Foreword

It is an honor for me to be asked to write the foreword for this important book, not only because I am a diehard believer in the power of teams and unions but also because I believe that competition can coexist with fairness if we embrace the idea that everyone is entitled to the promises of a more perfect union.

As the executive director of the NFL Players Association (NFLPA), I serve the workers of a business that has been the nation's premier pastime for decades. The NFL is a multibillion-dollar business. NFL games consistently rate among the fifty most-watched television shows every year, and even regular-season games often outdraw the playoffs and finals of other sports.

The NFL is also a business that has had a labor union for over sixty years. As a result, NFL players enjoy good wages, work-related and postcareer health care, fair limits on hours to be worked, postcareer pensions, and health and safety guidelines far beyond the minimum requirements set by law. Some believe that the great benefits and salaries enjoyed by the players who work in this business are simply a product of a wildly lucrative business model. Worse yet, I am certain that most of the people who follow our sport never think seriously about how the players are paid and how they achieve their pensions, salary increases, and postcareer benefits.

But those in the labor family understand that none of this would be possible without those NFL players who made the decision to form a labor union. Those in the labor family also know that the NFLPA exists because a small number of dedicated people worked hard and sacrificed much to benefit a larger number of workers who may never give their efforts much thought.

It is for those reasons that I write this foreword for *The Future We Need*. The future well-being of all workers will depend almost entirely on how many of them are represented by labor unions. The simple fact is that as representation by unions has decreased in recent years, so have wages, access to safe working conditions, and fair pensions and benefits.

There are two persistent lies used to suppress progress among working people. The first lie is that as productivity increases and as business grows more profitable, financial success will trickle down to increase the wages and benefits of those who do most of the work. The second lie is that profitability will be inhibited when workers form a union, a team to improve conditions in their workplace. One need look no further than the labor-management relationship in the NFL to recognize the falsehood of both assertions.

It is simply not true that the wealth generated by professional football automatically trickled down to benefit the players. They got their fair share only when the NFL was forced to bargain after years of contentious battles between players and team owners. For decades, the NFL did not recognize the player's union. (By the way, is it not ironic that so many people who support teams on the field are willing to do everything, legally and illegally, to prevent people from forming teams off the field? Can values like teamwork and mutual support be just as powerful when it comes to addressing issues in the workplace?)

As a result of management intransigence, dozens of players were forced to risk their jobs by suing the team owners in federal court. The lawsuits began in 1945 and continued unabated until 1993 when the players won a jury trial that broke the owners' de facto monopoly over pro football. Throughout those years, and despite the growing popularity of the sport, nothing was trickling down to the players. Like most modern multinational business owners, the NFL owners did not want to fairly share the profits.

However, in 1993 the first modern collective bargaining agreement was negotiated between the players' union and the NFL, essentially a sectoral agreement that covered all franchise owners in the league. And since then, the NFL has experienced nothing but unbridled success. In short, the facts show that the collective bargaining method of working through issues between labor and management has produced a far more profitable business model than the litigation and constant business disruption that existed during the decades of owner resistance.

The Future We Need exposes the lie that labor unions inhibit business development, suppress business growth, and decrease profitability. It also explains how we can organize workers into a cohesive team to help shape their own destiny. If every business in the United States operated according to the management-labor paradigm that defines the NFL and NFLPA, I am positive that everyone involved, from workers and managers to investors and senior executives, would be far better for it.

Non–sports workers deserve nothing less.

The lies we have been told go beyond falsehoods about the specific effect of labor unions. We have also been sold the false idea that there always has to be a loser for every winner, and that if you are on the losing end the reason is your personal ability or industry. Over the last forty years we have seen a tremendous increase in economic inequality simply because a small group of people believe that they must win extravagantly by ensuring that others lose perpetually. This is a false narrative, and one that is inconsistent with the best promises of a nation aspiring toward a democracy. The greatest promise of the United States is the promise of opportunity. If that opportunity is not equally available to everyone, then the promise of the United States and its potential greatness are falling short.

The Future We Need is also a timely lesson given the numbers of people taking to the streets in support of individual, civil, and human rights. There is a strong link between issues like voting rights and access to health care and the protests that arose after the death of George Floyd and the outburst of xenophobia, racism, and violence on display at the Capitol on January 6, 2021. We find ourselves witnessing yet another battle playing out as part of the United States' continuing democratic experiment. I believe that we can be greater only when we choose paths that build, support, and benefit us all. That is why I believe in unions. Accordingly, there is an unbroken and historical connection between the cause of civil rights and workers' rights. We experienced this firsthand when many opposed the collective action of players kneeling during the national anthem in response to police violence—as if their First Amendment rights no longer existed after they clocked into work.

This book is an important and necessary guide for those who believe in the sanctity and dignity history bestows on those who get up every day to do honest work for their families and themselves—and those who understand why it is equally important and necessary to resist and confront those who believe otherwise. It's a book for everyone who is still committed to the American Dream.

DeMaurice F. Smith

THE FUTURE WE NEED

INTRODUCTION
Who Rules?

Raquel works at an Amazon fulfillment center on the East Coast, stocking items that will eventually be shipped to homes throughout the region—everything from cans of soup to toilet paper. When the COVID-19 pandemic arrived in the United States, millions of families suddenly wanted to buy everything they needed without leaving their homes. As a result, Raquel found herself being publicly referred to for the first time as an *essential worker*. She is not yet sure whether it is a compliment.

Raquel is the sole provider for her five-year-old child and her mother, who has health problems. After the pandemic started, several of her coworkers were diagnosed with COVID-19 after the company failed to implement social distancing practices or provide personal protective equipment to employees. To protect her family's health, Raquel stopped going to work, calling in sick for as long as she could. But when her unemployment payments stopped, her student loans started piling up, and as overdue rent payments mounted, eviction loomed. How safe would her family be then?

Leonard lives hundreds of miles from Raquel in a midwestern city where he drives for Uber and Lyft and delivers food for DoorDash. When hailing a ride became dangerous to public health, Leonard found himself in a tough spot. Unlike Raquel, he was not considered essential, and he quickly lost all sources of income. When he applied for unemployment benefits, he discovered he was not qualified because he was not an employee. Despite having been a faithful, rule-following worker for all of the app companies he'd relied on, Leonard was now on his own. What would he and his family do?

The economy is not working for most of us. Too many people are forced to make impossible choices about whether to pay a utility bill, pay for a much-needed prescription drug, or put food on the table. Economic, social, and political shifts from plant closings to outbreaks of disease can devastate entire communities. If workers had a platform that allowed them to engage in decision-making within their companies, their industries, or the economy as a whole before a crisis arrived, they could avoid the kinds of impossible choices faced by Raquel, Leonard, and millions more like them. Why do US workers lack such a platform? In this book, we'll explore that question.

The prevailing political economy of the United States and much of the world is based on principles originally espoused by Southern slave owners—the paternalistic view that they knew what was best for their (enslaved) workers and that their liberty as individual landowners outweighed the rights of the working women and men who they claimed to own. This fundamental tension has defined our country from its beginning. Historian Eric Foner elaborates on how slavery sits at the root of modern-day conflicts in his book, *The Second Founding: How the Civil War and Reconstruction Remade the Constitution*.[1] The Reconstruction period was marked by attempts to build a multiracial US democracy. The Thirteenth Amendment to the Constitution abolished slavery and all forms of forced labor; the Fourteenth Amendment guaranteed citizenship to all those born in the United States; and the Fifteenth Amendment guaranteed the right to vote to Black men. Each included clauses empowering Congress to enforce these provisions, with the goal of ensuring that Reconstruction would be "the beginning of an extended historical process: the adjustment of American society to the end of slavery."[2] Many of the gains made by social movements from the 1920s through the 1970s were anchored in the same Reconstruction-era principles—women's suffrage, the New Deal, the Civil Rights Act of 1964, and the Voting Rights Act of 1965. These gains have been targeted by conservative judges and elected officials who have intentionally, systematically rolled them back, in many case seeking to restore pre–Civil War interpretations of the Constitution.

It naturally follows that the people fighting for dignity in the communities where systems of worker oppression descended from slavery have been in place the longest—namely Black and immigrant workers in the southern region of the United States and people of the global south—have some of the most creative approaches to undermining those systems and building, perhaps for the first time, a healthy democracy.

A healthy democracy is a system in which the majority of people have the ability and mechanisms in place to consult, confer, and collectively govern themselves. Democracy is not just a system of political practices. Democratic principles must also be applied to participation and decision-making in all aspects of our economic lives. While voting, lobbying, and other forms of policy and legal work are important forms of democratic participation, collective bargaining—both at work and elsewhere—applies democratic practices to economic relationships. Without both political *and* economic democracy, the whole system is compromised.

Collective bargaining, then, is fundamental to democracy. At its best collective bargaining is a system by which working people can exercise collective power in a way that directly confronts the owners of capital and reclaims a portion of that capital for working people and their communities. Collective bargaining allows everyday people to "practice democracy"—directly engaging in the decisions that affect their lives. Collective bargaining affects our lives beyond worksites as well. We all benefit when workers have a platform to prepare for a crisis before it comes. When the COVID-19 pandemic hit, essential staff in unionized nursing homes were better prepared to support aging residents, ultimately having 30 percent fewer COVID-19-related deaths than nonunion nursing homes.[3]

Unfortunately, the number of people in the United States who have been able to engage in collective bargaining has dramatically decreased in the last half-century. In January 2020, the percentage of US workers in unions hovered just above 10 percent, down from over 30 percent in 1954.[4]

The reason for this dramatic decline is threefold. First, power has shifted from national companies to multinational corporations and then again to hedge funds and other actors of finance capital. The result of this financialization of industry is that executives at the top are focused on maximizing profits without concern for the communities and workers creating those profits. The new global capitalists want to cut labor costs as much as possible, and because unions have the opposite goal of ensuring working people get a fair return on their labor, they must be eliminated.

Second, global executives have been socializing responsibility and risk while further privatizing the profits at the top. This is often described as *fissuring* the workplace, as it shifts responsibility for everything from labor practices to environmental costs to a series of intermediaries, contractors, subcontractors, and even workers themselves—misclassified as independent contractors and thus prevented from joining or forming unions.[5]

Last, and a stark reminder of the human role in the decline of union membership, is the growth of an active union-busting industry—including the use of legal firms to help companies prevent their employees from forming unions, coalitions to lobby legislators to weaken protections for workers attempting to organize and collectively bargain, and even the infiltration of business schools to turn what used to be basic courses in labor-management relations into propagandistic forums painting unions as bad for business.[6]

Because of these shifts economic democracy in the twenty-first century cannot be achieved solely on a practice focused exclusively on worksites supported by the legal framework of the National Labor Relations Act (NLRA). This is simply not enough on its own, even if it hadn't been systematically eroded to decrease worker participation in unions. Rather, organizers must explore a more expansive definition of collective bargaining that adapts to the context of global capitalism and all its features, including addressing the material and cultural needs of the modern worker. This means ultimately changing the very nature of what a union contract covers, broadening what individuals can negotiate over and who they can negotiate with, from their direct bosses to many other individuals with concentrated power in their sector or community. Company executives negotiate many contracts to formalize a myriad of different economic relationships. Why are workers limited to just one?

Workers have a stake in their ability to come together collectively not only as employees but also in the myriad of other ways working people play a role in the economy. Tenants, debtors, homeowners, consumers, and many others have joined together to directly confront and negotiate with specific forces of capital—corporations, banks, and elements of the state—to ensure dignified lives for themselves and their families. And some of the same forms of power used in a worksite context are also available in these arenas—in particular, the power to collectively withhold participation in an economic relationship in order to force concessions from those who seek to get rich through exploitation.

Collective bargaining is a means to an end, not the end itself. We don't tell people they have the right to elect a senator; we say they have the right to vote. Likewise, telling people they have the right to form or to join a union misses the point. People must leverage their power to organize and collectively bargain, whatever that needs to look like based on their economic relationship to other stakeholders.

Our ancestors were clear on this when they began embarking, from various positions, on the project of Reconstruction to build a multiracial democracy—politically and economically—in the United States. That project was never brought to fruition. Now we must complete the job. It is with this understanding that we, a southern Black woman and a woman descended from India, attempt to position collective bargaining as a critical pillar in the struggle for democracy, and not just in the current framework we know today. It is time to reclaim our country and the vision that so many of our ancestors intended for our future. It's not complicated. Those who exploit the labor of other people are not humanitarian. Those who defend the rule of a small minority over the majority are not populists. Those who carry flags of the Confederacy or deface the US flag are not patriots. We must stop legitimizing economic and political systems that do not center workers as leading partners, and we must pick up where we left off in advancing the ideals of Reconstruction.

The good news is that working people have what it takes to do this. In this book we emphasize the importance of centralizing the fight against white supremacy and patriarchy in building and expanding access to collective bargaining. And we do this by showcasing the creative strategy of Black workers, immigrant workers, southern workers, and workers from the global south—designations we are honored to share—as models to be scaled up in ways that viably challenge trends in today's global economy so that we can build a society that works for all of us. And we highlight these approaches, not simply in pursuit of collective bargaining but also to ensure we all receive a fair return on our labor, to support our families and live with dignity and even (dare we say it?) with joy.

In part 1 of the book, titled "How Did We Get Here?" we will take a look back at US history, particularly through the lens of labor movements. We will start, in chapter 1, by explaining the basic idea of *collective bargaining*. It is one of the most powerful tools that workers can use to assert their rights, share in governance of the institutions they are part of, and reshape rules, processes, policies, and systems to bring about greater fairness and better lives for all. Yet, as we will see, this powerful tool has become increasingly neglected in recent decades. How and why did this happen? The answer to this question is provided in chapters 2 and 3. As we will explain, at one time the US labor movement helped lead the battle for democratic reforms. It produced valuable breakthroughs in our workplaces—especially the creation of guarantees that were supposed to protect the right to collective bargaining. But labor won limited victories, meaning that the fight for economic democracy was only half-won.

How did the labor movement fall short? We will also address this question. The reasons are complex but include the narrow focus of labor leaders (largely ignoring issues outside the limited topics included in workplace bargaining) and their willingness to exclude too many people: people of color, women, immigrants, the poor, and the otherwise disenfranchised. These mistakes left working people vulnerable to divide-and-conquer strategies. The rich and powerful have used these strategies to impose a highly effective reactionary program on our country. Among other structural assaults, they have largely crippled the labor movement.

Over time, social and economic trends (including the United States' changing demographics, rising costs of education and health care, the evolving nature of work, globalization of markets and supply chains, and climate change) have made rule by the rich and powerful increasingly oppressive and intolerable. The forces of global capital that ultimately drive these trends have powerful media empires at their disposal that try to conceal the realities of what is happening. But even these propaganda factories cannot completely blind ordinary people to the dire trends unfolding in their own neighborhoods. Every year, more people realize the depth of the crises we face. Something has got to give!

We have seen that the labor movement of the twentieth century did a lot, within its own limitations, to improve the circumstances of working women and men in the United States. But mistakes by labor leaders and changing conditions have left workers vulnerable to a powerful counterattack by the Right. To fight back effectively against the unjust system we face today, we need a new kind of movement for organizing and collective bargaining.

In part 2 of this book, titled "The Building Blocks of Economic Democracy" we will offer some frameworks through which we might create the movement we need. We start in chapter 4 with an articulation of why collective bargaining in the workplace is worth the fight. Here you will meet the first of many worker leaders we were able to talk to in researching this book. Rubynell Walker-Barbee, originally from Detroit, was shocked to find that her coworkers in Atlanta were unaware of their right to form a union. We move on in chapter 5 to discuss the need for a movement that reaches beyond the workplace, representing us as *whole people*—not just as workers but as citizens, consumers, parents, patients, students, migrants, and more. (In this chapter, Kimberly Mitchell, a retail worker in Washington, DC, makes her case for being more than just a worker.)

And in chapter 6 we discuss the need for a movement that includes and organizes *all people*—one that fights against white supremacy, patriarchy, xenophobia, homophobia, and all other strategies of exclusion, division, and oppression. By failing to practice this strategy of inclusion, parts of the twentieth-century labor movement allowed itself to be robbed of much of the power derived from true solidarity. The twenty-first-century movement must not make the same mistake. Lidia Victoria of Tar Heel, North Carolina, explains how she and her coworkers won by centering a multiracial struggle for dignity at a Smithfield pork processing plant. And Sanchioni Butler explains how her women's liberation movement happened on the shop floor of an auto-plant in Dallas, Texas.

Last, we need a movement that does not get bogged down in partisan divisions but instead builds organizations based on *shared values*—which are just as likely to be found in the so-called red states of the South and Midwest as in the blue states states of the West Coast and Northeast that labor organizers and other progressives have traditionally considered more fertile ground for organizing. This is the primary discussion in chapter 7, where we meet Allyson Perry and Heather DeLuca-Nestor, two West Virginia teachers who did not see the political leanings of voters in their red state as a barrier to organizing.

Each chapter of part 3, "The Way We Win," explains a different aspect of the new movement we need to build. Bettie Douglas, a fast-food employee from

St. Louis, shows us why we need a movement that engages the *ultimate profiteers* in the new global marketplace, targeting and forcing to the bargaining table the individuals and organizations that control the international corporations that now wield most of the power over the lives of working people. Her story is complemented by the reflections of Cynthia Murray, a Walmart associate in Maryland.

We need a movement that uses organized bargaining power to establish *true economic democracy*, in the workplace and elsewhere—in our communities, our schools, our courthouses, and more. Deloris Wright, a domestic worker and tenant organizer in Brooklyn, illustrates the path for negotiating beyond a traditional worksite. And Jeff Crosby shares a lifetime of experiences that show us why we need a movement that will include the voices of working people in how changes in technology and economics will be implemented in our workplaces and beyond so that the rights and needs of humans outweigh those of any corporation or machine. Applying the principles of collective bargaining to all these arenas will give us a voice and equal power to assert and secure our rights against the wishes of global capital to oppress and exploit us. We will close with some discussion of how to apply these new and expanded frameworks to some of the more current debates surrounding the future of work—from automation to the gig economy.

Even more important—and, we think, exciting—we will tell the stories of individuals and groups that are already carrying out the hard yet promising work of pioneering these strategies—including our own stories. A single dominating narrative can rob people of their dignity. For far too long we have been comfortable with dominant narratives of who workers are and what they want. These imposed narratives often fail to reflect the breadth of diversity of our workforce and the complexity of our lives. As a result, we develop strategies that perpetuate or minimize exclusions, and we widen the gap between people's lived experiences and the solutions we promote. By bringing forward a diversity of voices and experiences in this book, we hope we will broaden perspectives and start the story of building worker power in a different place. Every story is powerful and provides us with great insight into pathways forward. These stories remind us of the importance of organizing people as their whole selves and the critical importance of building lasting power through collective action and institutions. They each give us a glimpse of what is possible when people can achieve agency, dignity, and joy in their lives.

Part 1

HOW DID WE GET HERE?

The first attempt of a democracy which includes the previously disenfranchised poor is to redistribute wealth and income, and this is exactly what the black South attempted. The theory is that the wealth and the current income of the wealthy ruling class does not belong to them entirely, but is the product of the work and striving of the great millions; and that, therefore, these millions ought to have a voice in its more equitable distribution; and if this is true in modern countries, like France and England and Germany, how much more true was it in the South after the war where the poorest class represented the most extreme case of theft of labor that the world can conceive; namely, chattel slavery?

—W. E. B. Du Bois, *Black Reconstruction in America*

COLLECTIVE BARGAINING
A Powerful but Neglected Tool

In 1968, sanitation workers in the city of Memphis, Tennessee, participated in one of the most historic strikes in our nation's history. These individuals, overwhelmingly Black, were paid poorly—between $1.60 and $1.90 per hour, with unpaid overtime often required. They were also treated with disrespect. They were given no uniforms, had no access to restrooms, and had no grievance procedure to address their legitimate complaints. In 1963, thirty-three workers were fired simply for attending a union meeting.

No wonder their primary rallying cry, the slogan they displayed on placards as they marched picket lines, was simply "I Am a Man." Theirs was a struggle for human dignity, which they realized was deeply intertwined with the ability to control their own destiny and to fight for fair treatment. And to gain that ability, they needed the power to organize a labor union—a right that, for those workers at that time, was not fully protected under the law. Neither the economic system under which the Memphis sanitation workers labored nor the political system that defined their rights recognized them as full and equal human beings—and that's what drove them to take desperate, dangerous steps to change their fortunes. Not just labor activists, they were freedom fighters in every sense of the term.

The 1968 strike was sparked when two sanitation workers, Echol Cole and Robert Walker, were crushed to death by a defective garbage compactor. After an angry meeting at a Memphis labor hall, 1,375 workers refused to go to work on Monday, February 12. As garbage piled up in the streets, the city government hired strikebreakers, almost all of them white.

The sanitation workers endured months of violence. Police squads used mace, tear gas, and clubs on peaceful marchers, and police shot and killed sixteen-year-old demonstrator Larry Payne. The violence culminated in the assassination of Dr. Martin Luther King Jr on April 4 while he was visiting Memphis in support of the striking workers.

The leaders of national labor groups were initially reluctant to support the strikers. Peter J. Ciampa, director of field operations for the American Federation of State, County and Municipal Employees (AFSCME), was quoted as saying, "Good God Almighty, I need a strike in Memphis like I need another hole in the head!"[1] But over time the determination of the workers forced labor leaders to change their tune. Walter Reuther, president of the United Auto Workers (UAW), donated $50,000 to support the workers' cause, and AFSCME provided organizing support.

Finally, on April 18, the city of Memphis yielded. It agreed to recognize the workers as members of AFSCME and offered wage increases and other concessions.

Today, workers all over the United States are following in the footsteps of the Memphis freedom fighters. Like their historic forebears, workers labor in circumstances that are grossly unfair, from inadequate pay and arbitrary schedules to dangerous working conditions. And like the Memphis workers, today's workers are taking serious personal risks in challenging the system that oppresses them because their right to organize in defense of their interests is still not fully protected. Many groups—in industries from meatpacking to farming, hospital work to domestic employment, fast food restaurants to grocery stores, transportation to delivery services—are not yet recognized as labor unions. Yet these organizations behave like unions, taking input from their members, making tough decisions about organizing strategies and tactics, and standing as one against those who seek to keep them divided and weak. And sometimes they win—not every battle, but in growing numbers.

The single most-important tool for claiming the human rights that the Memphis sanitation workers fought for, and that workers of today are demanding, is the ability to engage in *collective bargaining*.

You have undoubtedly heard of collective bargaining in the context of labor relations. The form of collective bargaining that most Americans are familiar with is what we call *worksite-based collective bargaining*. It's the process whereby a group of employees bands together to form a unit with the combined power to negotiate on equal terms with their employer. Employees from the Memphis workers in the 1960s to workers of today employed by Walmart, McDonald's, Amazon, a chain of nursing homes, or a local school district have all sought the right to engage in this form of collective bargaining.

In this book we will show that worksite-based collective bargaining, while critical, is not the only important form of collective bargaining. The workplace is far from the only arena in which people can benefit from banding together to assert and claim their rights. Collective bargaining is a powerful practice that people can use to transform the ways in which neighborhoods, cities, school and health-care systems, government agencies, and even multinational corporations behave. In later chapters we will explain how this can happen and offer examples that illustrate how groups of people around the country are putting this concept to work.

But because most people primarily associate collective bargaining with workplaces and with the efforts of labor unions to improve the lot of employees, we will begin our exploration of the topic by looking closely at how worksite-based collective bargaining works. In the next few pages you will learn some facts that may surprise you because the antilabor bias that permeates too many corners of our educational system and the mass media has given millions of people a badly flawed impression of how labor relations actually work in the United States. Understanding the realities of collective bargaining is an essential foundation to considering how this powerful tool can be used to improve the lives of people from every walk of life.

Collective Bargaining: What It Means and How It Works

Traditional worksite-based collective bargaining, at its best, is a system by which working people can exercise collective power and directly confront the owners of capital in a way that reclaims portions of that capital for working people and their communities. This type of collective bargaining has served as a direct mechanism to fight for a fair return on the labor working people invest into building, operating, servicing, or moving something. In this way collective bargaining allows everyday people to "practice democracy"—directly engaging in the decisions and choices that affect their lives.

As a result, worksite-based collective bargaining has provided an essential pathway to economic sustainability for millions of US workers, ensuring they can support themselves and their families and live decent lives with a manageable level of economic risk. In other democracies, the fundamental features of a social safety net such as health care, retirement income, and unemployment benefits are usually paid for through taxes and provided to people directly by the government. That's generally not the case in the United States. Therefore, for most of the past century, a union contract that embodies the results of the collective bargaining process has been the best tool for US workers to ensure they have access to these basic elements of a decent life.

When people talk about "union power" or "the labor movement" as a force in US society, the most important thing they're talking about is the power of unions to insist on collective bargaining to protect the rights of workers.

How, exactly, does worksite-based collective bargaining work? We can start our discussion with the kind of definition you might find in a dictionary:

> Collective bargaining (noun): the process whereby employees, identified as a bargaining unit, negotiate as a group, often through an elected bargaining committee, with their employer to determine wages, hours, and other permissible conditions of employment, resulting in a written agreement or contract that defines policy either for all employees of that employer or for those specifically represented by the bargaining committee.

Definitions like this raise more questions than answers for many people. What is mandatory for employers to bargain over? Who is counted in the bargaining unit? What is permissible to bargain over? There is an entire industry of lawyers, consultants, and policy advocates dedicated to clarifying questions like this and interpreting the law in ways that meet the needs of their clientele. For its part, the government provides some clarity through the National Labor Relations Board (NLRB). But even a scan of the NLRB website just raises more questions. For example, what does it mean when the NLRB site advises employers that they have the right to "bargain hard, provided you seek in good faith to reach an agreement"?[2] Can someone just explain collective bargaining all in one place?

Here's a basic explanation of what you need to know.[3]

What is collective bargaining? Collective bargaining is the formal process of negotiation between an employer and a group of employees—often with their union representative—that sets the terms and conditions of work.

Collective bargaining results in a collective bargaining agreement (CBA), a legally binding agreement that lays out policies agreed to by management and labor. Because of its role in governing the actions of both management and labor, a CBA is often referred to as "the law of the workplace." While every CBA is unique to a given labor-management relationship, most include provisions that address pay, scheduling, promotions, discipline, and job standards. CBAs also usually contain a grievance procedure, which provides a process for resolving disputes between management and labor over interpretation of the contract or regarding employee discipline or termination.

When does collective bargaining occur? Employees and employers engage in collective bargaining to negotiate new contracts and renegotiate existing contracts that have expired. For some this occurs annually. For others it occurs on a less frequent basis, depending on what was negotiated and agreed to.

In 2015 alone, an estimated five million men and women took part in the collective bargaining process, which was well above average. In 2021, the Federal Mediation and Conciliation Service (FMCS) received approximately 19,000 notices of expiring collective bargaining agreements, representing more than 1 million workers.[4] These are big numbers that show how common collective bargaining is. It's a proven method for reaching fair agreements between workers and employers, and it is used successfully in many organizations all the time. Yet only 7.4 percent of private-sector employees and 39.2 percent of public-sector employees are covered by a CBA.

Collective bargaining works. Unfortunately, only a small fraction of people are currently enjoying its benefits today compared to its heyday after the passage of the National Labor Relations Act (NLRA) in 1935. As early as 1963, at least one author referred to collective bargaining as "old before its time."[5] While some may echo this assessment to say that collective bargaining should be abandoned for other approaches, we think that at its heart it is very much worth keeping and expanding on.

Who can collectively bargain? Passed in 1935, the NLRA—also known as the Wagner Act—grants most private-sector employees the right to organize unions and collectively bargain. The Railway Labor Act (RLA) provides railway and airline employees the right to form unions and engage in collective bargaining. Between the NLRA and RLA, approximately 85 percent of all private-sector employees officially have collective bargaining rights. Some members of the private sector, including employees of very small businesses, agricultural workers, domestic workers, supervisors, and workers classified as independent contractors do not consistently have the right to engage in collective bargaining.

Collective bargaining rights for those in the public sector—that is, employees of federal, state, and local government agencies—are established by a patchwork of laws. Federal law offers many federal employees the right to engage in collective bargaining over a limited set of issues, and state laws determine whether state and local government employees can engage in collective bargaining. As of 2014, three states—North Carolina, South Carolina, and Virginia—expressly prohibit collective bargaining for all public-sector employees at the state level.[6] Though in 2021, Virginia allowed municipalities to loosen restrictions.[7] These laws are considered by many people in other countries to be inhumane. For example, the prohibition of bargaining is viewed by the nonprofit organization Human Rights Watch to be in direct violation of international human rights laws.[8]

What topics can employees bargain over? The NLRA—the law that applies to most private-sector employees—does not include a list of bargaining topics.

However, rulings by the courts and policies set by the National Labor Relations Board (NLRB; created by the NLRA) determine which subjects are covered. They divide bargaining subjects into three categories: *mandatory, permissive,* and *illegal.*

Mandatory subjects, broadly speaking, relate to wages, hours, pensions, health care, and working conditions—for example, measures to protect the health and safety of workers while on the job. Employers cannot refuse to bargain over these subjects, and negotiations may continue to the point of mediation if an agreement is not reached.

Permissive subjects are nonmandatory subjects of bargaining, meaning employers are not required to bargain over them. The requirement for a company to use union-made goods in its own operations is an example of a permissive bargaining subject.

Finally, *illegal subjects* are those that would violate any law. These cannot be bargained over, even if both parties agree. So, for example, a provision that requires discrimination based on a person's sex would be illegal.

This is the current framework that governs collective bargaining in the workplace. Later in this book we will share bargaining strategies that can help workers go above and beyond what is mandatory or permissive. We will explain the importance of bargaining over issues that violate laws we consider to be unjust, such as laws restricting protections for immigrant workers.

How does collective bargaining work? The collective bargaining process is similar to everyday negotiations between other parties over other topics—for example, the process of negotiating a merger between two companies. Bargaining commonly begins with employees coming together with their union to determine and prioritize a set of issues to raise with their employer. A bargaining committee made up of employees and union representatives then meets with management at the bargaining table, presenting a series of proposals and explaining the intention behind them. Management responds with its own proposals and counteroffers. The sides typically begin to reach agreement on some proposals while trading counteroffers over unresolved issues. The length of the bargaining process and the number of rounds of offers and counteroffers varies depending on the complexity and number of bargaining proposals.

In some instances, companies and workers engage in interest-based bargaining (IBB), a practice where neither party comes to the table with proposals. They instead meet for conversations aimed at finding solutions that work for both sides. IBB is often used in negotiations between employers and employees of nonprofit organizations, where both sides share common values.

Collective bargaining in the United States is typically a decentralized process, occurring between a single employer and its employees. However, in industries like hospitality and trucking, employers and unions sometimes engage in regional or industry-wide bargaining, where a CBA covers employers in a specific city or across an entire industry.

In the construction sector a project labor agreement (PLA) serves as a pre-hire collective bargaining agreement, establishing the terms and conditions of employment for a particular construction project. PLAs are negotiated between a coalition of building trades unions and a general contractor. Typically they require all the contractors on the project to pay fair wages and to contribute to joint labor-management health, pension, and training funds.

What role do unions play in collective bargaining? The collective bargaining process needs a vehicle through which it can happen. For most working people that vehicle is a union.

Employees join together to form a union, either through an election of the majority of employees or by the majority of employees signing authorization cards saying they want to be recognized collectively as a union.[9] The latter process is often referred to as *card check*. Once most employees express support for unionization, they form a new union or join an existing one.

Union members then pay dues to fund staff and infrastructure to support their interests. The infrastructure most often connects them to union groups in other places representing workers at similar employers or those doing similar work. These separate union groups are called *locals*. Collections of union locals make up regional and district councils, state organizations, and national and international unions. Furthermore, these national and international unions form federations and local labor councils throughout the country. The biggest such labor organization in the United States is the American Federation of Labor and Congress of Industrial Organizations (AFL-CIO). All these labor organizations at the regional, district, state, and national levels seek to represent the interests of working people, particularly, though not exclusively, in the political arena. When the federal Bureau of Labor Statistics defines the number of union members in the United States, it is talking mostly about people who relate to these institutions.[10]

What happens when management and labor do not agree? If, after legitimate good-faith negotiations, management and the union cannot reach agreement on one or more mandatory subjects, they are said to be at an impasse. Because the NLRA requires both sides to negotiate in good faith but does not force either side to agree to a proposal with which that side disagrees, when the two sides reach a legitimate impasse, management may unilaterally implement a final offer. Alternatively, both sides can agree to engage in a mediation process where a federal or private mediator or arbitrator helps the parties work toward an agreement.[11] Labor or management may also try to exert economic pressure to force the other side into agreement.

In the private sector economic pressure typically occurs in the form of a strike, when workers withhold their labor and negatively affect a company's ability to function, or a lockout, where employers prevent workers from working and in some instances replace them with nonunion workers.[12] Since the passage of the NLRA, the threat of legally protected work stoppages has often pushed the sides toward agreement. Additionally, the decrease of union density and power and the increase in using permanent replacements for striking workers have made strikes and lockouts less common in recent decades. However, there has been a recent uptick in strikes, with more strikes occurring in 2018 than in any single year since 1986.[13] And the fall of 2021 saw so many worker-led disruptions that it was dubbed "Striketober" in the mainstream media.[14]

Unlike in the private sector, many public-sector employees do not have a legally protected right to strike. Federal law allows the government to fire striking federal workers, while state and local laws vary on whether state and local employees have the legal right to strike. Some states, like Pennsylvania, prohibit strikes by emergency workers (police officers, firefighters, and prison guards) but offer them access to a binding arbitration process for unresolved bargaining issues to guarantee that the parties reach an agreement.

This patchwork of rules results in varied treatment for different categories of public workers. President Reagan famously fired striking air traffic controllers organized with the Professional Air Traffic Controllers Organization (PATCO) in 1981, a fight that ultimately led to the creation of Jobs With Justice. By contrast, many government employees have gone on strike without suffering such a penalty, such as the Chicago Teachers Union in 2012. And while not officially on strike, many Transportation Security Administration (TSA) employees and air traffic controllers slowed down work by calling in sick during the federal government shutdown in January 2019 to protest having to work without pay.

The Power of Collective Bargaining

In the twentieth century the spread of collective bargaining has lifted wages for working people as a whole; given many families access to programs that supply basic human needs like retirement, health care, and paid leave; and helped to democratize once-tyrannical workplaces by providing a clear set of policies along with the ability to enforce them through a process that enables employees to file grievances. Maybe most notably, and certainly to the deep dismay of the wealthiest, collective bargaining has acted as a means for redistributing wealth and ownership, directly challenging the drivers of inequality in society. Collective bargaining significantly increased upward mobility in the United States in the mid-twentieth century.[15] This trend was catalyzed by unions, by other movements of working people, and by the passage of laws protecting workers' rights. Collective bargaining played a key role in enabling many Black and Brown people to escape poverty and attain economic security in the United States.

Collective bargaining, in its many forms, allows working people to directly confront the corporate actors behind inequality and ensure that working families can shape their own social and economic futures. Like voting, collective bargaining is a way that we exercise power in a healthy democracy. It is not simply about the right to join a union but rather the ability to have a say in how your worksite or industry is governed.

To fulfill its true potential, collective bargaining should be seen as a gateway to democracy in the entire economic arena. Yet, as mentioned earlier in this chapter, for all the good it has done for so many, traditional collective bargaining is having trouble keeping up with the needs of workers, especially given the form of capitalism that we face in the twenty-first century that is characterized by financialization, fissured economies, and a widespread distrust of institutions that used to represent the heart of our democracy. We need not only ensure that collective bargaining is accessible to workers in this climate but also deepen its effect if it is to become an impetus to the revival of democracy.

WORKPLACE DEMOCRACY DOES NOT HAPPEN BY ACCIDENT

A Story of US Labor Movements

To fully understand the important role of collective bargaining in our national life, it's important to know something about collective bargaining's history. How and why do we enjoy access to collective bargaining in some arenas today? Why do we lack it in many others? What does experience tell us about how the benefits of collective bargaining can be spread more widely? History helps us answer all these questions.

However, books and articles about the history of collective bargaining, and the US labor movement more generally, tend to focus on big institutions like the AFL-CIO. These institutions are important and definitely deserve attention. But it's important to start with some of the earlier attempts of working people to organize and collectively bargain in the United States, long before any legal framework existed to protect them from angry employers or to offer guidelines on how they could safely join forces.

Consider, for example, the story of the Black washerwomen of Atlanta who organized themselves during the 1880s. They were organizing in extremely precarious conditions. Slavery was a recent memory. They knew people who had fought in the Civil War—on both sides. Many of them were single mothers or at least the sole income-earners for their families. There were more Black washerwomen in 1880s Atlanta than white male laborers, and the conditions were terrible. These women worked long hours, had to use dangerous chemicals like lye, and suffered the abuse of employers who still saw them as property to be treated as they liked. Their pay amounted to less than $10 per month.

In July 1881, twenty of these women joined together to form the Washing Society, a union of laundry workers seeking better pay and conditions. Without any kind of handbook, they started organizing. Given that each of them had several employers, all private and individual families, they targeted the city itself, seeking labor standards like a uniform pay rate of $1 per twelve pounds of wash. This goal was not unlike the area standards agreements common among modern construction and building trade unions or the domestic workers' bills of rights that have been won in several states by modern nannies and domestic workers.

With the help of local Black ministers, the members of the Washing Society held a mass meeting, organized door-to-door canvassing, and called a citywide strike in support of their goals. White laundresses, who made up less than 2 percent of the total, also supported the effort. Within three weeks, membership in the society grew to three thousand.

The city government struck back, arresting strikers. The government also sought to impose fines disguised as "membership fees" on the Washing Society's members. But when cooks, maids, nurses, and hotel workers joined the strike, the government capitulated. They withdrew the fines and accepted the washerwomen's salary demands.[1]

These women were not the first group of seemingly powerless workers to organize themselves into an effective force for change. Just two decades earlier they had lived through what many describe as the largest general strike in US history. This was the mass refusal to work by Black enslaved people in the South, midway through the Civil War, accompanied by an exodus of many of them from the Southern plantations in an effort to escape to the North. This concept was first articulated by W. E. B. Du Bois in his groundbreaking 1935 book *Black Reconstruction in America*, and it has since been taken up by other historians who regard the general strike as a turning point of the war. In the words of Erik Loomis in *A History of America in Ten Strikes* (2018), "The slaves freed themselves. . . . They did not wait for Abraham Lincoln to free them. Rather, they took their lives in their own hands through withholding their labor from their masters, fleeing to Union lines, and forcing Lincoln and the North to recognize the new reality of their lives."[2]

These and other pioneering efforts were crucial building blocks in the foundation that would go on to support the institutions of organized labor that would later help codify the practices of organizing and collective bargaining in the United States.[3] They illustrate the core truth that the right to organize and demand collective bargaining is not established by benevolent government officials or forward-thinking employers. That right exists only when working people themselves gather together and use their collective strength to force the rich and powerful to acknowledge it.

The Divergent Aims of Organized Labor in the Early 1900s

Over the past century and more, working people in the United States have attempted to assert their power to negotiate on an equal footing with employers and industry leaders in a variety of ways. Some of the organizing groups they launched in the early years of the twentieth century were racially and ethnically inclusive, while others were not. Some centered their struggle on the aim of expanding democracy to industry, while others were more interested in creating a pathway for workers to eventually become bosses in their own right. Some emphasized the need to place the struggle for workers' rights in the broader context of an ongoing battle between classes whose interests are fundamentally opposed, while others downplayed this theme. Some sought to enlist the help of the federal government in defining and defending workers' rights, while others opposed government involvement.

Still, leaders of the US labor movement in the early years of the twentieth century had some basic beliefs in common. All saw it as their role to develop free-thinking men—and sometimes women—who were capable of self-government. And they all believed that the power and voice of organized workers was at the heart of a healthy democracy. Thus these labor leaders all shared a handful of fundamental goals—goals of fairness, equality, and democracy that remain valid and urgent in our time. That means the insights to be drawn from the different paths these early labor leaders followed in pursuit of those common goals can inform our own strategic thinking today.

The early Knights of Labor skirted most notions of a struggle between a working class and a corporate class, seeking instead cooperative ownership that they believed would eventually make every man his own boss, hearkening back to the yeoman farmer and jack-of-all-trades craftsmen of US folklore. Leon Fink, who wrote extensively about the Knights, notes that they "did not self-consciously place themselves in opposition to a prevailing economic system but displayed a sincere ideological ambivalence toward the capitalist marketplace."[4] Less organized for worksite and industrial struggles, the Knights sought large-scale societal changes beyond the worksite, mobilizing their large membership in campaigns to generate political and legislative opportunities, often building across racial lines and around common interests. (As we will discuss later in this chapter, the Knights were leveraging what we call *associational power*, one of the kinds of power that working people may have at their disposal.) According to Clayton Sinyai in his book *Schools of Democracy*, the Knights "were fully devoted to educational and cooperative activities and eschewed industrial conflict whenever possible."[5] They were not interested in negotiating with managers because they saw themselves as future owners of their own enterprise. They focused instead on preparing their members for that ideal future, building broad-based solidarity across sector and even race and prioritizing legislative and regulatory gains that could strengthen their cooperative experiments.[6]

The Industrial Workers of the World (IWW), or Wobblies, however, were keen on the necessity of class struggle. Any government that elevated the interests of the capitalist class as equal to workers was not only undemocratic but illegitimate. They sought the complete capitulation of capital to the working class. Again, from Sinyai: "There is but one bargain that the IWW will make with the employing class—complete surrender of all control of industry to the organized workers."[7] Without this there was little to talk about at the bargaining table or in the halls of government.

Then there were the early craft unions. The craft union movement, championed by the American Federation of Labor (AFL), believed in organizing employees based on the specific craft or trade that they practiced. Craft union leaders like Samuel Gompers (who founded the AFL) and many union members took pride in the skills they'd developed. They liked to see themselves as their own masters, feeling that they controlled—or should control—their own labor based on their own rules and conditions. Any suggestion that positioned them in a class of laborers in contrast to a class of owners constituted servitude to them. Thus they resisted the concept of solidarity among workers of various crafts or trades. More specifically, in an era when chattel slavery had only recently ended in the United States, they did not want to be associated with formerly enslaved Black workers, either in theory or in practice. This prideful attitude was deeply infected with racism and patriarchal attitudes, as reflected to this day in the use of terms like *brotherhood* to describe organizations of workers—themselves referred to as *craftsmen*. Many craft union organizers used color and gender to define who was fit to govern themselves.

Having survived several decades of attacks, the craft unions also tended to keep the government at arm's length, seeking instead to govern their own skill sectors and control the flow of labor in and out of an industry using their power to control the specific skills within a given labor market. And the craft unions saw government intervention for either capital or labor as paternalistic and undermining their ability to govern themselves as full citizens. Any form of government intervention was a challenge to union members' masculinity. And the various brotherhoods were simply not interested in that. Woodrow Wilson, a candidate in the 1912 presidential race that included Theodore Roosevelt, William Howard Taft, and socialist Eugene V. Debs, aligned himself with this general sentiment when he said, "If any part of our people want to be wards, if they want to have guardians put over them, if they want to be taken care of, if they want to be children, patronized by the government, why, I am sorry, because it will sap the manhood of America."[8] Wilson was far from the most left-leaning candidate in that election, and his partnership with the labor movement was tenuous. He distrusted the collective power of unions but eventually found an alliance—in part because of this patriarchal sentiment.[9]

Early railway unionists, by contrast, recognized the need for government oversight over the federal rail system that employed them. Without the support of the AFL, Eugene V. Debs and other young railroad unionists had witnessed government force being used to defeat rail worker activities.[10] If the same force could instead be used to ease tensions and get rail carriers to the bargaining table, why pass up the opportunity?

Ultimately both railway unions and carriers pushed for the Railway Labor Act (1926), which opened the door for the government to mediate when negotiations between the two broke down and granted railroad employees the right to select representatives free of employers' interference or coercion.[11] Yet this guarantee came at a dangerous cost that continues to haunt us today, since the act required rail unions to give up their right to strike.

The first lesson network leaders learn in the Jobs With Justice training is, "Never give your power away." By bargaining away the right to strike, the early rail unionists and others after them essentially broke this golden rule of organizing.

While workers were battling it out in the streets and on the shop floors of the country, a simultaneous battle of ideas was in full swing among various thought leaders. One side in this battle was represented by the 1915 *Walsh Report of the U.S. Commission on Industrial Relations*. As historian Joseph A. McCartin wrote in his book *Labor's Great War*, "Not since Reconstruction had the report of any federal body seemed more radical."[12] The ideas of this report built on the spirit of Reconstruction and the constitutional amendments of that period; they suggest that the salvation of the grand US project of building a multiracial democracy would depend on the country's ability to expand democratic practices to industrial relations between labor and industry leaders.

The Walsh Report was countered by business interests and progressives alike. This ultimately translated into a middle-of-the-road solution that stopped short of industrial democracy, positioning the government as an impartial mediator and attempting to find legislative solutions to labor unrest. Instead of elevating workers' collective power to democratically govern their sectors alongside industry leaders, the prevailing school of thought was to maintain labor peace legislatively at all costs—including eventually suppressing worker power. Even Wilson's relatively milquetoast solutions for labor peace led not only to new critiques but also to a new alliance between Republicans and southern Dixiecrats intent on removing union and government "interference" from industry. Perhaps Wilson's own middle-of-the-road approaches even made it easier for one of the most reactionary governments to rise to power in the election of 1918.

As Mark Twain wrote, "History doesn't repeat itself, but it rhymes." The 2016 election of Donald Trump and reactionary Republicans in both the House and the Senate was a direct reaction to the administration of the first Black president, Barack Obama, and various attempts by the labor movement and government to better (i.e., albeit impartially) mediate conflict between labor and industry. Years of attempting to do everything but expand democracy to industry continues to erode US democracy, including through a growing distrust of unions, government, and other institutions where democracy was historically practiced. Yet again we find ourselves asking what we must do to save our democracy. To answer that question, we must look back in order to move forward.

The most important task of today's movement leaders is to continue the struggle for industrial democracy—establishing more pathways for workers to govern specific worksites and industry in general as stakeholders, equal at least to shareholders, investors, and other affected community members. We can no longer tolerate the hypocrisy of aspiring for democracy in society while allowing authoritarian rule in the workplace. The spirit of the US Constitution must apply everywhere.

Traditional collective bargaining practices produced results of real value for US workers. The practices tested real mechanisms for winning enforceable agreements that ultimately serve as the governing documents for companies or worksites. At the same time, twentieth-century unions extracted capital directly from corporations, using increased wages and member dues to resource and sustain the institutions democratically. These institutions ensured the contracts were implemented and enforced, either through legal processes or through direct action up to and including the withholding of their labor. Perhaps most important, these institutions gave everyday people the opportunity to practice governing themselves and their conditions—that is, to practice democracy. This is fundamental to the health of the country's overall democracy at a much broader level.

That said, it has been apparent for several decades that the current containers for practicing industrial democracy have been eroded and narrowed to the point of unrecognizability. They are no longer enough for today's generation of working people. As protection from the National Labor Relations Board (NLRB) became less effective throughout the 1970s and 1980s, working people tapped into other channels such as the Civil Rights Act of 1964 and Title IX to defend their ability to organize—and often with more success.[13]

The NLRA Creates a Legal Framework for Collective Bargaining

After extensive agitation from Black industrial workers, some union leaders made inroads into organizing around workers' shared interests against white supremacy. The leaders of what became the Congress of Industrial Organizations (CIO), such as John L. Lewis of the United Mineworkers of America, brought the vigor, discipline, and resources obtained through their days building the American Federation of Labor (AFL) to the controversial practice of organizing workers of all crafts into one union for a given industry instead of organizing them by skill set as the craft unions did. But having been cut off from the more conservative early AFL, CIO leaders also needed government support to level the playing field between their newly organized unions and employers. They found that support—albeit not always perfectly aligned—in Franklin D. Roosevelt, Robert Wagner, Frances Perkins, and other New Deal political leaders of the time. After learning the hard way what it meant to pass great laws without the means of enforcing them in the National Industrial Recovery Act (NIRA) of 1933, the union-government alliance heralded the passage of the NLRA in 1935, crafted by US senator Robert Wagner of New York, which included the creation of the NLRB to enforce it.

Most notably, the NLRA defined a process of exclusive representation whereby if more than 50 percent of workers voted for a union in an election, that union was the recognized bargaining representative for them in the eyes of the NLRB, and the government pushed companies to negotiate with them. While Gompers's followers cringed, this was generally okay with the industrial unionists. Up to this point, industrial union leaders had good experiences of the government as a third actor in labor-industry relations. The International Ladies Garment Workers Union (ILGWU) had some of the most success with tripartite industry standard-setting that turned sweatshop jobs into respectable career ladders in a short amount of time.[14] The statute forbade employers from firing, discriminating against, or otherwise punishing workers who attempted to exercise their collective rights.[15] When a majority of employees agreed to come together in a union, the employer had to bargain with the union in good faith.[16]

This package of rules and enforcement mechanisms became the primary framework for collective bargaining in the United States and is still the dominant basis of what is in use today. Other laws passed around the same time helped further shape the economic landscape of the modern United States, including Social Security, unemployment insurance, and the Fair Labor Standards Act, which created both the forty-hour workweek and a federal minimum wage.[17] As labor law scholar Kate Andrias has shown, the Fair Labor Standards Act of 1938 allowed for the formation of tripartite union-employer-government committees that provided the scaffolding for sectoral bargain in some industries (at least until that provision of the law was repealed in 1949).[18] These laws, along with later victories such as the Civil Rights Act of 1964 and other federal regulations, filled workers' armories with tools to counter exploitation and discrimination from employers—all in the name of strengthening our democracy.

At the time, the NLRA was indeed groundbreaking. And Robert Wagner's motivations went far beyond the desire to appease his union supporters. As Sinyai observes, "Wagner was concerned about the private power accumulated by the large industrial firms and the threat this posed to democratic life. . . . Trade unions were essential *because* citizens were unable to participate meaningfully in forming national policy. If not in the nation's great matters, then at least on the shop floor, there was a venue small and modest enough that a citizen might participate intelligently in its direction."[19] As Wagner himself noted, "This is why the struggle for a voice in industry through the process of collective bargaining is at the heart of the struggle for the preservation of political as well as economic democracy in America."[20]

While far from achieving the full dream of industrial democracy popular in the decades prior, the era of collective bargaining launched by the passage of the NLRA did open pathways for millions of Americans to family-sustaining jobs, home ownership, retirement security, vacation time, career advancement, and myriad other benefits. While not covered by the NLRA, collective bargaining in the public sector has been a key vehicle for women and communities of color to achieve more equity, combat low wages and discrimination, advance in their professions, and secure the freedoms, opportunities, and rights previously only available to a privileged few.

But as Charles Heckscher so eerily predicted back in 1988 in the first edition of *New Unionism*, ". . . this form of unionism, common as it is, and as effective as it has been in the past, is not the only form of worker representation. It is now possible and essential to build a more flexible system for expressing the concerns of employees."[21] In modern practice, collective bargaining is not monolithic. Organizations of workers have approached the question of how to build worker power, when to negotiate, and whom to negotiate with in many different ways. Today unions continue to occupy different areas of the economy and exercise different forms of power, with varying amounts and kinds of leverage in engaging employers, industry leaders, and government. And these positions are as dynamic as the changing global economy we all live in.

White Supremacy in Organized Labor

White supremacy is a system of thought and behavior that presumes and perpetuates the superiority and privilege of white people in all aspects of society. For centuries it has been at the core of shaping life in the United States, especially economic life. And white supremacy has played a powerful role in influencing—and often distorting or even crippling—the ongoing quest for workers' rights.

As a result, organized labor has a huge image problem. Consider the perspective of many Black and Brown workers today, who experience labor unions in part via unionized government agencies like US Immigration and Customs Enforcement (ICE) and local police departments—both negative, violent forces that often terrorize these communities. Despite the history of these same forces busting union efforts in the past and present, organized labor still has a difficult time holding unions in these sectors accountable for their structural racism and its daily effect on workers of color.

The story of how the labor movement has grappled with white supremacy is a complicated one. Here is an example that illustrates some of the varied sides of this story.

Black workers employed by the Pullman Company to serve patrons of George Pullman's long-distance passenger trains organized the Brotherhood of Sleeping Car Porters. They were deeply reliant on tips, with many white riders still thinking that Black people should be paid based on the service they provided, not an actual wage—a remnant leftover from their status as property. This was no accident. As Maurice Weeks of the Action Center on Race and the Economy has noted:

> When George Pullman was hiring his staff of Porters following the Civil War, he purposely chose dark skinned Black staff, many of whom were former slaves, knowing that he could exploit them for wages and that they would play into the racial stereotypes and roles of the mostly White passenger base. Unsurprisingly, the porters faced horrible treatment in every aspect of their job. Passengers referred to porters as "George" or "boy" and worse, the job required nonstop work with virtually no sleep and the pay was abysmal. And even though this all occurred during what was a golden age for labor organizations starting to stand up for the rights of the poor and working class, the fact that porters were all Black at a time when Jim Crow was gaining its strong foot-

ing in the country left them mostly out of the conversation as far as major unions went.[22]

The porters union eventually won a charter from the AFL-CIO and promptly negotiated a collective bargaining agreement with the company that established, among other things, better wages for porters and maids, a maximum of 240 hours worked per month, and overtime pay for workers forced to go over that.

However, this success story was not shared by other Black workers. Many found themselves estranged from the more formal institutions of organized labor. Joining the dominant unions that were often led by white workers openly antagonistic to Black workers did not guarantee them more economic sustainability. And in many instances, joining predominantly white unions led to limited career mobility. Perhaps the best illustration of this also occurred within the rail unions. Many Black unions opposed the drive toward exclusive union representation, the idea that only one union can represent workers in any given workplace. Much like Black communities who opposed desegregation in schools because they feared that Black children would not get the same attention or opportunities as their white classmates, some Black rail unions saw exclusive representation as potentially trapping them in second-class conditions. In her book *The Workplace Constitution: From the New Deal to the New Right*, Sophia Z. Lee recalls one particularly telling moment in rail history, a pivotal meeting in Dallas in 1937 between Black rail union leaders—who represented all Black rail workers regardless of specific craft or position—and Robert Cole of the National Mediation Board, a federal agency created by the Railway Labor Act:

> The men meeting with Cole were leaders in the all-Black National Federation of Railway Workers (the Federation), an independent union that represented most of the line's coach cleaners. The AFL's all-White Brotherhood of Railway Carmen (the Carmen) had recently petitioned Cole's Mediation Board to take over representing the line's cleaners, both the Black majority and the Mexican American minority: hence the forthcoming election. The Federation would need a majority of the votes to remain the coach cleaners' representative; conversely, if the Carmen garnered more votes, under the Railway Labor Act, the Mediation Board would certify it as the coach cleaners' exclusive representative.[23]

Justifiably fearing that the election would not be free and fair, the Black union leaders attempted to delay it. But they lost that battle, and their fears were confirmed. In most railroad craft unions Black workers represented a small minority. As a result, more numerous white brotherhoods displaced independent all-Black unions, which thus lost the power to negotiate with employers.[24]

This experience of Black rail workers highlighted another tension that would persist in twentieth-century labor organizing—the tension between members-only bargaining, also known as *minority unionism*, and exclusive representation by one union. The desire for one union per workplace was not always the dominant framework.[25] And while having one union per workplace did decrease the ability of employers to fragment workers, it also had real consequences on Black workers and often subjugated the interests of others who were in the minority at the time.

Lessons from Labor History

Reflecting on this history, we can draw a couple of important conclusions about types of compromises that ultimately undermine the long-term success of organized working people.

The first lesson is that any deal that wins a collective bargaining agreement or some other concession from employers after compromising away the fundamental powers that workers use to enforce and maintain those agreements—particularly the right to strike—is a recipe for long-term disaster.

Note that the NLRA itself did not undermine the most fundamental source of power of workers and their organizations: the power to withhold their labor through striking. That power was the true source of labor's growing influence. Even in the heyday of the NLRA, government statistics in 1937 showed that while only 262,000 workers won union recognition through the elections process sanctioned by the NLRA, over 700,000 workers won union recognition by striking.[26] The moral is important: *Direct action is critical to improving the position of workers in negotiations with employers.*

Strong legal protections can help to preserve the right to direct action. But when those laws are challenged or weakened—as with the gradual erosion of the NLRA in recent decades, for example—unions with no freedom to strike will have little or nothing to stand on. This is why those seeking to minimize the power of workers began seeking ways to use the NLRA as a pillow to suffocate the mass action associated with class struggles, which they preferred to label "labor unrest."

One of the most effective early assaults by antilabor forces was the passage of the Taft-Hartley Act (1947). This act exempted millions of workers from NLRA protections. The same law also banned "secondary boycotts," pickets against companies besides the employer with which workers have a dispute, a direct attack on solidarity that workers could no longer use strikes and pickets to pressure the suppliers, purchasers, or contractors of the company that was mistreating them to improve that company's labor practices.[27] Taft-Hartley illustrates how quickly a federal government that appears to be firmly on the side of workers can be twisted in the opposite direction when workers themselves fail to be vigilant about not just winning the game but also changing the rules to protect and maintain those victories.

The second lesson is that without confronting both the individual and systemic discrimination present in our society and movements, working people will be vulnerable to the temptation to bypass the issues of people of color, immigrants, and women—ultimately weakening any agreement and creating a pool of unorganized workers who can later be mobilized to undermine whatever improved standards were won.

Most lawmakers who crafted the NLRA were not interested in addressing the needs of working people as whole people, as active participants in the economy through multiple channels. Thus they were unwilling to confront the problems of racial, ethnic, and gender injustice. While groundbreaking for the period, the New Deal laws included compromises reflecting the dominant societal beliefs in racism and patriarchy. Most notable, northern New Dealers compromised with southern white supremacists—the so-called Dixiecrats—to exclude protection for employees in sectors that employed predominantly Black and Brown workers. Shortly afterward, these same politicians also allowed states to undermine and even ban various protections for workers attempting to form unions. These compromises still impede organizing today.[28]

Accepting these compromises was a terrible price to pay for maintaining the unity of the Democratic Party, which had been built from a coalition of southern white conservatives and northern liberals. The implicit bargain became unsustainable with the civil rights movement of the 1960s. Democratic Party support for the Civil Rights Act of 1964 and related measures led, in time, to the wholesale abandonment of the party by racist southern whites and the subsequent realignment of the United States' two major parties.

These truths shed a different light on mainstream versions of labor history that focus mainly on giant organizations like the AFL-CIO and the federal laws they helped to pass.

One way in which our perspective on the story of labor needs to be modified is by broadening our image of US workers themselves. The first image that comes to mind for many when thinking about the US worker is a stereotypical union man, a strong white man wielding a pickaxe or a hammer while building one of the major industries of the twentieth century—steel, automaking, or mining. Yet seen through a different lens, the face of the classic US worker looks different. Through this lens you might see the Black washerwomen of the 1880s who organized and nearly shut down the city of Atlanta in order to increase wages and establish laundry work as an important sector of the economy. Or maybe your lens would zoom in on the Mexican agricultural workers in California who went on massive strikes in the 1930s for better treatment. It might include Black sharecroppers throughout the South who organized for better pay and access to their own land or the women garment workers in New York—all in addition to the white man with the axe.

Another way of broadening our perspective is to recognize the various forms of power that working people have at their disposal.

Working people can exercise *associational power*—power that stems from people coming together collectively through unions, organizations, and political parties to create the change they wish to see in the world, such as through elections, mass mobilizations, boycotts, and other actions. On top of this, working people in certain sectors have specific forms of *structural power*. Beverly Silver separates these into two categories: *marketplace power* and *workplace power*. Marketplace power results from tight labor markets—where workers control a set of skills that are in high demand and low supply. Workplace power is leveraged when a group of working people are strategically positioned to disrupt a company, industry, or sector's ability to produce goods or otherwise function and thus profit.[29]

While the ability of some workers to leverage power has decreased with our changing global economy, financialization, and the confusion created by the fissuring of the employment relationship, the ability of many other workers has actually increased, thereby creating opportunities to leverage our associational and structural bargaining power in new ways. For example, postal work was once a highly skilled job when postal employees were responsible for all levels of sorting, tracking, and getting mail delivered in timely ways. These workers had marketplace power. But as postal work has become more automated, this power has shifted. Work is no longer as highly skilled. Yet, postal workers are still strategically positioned to disrupt the now automated systems of mail delivery if they are so inclined.[30] They still have structural workplace power. Similar shifts evolved from skilled machinists' marketplace power to unspecialized autoworkers' workplace power and so on. The moral: *power does not necessarily go away. It simply shifts.*

Perhaps this became most evident in 2020 after the beginning of the COVID-19 pandemic, when US leaders began to publicly and consistently identify a category of sectors as "essential" to the economy. These sectors included health care, food/grocery services, food processing, transportation and logistics, e-commerce, and some manufacturing. In acknowledging this, government agencies and many others made clear the role many previously unacknowledged people play in the economy. And that clarity highlighted the structural power workers in these sectors have at their disposal to improve conditions in their worksites (such as through demands for hazard pay and personal protective equipment) and in their communities (such as through lower patient-to-nurse ratios and improved social distancing practices). In what has been widely called "the Great Resignation," first termed this way by Texas A&M University Psychology professor Anthony Klotz, many essential workers were able to leverage a tight labor market to simply leave their jobs and not work for anything less than what they deemed fair.[31]

The history of working people joining together in unions is rich and diverse, containing stories from all over the country led by women and men—some known but mostly nameless. All these people were able to improve their conditions by organizing together in unions—and unions in the broadest sense of the word as the rules noted earlier in this chapter had yet to be enacted—to improve their lives and opportunities for their children moving forward.

And, of course, the lessons from labor history that we've articulated also imply the validity of their opposites. Thus, when unions give away their power, workers' rights decay; when unions continue to maintain and build their power, they are able to preserve and extend their victories, steadily improving the lot of working people.

Furthermore, when white supremacy, patriarchy, and xenophobia are allowed to flourish, workers' rights suffer; when workers centralize the struggle against these forces, they are able to win stronger agreements that work for everyone and are harder to undermine using tactics that divide workers from one another.

Collective Bargaining Today: In the Workplace and Beyond

In the last two decades there has been a lot of discussion about the right to organize and join a union. The ability of working people to organize is certainly critical to any discussion of collective bargaining, thus protecting that ability to come together with others is important. Knowing this, those who disagree with the idea that working people can govern and set standards for themselves through unions have successfully put up many barriers to prevent people from organizing or otherwise coming together in unions. These range from limiting when employees can talk to each other and about what they can speak. Removing or getting around these barriers can take a long time and is often unsuccessful. So, the ability of working people to organize cannot be underestated.

Yet organizing unions is not an end in of itself.[32] Working people started to form unions to ensure their safety and to claim a fair return on their labor so that they could support their families and live with dignity and even joy. We often take it for granted that we can enjoy recreational time with our families, plan vacations, attend soccer games, take music lessons, or volunteer for a project we value. Everyone should be able to do these things without fear of losing income. And these are some of the goals that our movement's ancestors were aiming for—work, rest, and recreation. Organizing and collective bargaining were simply the tools they used to get there, tools that leveraged the shared power built through organizing.

Worksite-based collective bargaining is important because it empowers working people to get their fair share from the representatives of capital who run the institutions for which they work. But employment is not the only way in which ordinary people are impacted by capital. There are many other ways in which our lives are shaped by those who control most of the wealth in the world. And all these ways offer opportunities for using the power of collective bargaining to improve the fairness of the deals we accept.

The idea of using collective bargaining to achieve greater fairness in our lives beyond the workplace is not just a theoretical notion. It is actually happening in a growing number of locations and sectors. Tenants, debtors, homeowners, consumers, and many others have joined together to confront and negotiate with powerful forces of capital—corporations, banks, and government agencies—to ensure dignified lives for themselves and their families. And just as being organized, uniting behind shared demands, and the power to threaten and engage in strikes were the sources of growing worker power during the twentieth century, similar strategies can be used in these other economic arenas. In particular, the power to collectively withhold our participation in an economic relationship can be a powerful way to force concessions from those who seek to get rich on our backs.

Thus, while the New Deal policies that established protected practices of collective bargaining between employers and their employees helped to pull many working people out of poverty, they were never enough. The legal framework coming out of the New Deal presumed that employers and workers shared a basic interest in keeping commerce going. Thus, it largely ignored the underlying class tensions that drive employers to prevent workers from having shared power in the workplace.

The fact is that the NLRA was never meant to address the needs of working people as *whole people*—active participants in the economy through multiple channels. It was not designed to protect the majority's ability to participate democratically in the governing of the economy. Rather, it was established to keep commerce moving, thereby ensuring the success of US capitalism. The summarizing line of the original law in 1935 literally describes it as "An act to diminish the causes of labor disputes burdening or obstructing interstate and foreign commerce, to create a National Labor Relations Board, and for other purposes."[33] While Wagner did recognize the fundamental class tensions between labor and employers, the final act was not directly anchored in the Thirteenth Amendment to the Constitution, which is supposed to protect working people against "forced servitude." Nor did it focus specifically on protecting workers' ability to take action in order to level the playing field for negotiating with the owners of capital—employers and otherwise.

Furthermore, the NLRA was inadequate even on its own terms as an effort to guarantee worksite-based collective bargaining to US workers. Under the terms of the original law, millions of workers were not protected by the law if they wanted to participate in workplace collective bargaining, particularly formerly enslaved Black domestic workers and Mexican farmworkers. If they attempted to organize, they were exposed to the full wrath of their employers, which could be devastating. This was by design, as large numbers of these workers were concentrated in the southern United States, where the wealthy descendants of plantation owners saw the potential economic clout of Black and Latino workers as a direct threat to their profits and power.[34] Millions more had restricted access to collective bargaining despite being legally included under the NLRA umbrella, including service workers in jobs mostly held by women, such as waitresses and others dependent on tips for survival.

The willingness of New Deal leaders to limit the power of collective bargaining to the workplace alone—and, in fact, to deny even that power to a huge portion of US workers—grew directly out of the political pressures generated by the northern liberal–southern Dixiecrat alliance. The northern New Dealers may have wanted to pass a historic set of policies that would actively redistribute wealth from the rich to the poor, but their political bedfellows sought to do just the opposite. This made the NLRA vulnerable to efforts to weaken it, which employers and industry ultimately did through the Taft-Hartley Act and via the courts, leaving us with a framework that—though progressive for its time—no longer provides workers with the tools they need to meet today's economic and social challenges.

Today's battle to extend the power of collective bargaining beyond the workplace begins in a particularly challenging place because even in the workplace itself, the right to organize and demand a fair share of the rewards for our labor has been steadily under attack. Yet, this is the course correction we must inevitably make to build a healthy, equitable democracy.

THE GREAT ROLLBACK
Capital Fights Back

In the end, the Dixiecrats won. They outlasted Franklin D. Roosevelt, Robert F. Wagner, and other supporters of the New Deal reforms. They steadily chipped away at the gains everyday people had made, rolling back the broad intentions behind the Thirteenth Amendment, which abolished slavery and forced labor; the Fourteenth Amendment, which broadened citizenship; and the Fifteenth Amendment, which expanded the right to vote. In each case, these reforms were scaled back to the most narrow interpretations, making them vulnerable to further erosion in the spirit of protecting the individual wealth of a select few and holding onto the legacy of an economy built on white supremacy and slavery. Despite having lost the Civil War, the Dixiecrats carried the traitorous flag of the Confederacy into the twenty-first century, ultimately leading to the situation we find ourselves in today—a situation marked by extreme inequality between the rich and poor, state-sanctioned police violence against Black lives, the unlawful imprisonment of migrants from Mexico including the separation of children from their parents, and the concentration of power in the hands of those who prioritize the profits of a select few over the needs of the majority, whether in terms of work, health, or the climate. This does not a democracy make.

In the last few decades, antiunion corporations and their political allies have attempted to roll back not just collective bargaining, but also all that the early labor movement leaders accomplished. Their coordinated attacks on labor unions, worker centers, organizing rights, and other principles of labor protection have gutted the very sources of power that once helped to make working people equal, or nearly equal, at the bargaining table.

The deliberate war on labor has been aided and accelerated by a number of economic trends and transformations that have changed the structure of society. Nicholas Lemann, a scholar who has explored the reason behind the decline of the American Dream, investigates the move from an institution-oriented society shaped by managerial capitalism to a transaction-oriented society as a result of shareholder capitalism. As Lemann explains in his book *Transaction Man: Rise of the Deal and the Decline of the American Dream*, the concentration of economic power in the early twentieth century led to intense debate about how best to constrain it, resulting in an institution-based order with a bigger government and corporations as its anchors. Twentieth-century collective bargaining was designed and implemented during the time of managerial capitalism.[1]

But over time, dissatisfaction and disagreements with government and corporations emerged that led to the rising influence of financial markets, resulting in the more transaction-oriented society we live in today. Increased financialization means investors gamble with companies and other economic entities in order to maximize profits with little or no consideration for their impact on wages, safety, healthcare, retirement, or any other social needs. Proponents of financial markets and many corporate boards are obsessed with maximizing shareholder value and see anything that delays "progress," anything that involves negotiation and compromise, as problematic—including labor unions, local governments, legal constraints, and interest groups. Shareholder capitalism has given rise to new instrumentalities such as hedge funds and private equity firms that have upended managerial capitalism and replaced it with a system that is more predatory, greedy, and antiunion.

There are many other economic trends that have led to the decline of collective bargaining and unions. The rise of globalization is one such trend. The ability of global corporations to easily outsource production tasks to countries around the world where workers' rights are few, governmental regulations are scanty, and wages are minuscule puts intense downward pressure on workers in the United States.

Another powerful antilabor trend is the growing prominence of contingent work—work that is subcontracted, temporary, part-time, or otherwise precarious. Today, over one third of the US workforce is contingent—a whopping 42.6 million people.[2] And that does not include the undocumented and those in the cash economy. Contingent workers are often indirectly employed and thus cannot negotiate with their "real boss"—the companies and executives who are setting the terms of their work, dictating standards for their industry, and shaping the laws that regulate how business is done. Some are *mis*classified by employers as independent contractors, which means they fall outside of the legal framework of the NLRA and are therefore denied the right to collectively bargain.

Many contingent workers may have a direct employer in a sector that is so fissured that they face an impenetrable labyrinth when seeking to determine who is responsible for their conditions during negotiations.[3] Nor can contingent workers fully access what is left of the social safety net—most are ineligible for unemployment insurance, for example. And these workers can generally be sourced from anywhere, lacking the stability and security of a local labor market. As a result, bargaining power, wages, and working conditions all spiral down. It is worth noting that the growing power and influence of the finance sector is connected to the fissuring of work, as corporate boards seek to maximize profits for shareholders.

Congress has yet to evolve labor law to deal with this new twenty-first-century workplace.[4] Indeed, the forms of collective bargaining protected by the NLRA do not work well in industries that involve gig work, temp work, subcontracted work, residential construction, entertainment, and other forms of the fissured workplace.[5] When companies have few long-term staff, traditional organizing of the workforce through an election campaign with the goal of getting most workers to support a union rarely works. And in many instances, the project will be over before a representation election can occur.

The transformation of the US workforce from overwhelmingly direct to increasingly contingent comes with two additional shifts: the rise of long-term unemployment and the linking of local and global economies. In combination, these trends pose a major threat to workers' ability to build power and win access to a dignified life.

Meanwhile, organizations that are supposed to represent the rights of workers, including unions, have become less active and effective in defending those rights. While many workers did not give up their power to strike, they did give the government increased authority over decisions previously decided directly between unions and employers. And over time, the NLRA and the NLRB that administers it, has proven susceptible to the political pendulum—often swinging heavily toward the side of business.

As a result, the Right has been able to attack prolabor regulations with increasing success. Formal and informal organizations of industry leaders have found ways to undermine labor protections, both legislatively and through the courts. Simultaneously, corporate leaders invested in a robust union-busting industry to help employers avoid and even destroy unions. And a series of decisions by the NLRB and the courts continued to put working people at an extreme disadvantage, with management typically resisting union organizing and bargaining efforts, often through the undisclosed efforts of union-busting hired guns.[6]

With the odds stacked against them, it's no surprise that fewer and fewer efforts of working people to organize unions today result in a collective bargaining agreement.[7] At times, the NLRA has become largely a tool used by employers against workers seeking fair compensation or challenging employer retaliation. This shift has led to current union rates that are lower than they were in the years *before* the NLRA was first passed.[8] These were years when working people had no formal legal protections, but when they understood and acted on their power to withhold labor to ensure equality in negotiations with employers.

Antilabor Means Antidemocracy

How did this cascading series of changes happen?

It happened because a philosophy that has always had its advocates in the United States—a strain of thinking that has always been influential among our national leaders—has been allowed to achieve an alarming level of dominance in US discourse.

There have always been some who are threatened by democracy and who disagree with the rule of the majority, seeking to limit the majority's participation in decisions at all levels to prevent them from threatening the wealth and private property of the select few who have it. Today, this antidemocratic philosophy is in the ascendancy. And it has its roots deep in US history.

Historian Nancy MacLean is one of many scholars who have explored the intellectual connections between today's radical libertarian Right and the leaders of what would become the Confederate States of America, a treasonous attempt to create an independent nation based firmly on the institution of slavery. For leaders such as John C. Calhoun, the famous antebellum senator and vice president from South Carolina, "liberty" meant the freedom to hold others in bondage and to exploit their labor without payment, while those who sought to impose a measure of democratic control on such oppressive behaviors were threats to that liberty. As MacLean notes, this strange definition of liberty meant that "a man whose wealth came from slavery was a victim of the government tax collectors, [and] poorer voters were the exploiters to watch out for."[9] This twisted ideology was the foundation of Calhoun's attempts to crush democracy's threat to economic liberty.

Calhoun and other Southern slaveholders like him had good reason to fear democracy. While spending time in his native Charleston where he directly enslaved many Black people, Calhoun and other white people—slave-owning or not—were outnumbered by a Black majority that would endure from 1820 until 1910.[10] If these enslaved people had been free to represent their interests against those of the white minority, the economic system of slavery that built the wealth of Calhoun and countless other would be at risk. As Nancy MacLean goes on to note, Calhoun and others recognized "the cold reality that they were practicing a type of capitalism that would not pass democratic scrutiny much longer if majority opinion was allowed to prevail in Washington."[11]

Calhoun was not alone in his fears. Antimajoritarian bias is written into Article V of the US Constitution, granting equal suffrage to states not people. In other words, each (nonhuman) geographic region defined as a state has a vote, but not each individual (human) within it. As Harold Meyerson cleverly articulates, "This is about Boise versus Los Angeles. It's not about 100,000 Americans outvoting ten million."[12]

Today, of course, the system of chattel slavery that Calhoun and other Southern white landowners depended upon no longer exists. In its place is a modern capitalist economy that is no less exploitative—particularly for Black and Brown workers employed disproportionately in low-wage sectors. Many people got a wake-up call when these workers, previously ignored or humiliated, were deemed *essential* workers during the COVID-19 pandemic and forced to work in dangerous conditions, sometimes without proper protective equipment or other safety measures. Yet this kind of treatment is not surprising considering that enslaved Black workers were also *essential* to building capitalism in the United States. Because the capitalist system continues to benefit the wealthy few at the expense of the struggling many, those who today identify with and defend the interests of the powerful share the same antidemocratic bias that Calhoun and his slave-holding contemporaries embraced.

Advocating a frankly antidemocratic philosophy would be difficult today. Therefore, today's anti-democracy champions rely on a variety of obfuscating tactics. One of the most popular is to confuse the population by equating the health of the capitalist economic system with the health of democracy. This logical sleight of hand is quietly employed not just by politicians and pundits but also by many in the mainstream media. As a result, millions of ordinary people are fooled into thinking that if Wall Street is doing well, we must all be doing better. However, as economist Thomas Piketty showed in his book *Capital in the Twenty-First Century*, a fundamental tension between capitalism and democracy is inherent to our economic system.[13]

Another way to justify the antidemocratic nature of our capitalist system is to ally it to religion. An array of popular religious institutions, particularly among Protestant evangelical denominations, preach some form of the so-called prosperity gospel, which presumes that wealth and success are God's reward to the faithful.[14] The natural corollary is that people who are poor or struggling are not victims of an unfair system but are simply undeserving of success, either because of their moral failings or because they simply aren't smart enough. In the same vein, a lifelong wage earner who has never risen to the level of a capitalist exploiter is in that position due to his or her own failures.[15] Under the circumstances, it is natural to want to turn over the reins of government to billionaires, whose wealth clearly demonstrates their personal superiority to the rest of us.

Yet another tool used by elements of today's Right to undermine the rights of working people without explicitly acknowledging their antidemocratic goals is the use of racist, patriarchal, and xenophobic rhetoric to divide the opposition. This is perhaps the most obvious way that the modern conservative movement draws inspiration from the white proslavery leaders of the old South. As seen throughout history, the operators of global capital, who have representatives in both US political parties, use the system of white supremacy and structural racism to keep working people disorganized and isolated from each other so that they do not disrupt the ability of the capitalists to continue to concentrate resources among a tiny select few—often characterizing white workers as the productive "makers" in society and everyone else, particularly Black and migrant workers, as the "takers."

Building on this legacy today, corporations and their union-busting consultants have actively used the tropes and emotions associated with white supremacy to discourage working people from joining forces across racial and ethnic lines. They paint the union not only as an outside or alien force but as an institution that could only benefit workers of color. Such strategies led to union defeats in 2017 at Boeing in South Carolina, where workers attempted to organize with the International Association of Machinists and Aerospace Workers (IAM), and at Nissan in Mississippi, where workers sought recognition with the UAW.

Unions aren't the only democratic organizations that have been targeted by the Right. Students are another popular target. For example, many of the same groups aggressively fought student fee autonomy—the ability of students on campus to have democratic control over how their student fees are spent—in an effort to break up democratic organizations in colleges around the country. Similar antidemocracy forces are behind the hyperregulation of nonprofit organizations.[16] For instance, in a report commissioned by the US Chamber of Commerce, Jobs With Justice (JWJ) and a handful of nonprofit worker centers were targeted as organizations that should be categorized as unions despite the fact that they do not represent workers in relationship to their employers.[17] The Chamber's goal was to bog the organizations down in the time-consuming administrative work forced upon unions in order to make it more difficult for JWJ to advance its core campaigns and program work.

In these and similar attacks, the Right has targeted poor people, communities of color, and the organizations that work with them using so-called dog whistles to divide voters from each other and demonize those the Right seeks to limit.[18]

In addition, antidemocracy forces have worked to undermine political democracy through direct efforts to twist the results of elections. The amount of money that corporations can spend to influence elections has skyrocketed in the last half century. The trend began long before the *Citizens United* court case, which consolidated right-wing gains by giving legal free-speech rights previously reserved for humans to corporations.[19] And when throwing money at like-minded candidates has not worked, the radical Right has sought to limit the number of people who can vote through false claims of voter fraud.[20] These claims are used to justify policies that make it more difficult to vote, such as voter ID laws, and that blatantly exclude some individuals from voting altogether, including people who were once incarcerated but have since re-entered society. In all these ways, the Right has contributed to the United States having one of the lowest voter participation rates in the developed world.[21]

Riding this wave, people like former Wisconsin governor Scott Walker and the Koch brothers would have us believe collective bargaining is in its final death throes. Walker himself certainly did his part to kill it. His success in introducing policies to strip bargaining rights from public-sector workers in Wisconsin led many other midwestern states to adopt policies making it a lot harder for working people to form unions.

The Right does not deserve all the credit (or blame) for the current field of play. Some would argue that the NLRA committed the structural error of letting government off the hook by giving unions and employers responsibilities that should have been held by federal agencies. Labor historian Lane Windham, for example, observes that "in depending on unions to do the negotiating for a social wage, the U.S. had inadvertently given employers in the U.S. a higher incentive than employers in other nations to fight union organizing."[22] European labor strategists chose a different path. They seized the period following World War II to demand, and win, stronger government protections for workers and improved social programs. This left European unions free to expand the scope of bargaining to address workers' role in business and production decisions as well as directly manage the labor market.[23] Similar approaches persist throughout Asia, Africa, and Latin America. Could such an effort have succeeded in the postwar United States? We may never know—but it might have been worth a try.

The progressive movement in the United States also bears a share of the responsibility for our current dilemma. Until recently, the US Left has not been consistent in maintaining pressure on the government for a social safety net that includes many of the issues unions bargain over—health care, retirement, sick time, paid leave, and other benefits. Most unions have certainly fought hard at the bargaining table for these things—creating a significant economic benefit to being a union member, the *union value*. But this has also created a significant divide between union workers and nonunion workers who have been left to fend for themselves.

Meanwhile, union density in the United States has hit rock bottom.[24] As a result, the best unions can do is to win decent benefits for a small section of the working class—namely, their members. It's a dynamic that pits the interests of organized union workers against those of the unorganized majority. Unintentionally, unions have thus played into the same divide-and-conquer strategy that underlies the Right's appeals to racism, patriarchy, and xenophobia.

This, then, is the current state of play in the long-term battle for collective bargaining and economic democracy—not just in the workplace but in every area of our lives. The picture is a troubling one. The important question now is, how do we intervene to push back against the existing system that isn't working for most of us and lay the foundation for a truly equitable democracy? We'll begin to answer that question in the next part of this book.

Part 2

THE BUILDING BLOCKS OF ECONOMIC DEMOCRACY

A nation of passive observers watching others make decisions is a nation that will succumb to anger and resentment—witness the United States.

—Yoni Applebaum, "Losing the Democratic Habit," *Atlantic*, October 2018

Erica Smiley. Portrait by Gwenn Seemel.

PROFILE OF THE AUTHOR
Erica Smiley: In Exactly the Right Place

I used to feel like an imposter in the labor movement, coming from North Carolina and not knowing what a union was until I was in college. This is all strange when you consider that I was only sixteen when I was a part of my first labor struggle. I just had no idea that's what it was. When Black K-Mart workers in Greensboro, North Carolina, asked for help in 1996 to combat what they felt was racial discrimination, I was simply a youth in one of the churches that answered the call. As St. James Presbyterian joined others in boycotting, I watched as our congregation collectively escalated toward more collective direction action—including civil disobedience at a local golf course. And ultimately I saw 550 K-Mart Distribution Center workers negotiate with the company and win.[1]

I didn't know workers were trying to form a union, or that they sought to negotiate with the company in an ongoing way to address issues beyond these immediate concerns. And yet that is exactly what they were doing—in one of the states with the lowest union membership rates in the country. So nearly ten years later when a colleague asked me why I was going to work for a local of the SEIU in Baltimore, it felt like a no-brainer to reply that, after a few years at a reproductive justice organization, I was *returning* to the labor movement. But she didn't see it that way. Her reaction was skeptical, and she wanted to know what experience I'd previously had with the labor movement. Who else had I *worked* for?

Of course, up until that point I had not worked directly as staff for any union. Certainly I had organized in various communities. I had supported taxi drivers in Northern Virginia after the crises following the September 11, 2001, World Trade Center and Pentagon attacks with an organization known at the time as the Tenants and Workers Support Committee. I'd fought for a living wage and other local changes as a part of another community organization in suburban Maryland. I'd supported the Washington Teachers Union and a plethora of parent and student organizations to improve health education curricula, support home childcare providers in Alexandria, and support building service workers in Chapel Hill while in school. But I had never, until that moment, worked directly for a union.

So, to her, I was not in fact returning to the labor movement but merely entering it for the first time. The leadership of the union local (mostly white at the time) agreed, and the translation was that I should, naturally, start with the basics—implementing a strategy that other staff organizers came up with to mechanically engage workers (mostly Black women) providing home-based care for children in Baltimore—often in homes where their row house was the only occupied residence on a street of hundreds of abandoned homes, women I could have known my entire life. I enjoyed the work, but at some point, once the higher ups felt we had a critical mass of workers organized, I had to hand it off to smarter people. And I didn't like that.

Even though my lead organizers recognized what I brought to the table and were actually quite supportive, this one conversation and the experience I had in Baltimore really set me back. What was I doing here, acting like I knew how to talk to people? I had never been a paid organizer. I was an imposter in the labor movement.

It took over a decade to recover. And in the process, I was transformed.

I realized how so many people have had similar experiences, this subtle experience of being an outcast. For example, as a child, despite my understanding that I was obviously Black, I was questioned by other kids of all races about what race I was and why did I "talk like that"? I never seemed to fit into one group. I was always a bit of an "other." And yet I directly experienced the racism of being Black. In the summer between second and third grade, I was tracked into a remedial summer school program for kids who had been held back—mostly Black—as opposed to the summer enrichment program I was actually supposed to be in that was far more diverse and included white students. I'd been profiled and tracked. And I learned that the only thing that could stop it was direct action, in this case my mom being late to work to come directly to the school and confront the administration.

Likewise, despite always knowing that I was a girl, many found it confusing that I had a deep voice, was good at sports (I was devastated when I learned I could not be in the peewee football league), and hung out with a bunch of guys. My parents did not expect their youngest child and only girl to act like this. I still think my mom thought that since she was a beauty queen—literally the first

Black woman to compete in the Miss Suffolk Virginia pageant in the 1970s—that I would somehow follow suit. The reality could not have been further from the truth. And she and my dad had to adapt. I could only be who I was.

Others were less flexible. One kid in particular, Nick, he really didn't like how much I thought of myself, and he showed me by punching me dead in the eye on the playground. I beat him up pretty bad after that. But I was horrified to face the wrath of my mom when she came to pick me up. But she did something strange. She walked over to Nick and gave *him* a talking-to. And later at home, she spent an hour lecturing me on how never to let anyone hit me. "If you have to fight, you have to fight. But don't let anyone run over you," she said. Well, shocked does not begin to convey how I felt about all of this. I was proud but still a little scared. I was also a little relieved. I felt like Ralphie in *A Christmas Story* when his mom downplayed the fight he had been in with Scott Farkus to his dad when he and his brother Randy both knew he was a goner. I was going to live! And yet I began to understand this new weight on my shoulders. What did it mean to fight? I was nine.

I was an "other" when I grew up and eventually moved to DC and later to New York. There I experienced some who would talk about Black people in the South who stayed and didn't migrate to Chicago, New York, and the big cities as if they were dumb, backward-thinking negroes. Of course, I was a walking example of how wrong they were. I'm from a family of individuals that were born, bred, and died in the South and had a lot of success. I remember years before when leaving my grandmother's funeral with my mom, she reminded me that sometimes the people who need your help the most are those you've left behind. You see, my mom is from a farming family in Suffolk, Virginia. And like my dad who had grown up in Mississippi and now worked as a professor, my mom was the one who *made it*. My parents were successful. They *made it*. And at the time of this conversation, I'd left North Carolina to be a hotshot organizer, and I was *making it*.

I witnessed this "othering" of people who have not had the opportunity to be a part of the elite club of US union members, let alone work for one, or any other organization that seeks to position directly impacted people in ongoing decision-making about their work or community lives. This is one of the many mentalities and cultural behaviors that is keeping the ranks of organized labor so small.

At some point I guess I'd finally had enough. I decided I was just going to do it my way, whatever that looked like. I was going to make my own path. I was going to own my self-determination, the ability to set my own vision and dreams and access a pathway to meet or not meet them, individually and collectively, and not let anyone define me. I didn't want to be limited. I wanted to dedicate my life and my organizing to not just one aspect of my identity but to anything that was going to help me build a better life for my family and my community. I knew that path would take me far beyond any one identity.

Self-determination is what we're trying to strive for through democracy. Everyone has to be able to show up as who they are, and to weigh in. Voting is one version of that. But real deliberation is also important, whether it's the governing body of your church, the labor-management committee at your worksite, the local city council, or even the governing body running the local library. We should all be in active deliberation for what we want to see happen in the world. And that can only happen, really happen, through democratic practices.

Identity is useful insofar as it brings us together around our shared values and helps us understand each other. But it is not useful when it siloes us off from each other. That's not to say we don't sometimes need safe spaces to reflect on ourselves and the way forward. But that cannot be the entire strategy.

Nearly all working people have experienced exploitation at the hands of capital—whether from their employer, landlord, financier, or some other predatory agency. And millions of them have joined with others in attempts to do something about it—such as school service workers like Rubynell Walker-Barbie in Georgia, who won $8 million in back wages from the state in 2013; the victory of immigrant recycling workers at Tito's contractors in Maryland who ultimately won their union election with the International Union of Painters and Allied Trades District Council 51 in 2013; or the victory of Allyson, Heather, Jacob, Amie, and other West Virginia educators at their state legislature.[2] Are the women and men who led these struggles not twenty-first-century labor leaders?

Our generation will not strengthen the twenty-first-century labor movement by solely acknowledging the needs of those who still have access to twentieth-century mechanisms of collective bargaining, those defined as union members by the US Bureau of Labor Statistics. These individuals are included. However, the twenty-first-century labor movement is and will continue to be made up of all of the individuals in active struggle for their dignity against the 0.01 percent of the population who would tread on it just to make an extra dollar. The twenty-first-century labor movement is made up of people who do not have access to the protections of the previous century and who are not simply fighting for access but hoping to expand on what was won in the last one hundred years and evolve it to the current moment.

Now sitting at this pivotal moment in the history of US labor, I have never been clearer that I am exactly where I am supposed to be. I found my people at Jobs With Justice among millions of others who seek a new foundation on which to build their futures. We, of the race of people whose forced labor built the foundations of capitalism and the modern economy. We, of the people who ran one of the first US industrial labor organizing demands—for the abolition of chattel slavery. We, of the people who organized sharecroppers' unions in the most dangerous of conditions. We, the washerwomen who threatened to shut down the city to secure a better life for our families. We, who know what it means to organize in the harshest conditions and win. We are not simply the ones we have been waiting for. The stories and efforts of heroic leaders and communities in this book demonstrate that we in fact are the ones who have been waiting for everyone else to catch up.

Regardless of where the groups in this book started, they all did just that—they started. And together they are building a path for themselves, asserting that "we can build a more democratic and economically just society of the twenty-first century." And embodying that mantra, Sarita and I took a leap in writing some of it down.

WORTH FIGHTING FOR

Collective Bargaining in the Workplace

The labor movement is not dead. In fact, unions and other organizations of working people are actively evolving to meet the needs of the modern worker and the environment she operates in.

In this chapter we will focus on some of the battlefields of this fight. If we hope to improve our chances of expanding collective bargaining beyond the workplace, we need to do a better job of protecting our home turf—the workplace itself.

While we have seen how some specific failures by organized labor have made unions and the people they represent vulnerable to new kinds of attacks by entrenched power, we have also seen a renewed willingness by workers to make use of their most powerful defensive tools, including walk-outs, wildcat strikes, and other direct actions.

There were more workers on strike in 2018 than in any previous year since the mid-1980s.[1] In addition to educators, who made up the majority of these strikers, 1,400 employees of Frontier Communications in West Virginia went on strike with CWA, followed in June by AT&T employees throughout the Midwest.[2] Later, UNITE HERE's hotel workers were also fed up enough to take action. In Chicago, six thousand hotel workers at twenty-six area hotels walked out to demand year-round health coverage, while over 7,700 workers struck against Marriott Hotels in eight cities.[3] November saw fifteen thousand healthcare employees walk out on the University of California Medical Centers throughout the state in a three-day work-stoppage, not to mention the twenty thousand Google employees who walked out over sexual harassment.[4]

In the early part of 2019, over thirty-one thousand grocery workers at Stop & Shop stores throughout New England walked off the job to protest the company's proposed cuts to health care, take-home pay, and other benefits. Supported by many community residents, these striking workers managed to win an agreement that preserved healthcare and retirement benefits, provided wage increases, and maintained time-and-a-half pay on Sundays.

This trend toward increased labor activism is likely to continue. The COVID-19 pandemic in 2020 only exposed existing repression, angering more workers to take action in defense of their livelihoods and their lives. And in 2021, over five million workers were in contract negotiations.[5] This led to the historic moment known as *Striketober* in October 2021.

The business executives who seek to maximize profits with little or no consideration for human and community needs understand that when working people organize, take collective action, and attempt to vote or negotiate together, it represents a direct threat to their goals—which is why they are determined to do whatever it takes to stop it—including making us believe we are obsolete.

Andrew Puzder, fast-food-chain executive and Donald Trump's one-time pick for US secretary of labor, went so far as to suggest getting rid of workers altogether after workers in the industry began organizing for and winning minimum-wage increases. When discussing the issue with *Business Insider*, he spoke about how he longed to replace humans with machines, noting that "they're always polite, they always upsell, they never take a vacation, they never show up late, there's never a slip-and-fall, or an age, sex, or race discrimination case."[6]

In the past fifty years, corporate leaders like Puzder have reorganized their companies to more efficiently exploit the human labor and natural resources of the Earth in devastating ways. National industries have given way to multinational production chains, just-in-time manufacturing and compulsive labor migration patterns that maintain the companies' mobility and nimbleness. Employees have been reclassified as independent contractors and entrepreneurs to minimize the responsibilities of large corporations who control their workday.

In the public sector, as noted in chapter 1, collective bargaining rights are inconsistent. Federal law offers many federal employees the right to engage in collective bargaining over a limited set of issues, and state laws determine whether state and local government employees can engage in collective bargaining. As of 2014, three states—North Carolina, South Carolina, and Virginia—expressly prohibit collective bargaining for all public-sector employees.[7] But again, Virginia allowed municipalities to loosen restrictions in 2021.[8] Collective bargaining rights were further undermined in January 2018, when the US Supreme Court overturned the ability of public sector unions to collect agency fees from all the public employees that benefit from the work of the union.[9]

During the COVID-19 crisis, public sector unions were additionally threatened by the promise of massive layoffs and furloughs at the state and municipal levels of government. And yet public sector unions continued to organize, perhaps more energetically than before.

While we will share new strategies for organizing and collective bargaining beyond the workplace in later chapters, it's urgent that we simultaneously defend our ability to collectively bargain in the workplace. In truth, many of the strategies to expand bargaining that we highlight will not work unless we secure this first.

Rubynell Walker-Barbee. Portrait by Gwenn Seemel.

Profile of a Modern Worker:
Rubynell Walker-Barbee: "Make Them Do It"

Rubynell Walker-Barbee is one of the many Black women who was personally impacted when unemployment benefits were suddenly denied to school workers in Georgia. Hailing from union-dense Detroit, she was shocked to find how little her Atlanta food-service coworkers understood about unions. Her story illustrates the difficulty of organizing and ultimately establishing a union workplace.

It was like a tornado had hit us. Here we all were, ready to end the school session thinking that, if nothing else, we were going to get unemployment while we waited to be rehired in the next semester. It was never all that much, just enough to help some of the women keep their lights on until they were called back. But come to find out, Mark Butler, the head of the Georgia Department of Labor at the time, decided we weren't going to get unemployment benefits anymore. We had no choice but to do something. And we had to do it together.

I grew up in Kalamazoo, Michigan, with ten sisters and five brothers. I was smack in the middle. My parents migrated there from Mississippi, a town called Okolona near Tupelo. We were a close family. My mom stayed at home, and my dad worked at restaurants and swept houses. He did the best he could. He was sick a lot because he had been shot before. He'd come up hard. His mother died when they were all babies, and there were eleven of them. His sister, who was thirteen at the time, took on raising them. I don't know how she did it. And I really don't know how my parents did it either, raising all of us. I would never have known it if we were struggling though. We always had nice clothes. We always had food. My mother would always say, "God will provide." And that's the way we lived.

I started working when I was twelve. I had a full-time babysitting job watching my younger cousins. I would leave school by four o'clock and keep the kids until midnight, three little girls. To this day, I don't know how well it paid because back then the money went to my parents. My cousin's parents didn't pay me directly. All income was shared. It went to my parents. It wasn't my money. By the time I was sixteen, I had a job as a receptionist at city hall. And from there I went on to become a payroll clerk for the school system. I did that from ninth to twelfth grade when I finished school. That's just how it was. We all worked, come to think of it. And we all contributed. Maybe that's how we survived. We took care of each other.

Anyway, after I finished school, I wanted to travel and see what the world had to offer. I've lived in Nevada, California, Indiana, all over. I've always felt that before I let a city bury me, I'd rather move on to somewhere else. I eventually moved back to Michigan to take care of my mother when she had heart failure. I was there for nearly thirteen years caring for her. She passed away in 2005. And by February 2006, I'd moved here to Atlanta.

I had a sister in Atlanta, so I thought I'd try it out next. A friend of mine was in the military, and I took on watching her sons who were eleven and maybe thirteen. There were actually supposed to be three of them, but one of the boys was killed just before I got there. I guess you could say they were troubled kids. They probably just needed a little counseling or something. When I was with them, it was one of the first times I started thinking about the phrase "no child left behind" because they had so clearly been left behind. When they got in trouble at school, they were disciplined and eventually sent to an alternative school. No one thought to work with them or help them. I was always getting called into the school because one of them was being punished. I would talk to the principal, but I couldn't get any help. And I didn't want to stress their mother out because she was off in Iraq with the military. The youngest boy, he's in prison now. And like I said, he's been left behind.

I guess I've seen a lot of children left behind if I really think on it. I had a nephew that was shot. He was twenty-two. And another nephew was diabetic. He couldn't get the help he needed and kind of let himself go. He was also young. I had one nephew who was a notorious homebody. Once, he was at home waiting on his mother to finish cooking Sunday dinner. They say some of his friends came and got him because someone was fighting, but it was he who lost his life that day. So many Black boys gone too soon. So many children left behind.

I just don't think our system is set up correctly. People are going through all kinds of things. Some people are able to get out of it. Some people aren't. Growing up, I knew we were poor and that I had to work to get what we needed. But I had people in my life who were able to help me get to those goals. Some people need a little bit more attention. Some tragedies keep a person wrapped up in the trauma. That guy begging under the bridge, you don't know what he's been through. Some people need help to get out. It takes a village. And our system isn't always designed to help them survive the trauma they've had.

Still, as always, I keep it moving. I started working in food service at Morehouse College after I retired. I like working, and I like to keep busy. I became a manager at the Chick-fil-A on campus. I enjoyed the work. I was close to a lot of the students who came through, my grandson being one of them. He graduated with a 3.8 grade point average and recently got married. I'm so proud of my grandchildren.

However, that is not all I saw while working there. I worked hard. But when it came time to reward me with a raise, they offered me two cents. What in the world did they think I was going to do with just two more pennies? They brought me into the office, sat me down, and told me, "You've been here for three years. You've been doing a great job. We really appreciate you. We're going to give you a raise of $0.02." That's no reward.

Then I started asking around and realized that some people I worked with weren't even making the minimum wage. They were working the grill in these hot conditions, and they weren't getting paid fairly. And when you got things straight with one general manager, you got a new one. The company was always changing general managers. I think I had three general managers over the course of a year at one point. I started getting more involved with my coworkers after that.

Now, remember, I come from Michigan. There was always a union you could join. I've been a member of several unions over the course of my working life. So, despite the different rules in Georgia, I started organizing. We organized with the SEIU and won a collective bargaining agreement with our employer that laid out policies in a clear fashion, including how and when to apply wage increases. We all had copies of the contract and kept the little booklets in our pockets in case the next general manager was confused. Our workplace now had rules, and together we could enforce them.

It didn't solve everything, though. For example, unemployment was a part of the job. At the end of the school year, our managers would give us our layoff note and our unemployment number at the same time. It's not like we had the option of getting paid over twelve months instead of nine like some teachers do. And to be frank, unemployment doesn't exactly *pay*. It just keeps you from going under. But this came with the job. It was the business model—hang out for a couple months with no pay, then come back. That's what we were told to expect.

That's why we were so shocked when it was taken away. It broke my heart to hear some of the stories. I was lucky. I had retirement and savings, and I was not responsible for feeding anyone but me. But some of the women there were caring for children all by themselves. It was a disaster, almost like a tornado had hit. People were losing their homes, their vehicles, their ability to put food on the table and pay for their prescriptions. We paid unemployment insurance, but we can't access the benefits? Yet again the system showed its cracks and tried to leave us behind.

And it wasn't just us at Morehouse. Food service workers throughout the state were struggling—union and nonunion. We knew the only way to fix it was to come together. We started to meet around the city and in the West End. Churches would take offerings for the women struggling the most, and we would have dinner at the meetings so everyone could eat. We started to organize ourselves to confront legislators and different agency representatives at the state level. We held a rally outside our worksites. We even went directly to Mark Butler's house and saw how he and his family were enjoying their time comfortably while our families suffered.

I guess we hit someone's nerve because the governor overturned Butler's decision. School workers got $8 million back in unemployment benefits. It felt like we'd gotten backpay after our wages had been stolen. It was a huge victory!

But again, it did not fix the whole problem. The trauma you experience doesn't simply end after the trauma is over. It takes a lot more than that to keep all of us from being left behind. When a tornado hits, you might lose your home, your pictures, all of the things that have made you who you are. And now that's gone. For many women, after the tornado of losing unemployment, that was all gone. They're still traumatized. They still need help.

And the business model is still the same. Annual unemployment comes with your annual layoff notice. That's why our union is so important. We need these jobs to be good, family-sustaining jobs. None of us can do this by ourselves. We might get on each other's nerves sometimes, just like any family might, but we have to stick together. Only together can we hold our employers accountable to the rules and policies to which we all agreed. It's so few wealthy employers, and so many of us who work. They're not just going to volunteer to pay us more money out of the goodness of their heart. We have to make them do it. If the manager calls one of us in, we can ask someone to go with us to ensure everything is done by the booklet. We can negotiate more hours before they hire people on a temporary basis. And if our unemployment is taken away, you better believe we'll be ready to fight for it.

Rubynell's story shows how much goes into organizing a union in a workplace. Service workers had to overcome their fears while living through a real-life economic nightmare. But they persisted. And it was worth the fight.

BEYOND *WORKERS*
Organizing Whole People

Organizing people *as workers* is not enough. As the strategies deployed by capital change, the specific mechanisms working people access must also change to apply to all the ways in which humans relate to capital.

Economic democracy in the twenty-first century cannot be achieved solely within a framework focused exclusively on worksites. Rather we must explore a more expansive definition of collective bargaining that adapts to the context of global capitalism and all its features, including addressing the material and cultural needs of the modern worker—who, shockingly, does not solely identify as a worker but sees themselves as having a diverse array of identities. The understanding of workers as whole people must fundamentally shift our strategies and how we think about what collective bargaining can entail. This inevitably changes the very nature of what a union contract covers, broadening what individuals can negotiate over and who they can negotiate with—from their direct "boss" to the individuals with concentrated power in their sector or community.

The fact is that everyone needs to negotiate with capital every day, whether they are at work or not. Working people have a stake in decisions made not only at their worksite but also in the economy overall. Those who oppose worker empowerment are clearly aware of this. What happens to workers on the job is intimately connected to what happens in their communities, in their schools, and in their lived environments. It is also intimately connected to their gender, race, ethnicity, ability, and citizenship status. The same forces that are weakening worker bargaining power and making work more precarious are also undermining public institutions like schools and mass transit, profiting from rising household debt, and shaping policies that are contributing to climate change and environmental injustice.

Improving workers' lives on the job cannot be separated from improving their lives when off work.[1] They have a stake in their ability to come together collectively not only as employees but also in the myriad other ways working people play a role in the economy—such as account holders in banking and finance, consumers, renters, and debtors. As a natural consequence, some of the most successful worker organizing in recent years has in fact occurred at the intersection of several identities, not just within the single identity of worker or employee.[2]

The notion of "intersecting identities" invokes the term *intersectionality*. Coined by Black feminist scholar Kimberlé Williams Crenshaw in 1989, this term may seem like a vague piece of jargon with little direct connection to the lives and struggles of working people. In reality, intersectionality is a straightforward description of the complex challenges real-life people are facing every day.

To understand what *intersectionality* means in practice, let us consider the following "Profile of a Modern Worker." It is the story of Kimberly Mitchell, whose life exemplifies the way ordinary workers are buffeted by powerful capital-driven forces not just in the workplace but also beyond—as well as the ways in which they are fighting back.

Kimberly Mitchell. Portrait by Gwenn Seemel.

Profile of a Modern Worker:
Kimberly Mitchell: More Than Just
a Worker

Kimberly Mitchell is a union organizer and labor rights activist who is acutely aware of the intimate connections between her identity as a worker and the struggles she faces in every other aspect of her economic life—as a single parent, a consumer, a homeowner, a small-business owner, and more. Starting out as a retail clerk in Washington, DC, in the 1980s as a Black woman, her story is one of millions that illustrates why progressive organizing today must address the whole person, not just the slice that we bring to the workplace.

I've always been self-sufficient and ambitious. I've always wanted more for myself.

I grew up in Washington, DC. I have many fond memories of my family, especially in the 1970s. In her best days, my mom was a club owner and successful entrepreneur, and my dad worked in Mayor Marion Barry's administration running the DC Mayor's Command Station. He was loved by his team and respected in the community. Because of these recollections, I often have thought that I got my social consciousness and entrepreneurial spirit from them.

These good times didn't last, though. In the 1980s, DC became toxic with drugs, overrun by crime, and was the murder capital of the country. My mom had a nervous breakdown, and my family thought I'd be better off with Dad. But my dad suffered with his addictions. In watching them both, I learned a lot about life—including some examples of what not to do. Mostly I was determined not to make the same mistakes. When life became too much, I moved in with my grandmother. At a young age, I believed that God had a calling for me.

I always had a part-time job, and I made sure that whatever I needed I got. That is how I got into retail. I worked at Bradley's my last year in high school. As a student at H. D. Woodson High School, I called out policies and procedures that were not right for the student body. As a result, I was elected student-body president. The principal pulled me aside and told me that my peers must really respect me to have elected me. I didn't really understand what he was saying at the time. But it always stuck with me.

All my peers were graduating and getting jobs with the federal government then. But no matter how hard I tried, I couldn't get one of those jobs. So I stuck with retail. I didn't want to live in my grandmother's house anymore after my dad moved in. I wanted something different. But to move I needed a real job. Upon applying for a manager position, I was hired as the assistant manager at a shoe store. I bought a car with the income and convinced two of my girlfriends to move in with me. We got a nice townhouse in Maryland.

Those were great times. We struggled but we learned so much about life. I was nineteen and working six days a week. We all worked, but within two years, my friends' lives took another path, and they soon moved out. I guess you could say work saved me, or maybe it was my determination to take care of myself. Working kept me out of trouble, and my girlfriends and my coworkers had essentially become my family.

My grandmother helped to lay down a foundation for me. She taught me the value of being a homeowner. She also taught me how to take care of myself because nobody else was going to do it. Before my marriage, I bought a house across the street from her to be near her because I wanted to take care of her like she'd taken care of me.

For a long time, I didn't want children. I'd been taken away from my mom when I was nine and ended up at my grandmother's house, and I'd seen other women in my family not really take care of their kids. So I guess I just assumed I wouldn't be a good mother. But I eventually did get married, and I decided to have a child.

Up until this point, I felt like I'd done everything right. I'd gone to school. I had a good job. I had a family. I was living the dream. But there were cracks.

I remember trying to help my daughter get into a good private school. I had a little money, and I wanted to help her be more successful than I had been. My mom was like, "Does she deserve all that?" I didn't understand why she would say such a thing. That hurt. But my answer was, "Yes, we all do."

I also wanted to go back to school myself. But for some strange reason, I did not get the support from my husband. I didn't understand why he didn't want me to better myself. I wanted to start my own business, and I hoped he and I could start it together, but that did not happen.

After a while, I could not wait any longer. I realized that no one else could see my vision. What God has in mind for me is only for me. I woke up one day in bad health and realized that my husband and I were living a lie. I had to think of myself and my daughter. So I got a divorce.

We'd been living in a house in a neighborhood that was quickly gentrifying. I made a lot of money when I sold it after the divorce. What's strange, though, is that even though I'd lived in that area for a while, it didn't feel like my neighborhood. While I was walking my dog, I would look around and realize that all of the people around me were now white. They made me feel like I didn't deserve to be there anymore and that they had saved my neighborhood.

A few years later, my grandmother was diagnosed with throat cancer. Doctors told me there was nothing they could do and that I should take her home and make her feel comfortable. I took on caregiving responsibilities for her while still working my full-time job as a store manager. I didn't realize how hard it would be. I wish I had been able to spend more time with her and take better care of her. She passed within a year of her diagnosis.

I worked as the caretaker of an older European woman. She hated it when people asked her where she was from. I never understood why, until she finally told me it was because people never asked where I was from. I told her it was because I was Black—they just assumed I was from the United States. I had never thought about it.

Someone later asked me if I preferred to be called Black or African American. I had never thought about that either. It all made me think. My daughter's complexion is much lighter than mine. And sometimes people would walk up to her, right in front of me, and ask her where her mother was. And I would be like, "I'm right here!"

I thought about taking one of those home DNA tests. But I do not need a DNA test to tell me who I am. I can hear my ancestors. I know I am a strong Black woman, and I stand on my ancestors' shoulders.

At the time of my divorce, I was in school to be a skin therapist. My ex-husband sued me for my business, property, and money. I had to stop my business. It is hard being a single mom and a business owner. I had to leave school and go back to work for someone else because I needed a steadier income.

That's how I ended up at Macy's. I had gone to social services to get help while taking care of my daughter. They wanted to make sure I was looking for work. So I did. I found the job listing in the *Washington Post*. I went in for a make-up artist position. Even though I was qualified, I didn't want to be a manager. I wanted to have a peaceful life. I was still taking care of my daughter. But they pushed me to do it because they had a new counter open. Truthfully, this was ultimately good because that's how I got my higher salary, and my hours were good. But when I got the job, social services said I could no longer get food stamps because I made too much—about $15 an hour. So, I was essentially still working as a freelancer and a full-time manager in retail but getting less support for both.

Macy's was my first union job. I didn't really understand what the union did at that time.

Meanwhile my mom got sick with cancer. I was trying to figure out who I was, and I began to ask questions about my life. I asked my mom why she never came for me after I was taken away. I asked her about her life. I learned that she'd been a sickly child and had been in and out of hospitals. Later she'd owned several companies. I realized I'd gotten my entrepreneurial spirit from her and not my dad as I'd originally thought. We kind of reconciled as adults. But because my mom was sick, there was talk of moving her from her house to a nursing home. I had to tell her this during my lunch break. I hated the thought of it. Pop went to visit her in the hospital after I told her about the nursing home, and she died that night. That was the last time I'd spoken to her.

I had peace, though. My mom hated hospitals, and I knew she didn't want to leave home. She must have made an agreement with God that she wasn't going to live in a nursing home. And that's what gave me peace. Her death was a blessing because, even though DC had passed a law requiring paid family leave, I still couldn't figure out how to take more time off. There was no way I was going to be able to take care of her, as much as I wanted to.

I have owned a few homes in my life. While living in the home that I raised my child in, I almost got caught up in the housing bubble. I came across the Neighborhood Assistance Corporation of America (NACA). NACA was the first time I had seen anybody organize to help people.

I decided to refinance my mortgage. When I went to the bank, the loan officer was like, "Your credit is all right." And I was like, "Just all right?" For it to be over 760 for a single Black mom working retail, I felt like he was really disrespecting me. But I went with it because I assumed the best.

Later, when talking to a broker, I discovered that the bank hadn't given me a good rate. I'd been redlined. Not only that, they had also made me spend money that I didn't have on home improvements.

On top of that, I'd had flood insurance through a federal program. It cost around $560 per year. Chase Bank said I didn't need it, so they canceled it. When I refinanced, I was trying to get out from under Chase Bank, given their involvement in the housing bubble and their predatory practices. But then my new mortgage was bought out by, guess who? Chase Bank. And I found out I really did need flood insurance, but I was no longer able to get back into the federal program. So I had to pay more, a whopping $1,200 per year.

After being in the house I realized that the contractors hadn't been honest with me either. The house flooded—a lot. Before I'd moved in, I'd asked them about why they were doing certain things like putting up greenboard. Was there water damage? They said no, and I believed them. I called to get the gutters fixed, thinking it would help a little. But when I got home from work, I found that the contractors had replaced every last one of my gutters, without ever talking to me or getting me to sign anything or giving me an estimate. And they were looking for payment.

I was so angry. I felt like, "I'm doing everything I'm supposed to do. I'm a single mom taking care of business. How come I can't have the American Dream?"

And then I found out my daughter was pregnant. I'm fifty-two and a grandmother. My daughter is still young. So I had to figure out how to take care of both of them. I asked my store manager if I could take time off to support my daughter in those first six weeks. I only had two weeks of vacation. My manager was like, "It's in the middle of the Christmas season!" I didn't know what to do. I asked God, "What are you trying to tell me?" It was just so many things.

I ended up selling that house at a loss to stay above water. And wouldn't you know, I moved back into my grandmother's house. When she passed away, she left it to me. And that's where I am now. On the surface you might think, "Wow, an inheritance!" But her house needed so much major work done to it—so much money to spend that I didn't have. It was then that I realized that the dream was never meant for me: as either a person of color or as a woman.

When I first ran into the union, I ran into a door.

I was with my friend at the Baltimore Harbor, sightseeing. There was this door that was all glass, and I tried to walk through it. Afterward I started getting these bad headaches. My head was hurting and I was scared to call in sick from work. I still needed money for everything else going on in my life. I asked my union rep at the store how I could get out of the union so I could get more money in my paycheck. And she was like, "Why would you do that? The union can help you out. Why don't you just go downstairs and fill out a family leave form?" And I was like, "Why didn't anyone tell me that before?" And she said, "The managers aren't going to tell you that." I realized that there was all this information that I hadn't known, and I started soaking it all up.

One day the union rep called and asked me if I was going to be at the union election. It turned out I was the only person who came from Macy's. So, they asked me to come out and be more active with the union. They invited me to speak to the city council about wages when they were trying to pass the Large Retailer Accountability Act. After thirteen years at Macy's, my hourly take-home had only gone up $4. I was excited to be a part of the union after that.

I started going to union meetings and getting active. And it was just in time. Things started changing at Macy's. The seniors who worked in the store were in a funk. And you know I really care about seniors because of my grandmother. I found out that the store had implemented all of these new computer systems for scheduling, signing in, and so on. Many of the older associates weren't able to do it. Then this program called "Schedules Plus" came out. It was a program that generates your schedules, and if you're late or don't have enough points, you lose your job. So the older store associates were at yet another disadvantage.

I felt bad about that, felt it wasn't right. I'd been there for thirteen years, but some people had been there for thirty or forty years, starting back when they couldn't even be on the floor because they were Black and had to be in the stockroom. They felt like after all they'd been through, they were back at the bottom.

So I wanted to help. I asked the union, "What do you need me to do?" I became a shop steward. I loved it. Then the union president called to ask me to be an executive board member, and I called my mom, and she was so proud of me.

You know, it's funny. My mom only told me she was proud of me for two things. The first was that she thought I was a good mom. And the second was that I was a leader in my union. I knew I was on the right path after that.

Now Macy's became my second home. I was even dating. At one point, the guy I was seeing asked me why I was letting the union organize me. He said I was doing all this stuff for free and not spending time with him. But it wasn't about the money. I remember being asked, "What would you do, that even if you didn't get paid for it you would do anyway?" And I said, "I would do my union work!" I was able to talk to people in the stores about things I'd been through and about what their rights were.

Of course it wasn't all easy.

When I was talking to coworkers in my own store, my manager got mad because she had to answer to the union. I told her we wanted a partnership, and she was like, "We don't need you!" And I was like, "Why not?" I mean, I also came from management and was even a district manager once. I thought Macy's was about "team wins," and she wasn't being a team player. I was super confused.

But I learned quickly. My manager thought she had put me in my place. She wrote me up for an entire year for questioning policies and procedures at a store rally. She claimed I was being disrespectful.

You know, the thing about this idea of "respect" is, it can be used against you in weird ways. I did not know what the word meant until I was much older. For me, it means I must have respect for myself by loving my mind, body, and soul and not letting anyone just say or do anything to me.

It's not good for workers to feel belittled. I don't want to be seen as the angry Black woman. But some people will see me this way even when I'm not because portraying me that way makes them look better. When I got written up, it was because I was supposedly being disrespectful for correcting a manager who was giving false information about store policy. And I wasn't angry or loud when I did it. I was simply clarifying the truth. But I guess they knew they were trying to mislead us. So, they're the bullies in this situation, but they say that I'm disrespectful to cover up for the fact that they are lying.

I wish I had figured it out earlier. It would have helped me avoid a lot of pain and heartache.

I was fearful of losing my job, and it paralyzed me for a short time. But my coworkers organized on my behalf and inspired me to be true to myself, and I continued to do the work that needed to be done.

Now I'm taking all of my power back. I'm past ready to take a stand. If you can't respect me as the person that I am, then I don't need to be here. Go ahead and send me home! I've had so many managers, at least twelve different managers. I have a new manager, a new floor manager, and a new operations manager. I told the union rep and the other associates, "These people come and go, but this is our house."

One year we went through the worst Christmas season. Hours were all over the place. I thought I would have a nervous breakdown. I kept getting confused about the schedule and started losing points. It was like someone was rolling dice to determine when each of us would work each day. Then, to top it all off, they decided they wanted us to work inventory from 9 p.m. to 6 a.m.

I started talking to the other associates about all this. The managers didn't know or care about Macy's policy. They looked at us like we were a bad boyfriend. But this is our house. We have a union contract that we really had to fight for. I told the other associates that I didn't care what they felt about the union. I asked them, "How do you feel about managers coming down here, constantly disrespecting us, telling us what they want to tell us? We have to reclaim our own space!"

It's important not to just let the managers do whatever they want. We need these jobs. Not everyone can just quit. Not everyone can retire. Pop is in his eighties and still looking for side work. And, frankly, there should be dignity in work. If you feel like you want to work for the sake of work, you should be able to work and be treated fairly.

We had enough people who knew they didn't want to do inventory, so I suggested that we should meet with store management and refuse to do inventory at those hours. I knew we had the power to ask for a meeting with management, but the meeting never happened. Instead of doing inventory, associates called in sick.

The word "worker" is not a good word to me. It can sometimes feel patronizing—like we're just sitting around, waiting for someone else to tell us what to do. I respect my local for letting members speak up on behalf of themselves and their brothers and sisters—because we are the union.

One of the union staff was having a planning meeting with other organizations and she asked me if I wanted to come. When I arrived at the meeting I was the only worker at the table. That happens because they sometimes have these meetings at lunchtime when workers can't be there. The timing and location are wrong. I told them, "I don't think you realize the importance of having the workers there." We are the ones behind enemy lines. Who better to help you plan and strategize to win this fight?

I don't want to be in an army where we were forced to sign up. I want to be in an army where we all volunteered and are committed. It's not just about pouring words and money into workers. One thing I like about my union is that they ask me what I want to learn. It's about meeting workers where they are and helping them to improve their situation, teaching them the importance of organizing work, and helping us develop into leaders. We all have to learn how to love up on each other if we are to make a difference.

Workers are ready to fight. I knew we were ready. I told the union that the workers were ready. It's the organizations that aren't always ready. We all have to get our timing right. And when the organizations miss that, the workers veer away. That's how we get divided by the Donald Trumps of the world, who don't want us to get together. They know that if we do, we are powerful and there's nothing they can do to stop us. They make us think that they have the power, but we do. We need to organize and not compromise—or else we will wake up again and look out the window and say, "What the hell happened?"

Now even the young people are standing up for their rights. They see the system for what it truly is. The seams are coming apart. It's up to unions and organizations like Jobs With Justice and the community and faith groups to help pull the world back together. We have the power and the people. We're angry. And we need to know how to channel that anger against those who are trying to harm us. Otherwise some of us will use our power the wrong way and end up in jail or, worse, dead.

If we're going to be known as workers, we need to be empowered by that. We need to have jobs that we're proud to do. Caretaking is important work. Having a small business is important work. Retail is important work. We should all be valued for what we do.

If all you see when you meet me is that I'm a worker, you're missing the entire point. I am a whole person. I should be able to exercise control of my life in all aspects—at work, in my home, and in relationship to the big banks and the large corporations who shape so much of our society. If we fail to see people like me as whole people, then we're losing good soldiers who could be in this fight with us, this fight for dignity and respect.

A Broader Definition of Collective Bargaining

Those of us who advocate a new approach to economic democracy—one that broadens our view of human beings and seeks to bring the benefits of collective bargaining to arenas beyond the workplace—are sometimes accused of throwing the baby out with the bath water. That's wrong. We recognize that there are a lot of practices from twentieth-century organizing and collective bargaining that are worth retaining in the twenty-first century. Most important, traditional collective bargaining practices have developed and tested real mechanisms for winning enforceable agreements, union contracts that ultimately serve as the governing document for many a company or worksite. These collective bargaining agreements also extract capital directly from corporations via increased wages and member dues, thereby providing resources that help to sustain unions and the democratic power they represent. As a result, there are mechanisms in place to ensure that the contracts negotiated through collective bargaining are implemented and enforced. In all these ways, traditional organizing and collective bargaining has given millions of everyday people the opportunity to practice democracy. This is fundamental to the health of democracy at all levels.

Yet despite all these benefits, it has been apparent for several decades that the current vehicles for practicing collective bargaining are no longer enough. Some of the reasons have been skillfully described by Charles C. Heckscher in the 1996 introduction to his book *The New Unionism*:

> In the 1930s the work force was dominated by the blue-collar skilled and semi-skilled who were employed in large bureaucratic organizations; the Wagner Act was designed for them. Since then what might be called the middle ranks of employees have more than tripled: managerial and technical workers now make up well over half the work force—more than the total of crafts, operatives, and service employees.

Heckscher goes on to describe another challenge that may be potentially even more important than the changing roles of the workforce. In his words, "cross-cutting identities of race, ethnicity, gender, religion, and other social categories have become increasingly important alternatives to older occupational identities of workers and managers."[3] In other words, a range of social roles and identities beyond just the role of worker must be considered and addressed if we intend to tackle the fundamental forms of oppression that continue to distort US society. As evidence, consider the fact that during the 1970s and 1980s, as protection from the NLRB became steadily less effective, growing numbers of working people turned to other legal tools, such as the Civil Rights Act of 1964 and Title IX, to defend their ability to organize—and often with more success.[4]

Advocates of traditional unionizing strategies are not the only ones who have been reluctant to embrace new models of organizing. Some moderate and progressive political leaders have also fallen into the trap of accepting a limited perspective on democratic principles and practice. Historically, many Americans have assumed that, for the average citizen, democracy means merely voting every year or two; making the occasional consumer choice that is supposed to have an impact on corporate behavior (such as buying organic produce at the supermarket); and, maybe most important, the right to be left alone, as reflected by the popularity of the Tea Party slogan, "Don't tread on me."[5]

Building a more powerful people's movement for economic democracy will require the spread of a more expansive view of democracy, one that moves past individual rights and into the realm of shared responsibilities. Repressive laws, policies, and practices only change when masses of people take aggressive steps to force that change, even when that entails reorganizing institutions built over the last century.

Collective Bargaining for the Twenty-First Century

The changed circumstances we have described demand an evolved definition for collective bargaining, applicable to the twenty-first century:

> Collective bargaining (noun): The process whereby working people take collective action in negotiating with any entity that has power over their wages, living conditions, and overall economic well-being in a way that produces an enforceable agreement that can be renegotiated as conditions change.

As we will explore in the chapters that follow, a range of organizations representing working people are already engaged in the process of bringing workers together to negotiate with those who have control over their shared conditions—not just employers but also landlords, bankers, merchants, government officials, and more. These groups are demonstrating the necessity and the value of creating new institutions and laws to support them. They are evolving the unions of the future.

But many are also being transformed in deeper ways, recognizing their efforts not simply as part of the struggle for union rights but also as part of a fundamental fight for our democracy. The more corporations and billionaires rig the rules to interfere with people's ability to collectively bargain and to participate in democratic action in many other ways, the nimbler and more innovative the modern labor movement must become—and in more and more places, and in more and more ways, this is exactly what is happening. Growing numbers of union and nonunion workers are discovering how they can build on effective elements of traditional bargaining to inaugurate a new period of organizational and movement growth.

Through it all, workers like Kimberly Mitchell and thousands of others are obeying the organizers' golden rule: They are *not* giving up their power. And against all odds, they are winning.[6]

ORGANIZING ALL PEOPLE

We Will Not Win without Destroying
White Supremacy and Patriarchy

Global capitalism created the situation we currently find ourselves in, with right-wing populism, both in the United States and around the world, exploiting the fears and insecurities of working people to maintain their hold on power and the riches it generates. Global capitalism has systemically deregulated one business sector after another, privatized public services for private profit, and turned the future itself into a commodity to be wagered on through financial speculation. But while these varied effects are ultimately driven by a single cause, the individual experiences of those who suffer the impacts often feel disconnected. It is important to look beneath the surface to understand what is happening. And one of the most important under-the-radar dynamics of the current era is the way white supremacy is being used to crush the spirits of *white* workers.

Divide and Conquer: White Supremacy as a Tool of Capitalist Dominance for White People

White workers are not immune to the destruction caused by global capitalism. Millions have experienced job loss, the lack of needed services such as health care, poor housing conditions, and limited educational opportunities. While communities of color are suffering from chronic conditions like diabetes and hypertension, white communities are suffering in growing numbers from "deaths of despair"—death attributable to drugs, alcohol, and suicide—and to the ravages of killers like heart disease and cancer. As a result, the mortality rates of whites with no more than a high school degree, which were around 30 percent lower than the mortality rates of Blacks in 1999, grew to be 30 percent higher than Blacks by 2015.[1]

There is no way around it: global capitalism has kicked the butts of white workers over the last several decades. And they have not gotten much help from either dominant political party.

The fate of Youngstown, Ohio, beginning in the late 1970s has been used by community organizer Kirk Noden to illustrate this dynamic and the way it has served the interests of those in power.[2]

Noden begins by explaining the implications on working people after steel companies and other manufacturing industries left Youngstown:

> In a place like Youngstown, that means not only an inability to get a well-paying job at the steel mill; it also means owning a house that has failed to appreciate in value for 20 to 30 years, in a city that continues to lose double-digit percentages of its population every 10 years. It is not just a stripping out of economic opportunity but a stripping away of identity for these communities. It is the sense of abandonment and perpetual decline that people feel mired in. Resources, jobs, decent housing, quality neighborhoods and schools are all in decline. It creates a "scarcity mentality" for White working-class people and others who live in the heartland.[3]

White workers initially fought back. Many joined with others in the community, including faith groups, private investors, and neighboring Black families to attempt to get federal support from President Jimmy Carter's administration to reopen the mills as community-owned, cooperatively run enterprises. But President Carter caved to the interests of US Steel and other corporations in hopes of getting reelected. Says Noden, "The impact of this betrayal on White working-class people was a universal distrust and dislike for institutions—none of which were able to defend their livelihoods or their futures. The unions didn't stay around to organize a new strategy for revitalizing Youngstown. They moved to another line of defense elsewhere, as they grew increasingly insular and focused on protecting their shrinking base."

Youngstown is emblematic of countless other communities where similar chains of events have played out. The tendency of corporate class leaders and their supporters in politics and the media to downplay the impact of the loss of manufacturing—or, worse, to accept it as a necessary by-product of globalization—continues to feed this feeling of betrayal among white communities. But it is the use of white supremacy by right-wing leaders that ultimately prevents white people from seeing global capitalism as the problem and instead aims their righteous anger at the wrong people, including Black workers, immigrants, refugees, and Muslims who themselves are also suffering under the same oppressive economic policies.

What Noden refers to as a "scarcity mentality" is coupled with a sense of entitlement that is encouraged by white supremacy—a sense that I, the white Christian male, should have a good job or government support, not "those people" who are different from me in race, ethnicity, or religion. Combine this mentality with rising social expectations for tolerance and even acceptance of those from different backgrounds and some white workers' sense of scarcity turns into outrage over the belief that they are threatened with extinction. Reverend J. C. Austin describes this reaction as "anger at feeling that the concerns and beliefs of White Christians, in particular, are being actively and intentionally displaced in our culture in order to favor those of other religions and racial/ethnic backgrounds."[4]

The election of Donald Trump in 2016 focused new interest on the plight of working-class white voters. Books like *White Working Class* by Joan C. Williams, *Hillbilly Elegy* by J. D. Vance, and *Strangers in Their Own Land* by Arlie Russell Hochschild were scrutinized for clues to the frustration of working-class white people. Many assumed these working-class voters had been responsible for Trump's victory. But exit polls consistently showed that Trump's base of support included more well-to-do white voters than working-class and poor whites.[5] Certainly white workers were part of Trump's base. But they were far from being the majority of that base.

Still, it is true that Trump capitalized on both the scarcity mentality and the racial resentment of working-class whites in winning his narrow election victory. Many white workers have been encouraged to feel that "those others" are cutting in front of them in the line to claim the fruits of the American Dream, somehow breaking the rules that whites have always followed. Many decided they needed a standard-bearer to stop all of this rule-breaking—someone like Donald Trump.

Leaders on the Left have not done enough to push back against this false narrative that too many white workers have absorbed. While labor unions have historically played an important role in mobilizing white workers against right-wing populism, they are much weaker today than they once were, and arguably many union locals did not take on race as aggressively in the 2016 election as they should have. And until recently, most progressive organizations had not done much to build membership in poor white communities or to change their thinking, often brushing them off with comedic quips about incest and missing teeth.

In reality, of course, the economic woes of white workers in towns like Youngstown are not caused by people of color, immigrants, or any other familiar scapegoats. In those same towns Black and Brown workers are struggling just as much, and usually more. White working-class levels of wealth have stagnated in recent decades. But if those levels were to remain fixed while people of color had the opportunity to grow their own wealth at current rates of increase, it would take more than eighty-four years for Latinos to amass the wealth that white Americans currently have, and 228 years for Black families to close the wealth divide.[6]

Racial divisions are not just irrelevant to the real problems victimizing white workers. They actively make matters worse for all working people. Consider, for example, the phenomenon known as white flight. Author Chris Arnade interviewed a woman named Maria Garcia about what happened when economic decline came to Gary, Indiana: "This street used to be filled with good neighbors," she said. "Then in 1981, people started moving out. They started seeing Black people coming in, and they said they would bring drugs and crime, so they left. . . . Racism killed Gary. The Whites left Gary, and the Blacks couldn't. Simple as that."[7]

As communities like Gary begin their decline, the remaining jobs often pay less than before. And the increasing number of lower-wage jobs in every industry makes it more difficult for many in manufacturing to keep wages increasing at the same pace as productivity. For example, transnational auto companies like Nissan and Volkswagen have focused their US manufacturing growth in the southern part of the country, where the remnants of Jim Crow and tough legal impediments to unionization prevent the overwhelmingly Black workforce from organizing successfully. Simultaneously, the base of the UAW throughout the Midwest, unable to avoid the downward pull of their southern peers, is struggling to maintain gains it won over the last several decades, forced to accept increased numbers of temporary and contract workers, regressively tiered wages, and cuts to health care.[8]

Immigrants, documented and undocumented, are also used by global capital to victimize workers in general. Immigrants are often concentrated in jobs that put them in precarious situations, in many cases recruited because of their vulnerability. While not fully protected by the NLRA, undocumented workers struggle to access remedies to help them recover stolen wages, overtime, and being paid below poverty levels.[9] And many holders of temporary work visas are bound to one employer who could threaten their families and their livelihoods if they step out of line. It is one thing to work a low-wage job. But what happens when that same employer can hold the threat of ICE or social services over the heads of workers to keep them from improving their conditions?

Yes! magazine shared the experiences of Mexican guest workers in the small town of Breaux Bridge, Louisiana: "Martha Uvalle and her co-workers at C. J.'s Seafood, a Walmart supplier, faced abuses many Americans imagine only take place in poorer, faraway countries: They were forced to work shifts of up to 24 hours, with no overtime pay; threatened with beatings if their breaks lasted too long; and, on at least two occasions, locked inside the facility to work. Some fell asleep at their workstations from exhaustion."[10]

Conditions like this drive wages down for everyone. Workers on all sides suffer as those in power play one group against another.

To their credit, some white working-class voters identified with Bernie Sanders in the 2016 primary elections. In Michigan, a high-union-membership state, Sanders won 62 percent of white men and a third of the overall electorate according to exit polls.[11] But after the primaries, too many of these voters saw Trump as the only "outsider" politician left in the race. Their vote for him in November was a vote for change, any kind of change, even if it came in the form of reactionary solutions touted by the extreme Right against much of their shared self-interests with workers of color.

Lidia Victoria. Portrait by Gwenn Seemel.

Profile of a Modern Worker:
Lidia Victoria: Organizing Under
the Shadow of ICE

Lidia Victoria immigrated to the United States from the Dominican Republic, ultimately settling in North Carolina to work in meatpacking. She is an organizer who helped win the extended fight to gain legal recognition for a labor union at the Tar Heel, North Carolina, plant of Smithfield Packing, the world's largest hog-killing factory. This victory, ratified in a December 2008, vote, required a strategy that centered on the fight against white supremacy, including its impact not only on immigrant workers and workers of color but also on the white workers in the plant.[12]

I remember that day in 2006 when ICE came. It was just a regular day, nothing out of the ordinary. I'd transitioned from the chitterling room at the Smithfield Processing Plant to washing bones and checking the intestines to ensure we were compliant with USDA standards. My husband also worked at the plant on a nearby line, near the hearts. I vaguely remembered seeing the supervisor walk by with a Mexican worker I recognized. I didn't think much of it.

We got off work earlier than normal, around 2:45 p.m. On the way to our car I saw one of my friends who should have left before us but was still there. She was worried, and she asked me if I had seen her husband. And I remembered that I had seen him walking with the supervisor earlier that day. But I hadn't seen him after that.

My husband and I went home, and our phone started ringing. People knew that we were in support of the union, and so they called us to see if we knew anything about ICE coming to the plant. We didn't. My husband and I kept replaying the day in our heads. Had ICE been in the plant?

Then my friend called again and asked, "Ms. Lidia, do you know where Antonio is?" I told her again that I had seen him walking with the supervisor. But I didn't know where they went, and they didn't come back. And she said, "Okay, because his father is here, and the babysitter is calling me and telling me that he didn't make it to pick up the kids."

That's when I realized that something was happening. For Antonio to not pick up his children was unusual.

So we waited by the phone. We tried to believe it was nothing serious. It was just one person, right? But we later realized it was not just Antonio. ICE took twenty-six people from the plant that day. I'm still haunted by it. It was terrible.

I hadn't had this experience before. I came to the United States from the Dominican Republic in 1981. There were many people who left the Dominican Republic and came here during that time. My father came first, then he got visas for me and my siblings to follow. We were documented. We came through New York's John F. Kennedy Airport and settled in Passaic, New Jersey, where we lived for a little over a decade.

I finished school and started working. My father was working in a metal factory, and they were union. He always told me, "When you fill out the application to get a job, make sure that you put union, yes!" He knew about the *sindicatos* in the Dominican Republic—that's what we call unions there. He told me, "The union is like a lawyer who takes care of the employees. Even if you never need it, it's good to have." That made sense to me. You know the employers have all kinds of legal protection and insurance. We workers have to be our own insurance. So I joined the union at my job.

Actually, all of us, my brothers too, were in unions. It was common in New Jersey. In some places you couldn't work there without belonging to the union. And that's what I was used to. We had contracts that we had negotiated and the company respected them. Employers didn't interfere in our activities. I never worried about the boss because we had an agreement and we all followed it.

But that changed when I moved to North Carolina.

I had gotten married and had my two kids in New Jersey. And it just became too crowded. Meanwhile, my sister was living in North Carolina. She had a yard and space to park. I felt like it would be easier to settle my family there.

My first job was in Fayetteville at Perdue, where we processed poultry. There was no union. And supervisors did not seem to respect workers. I kept thinking, what's going to happen if a supervisor does something to one of us? I was there for just under three years before I left in 1995 to go work at Smithfield, processing pork.

When I got there, I was like, wait a minute! Perdue was fine. Everything was okay there. But Smithfield was a big problem. I was working in the chitterling room for over two years at first. Oh my God, I was piping and splashing all kinds of stuff. After a while, I got another position on the kill floor, doing a different job. I saw a lot of bad things. We were working in terrible conditions. It was hot and people fainted. Supervisors did whatever they wanted with employees. They called us names. They fired people for no reason at all, you know? They treated people so badly. I knew we needed a union.

I learned that workers in the plant had tried to unionize several times before. But they never won the vote of the majority of people in the plant. The company made everybody scared to vote yes even though they wanted to. It was easy for companies to cheat. In North Carolina, this was normal. And most of the workers who were from there were like, this is just how it is. We're going to take what they give us. And they would, you know?

But the need for a union didn't go away, and workers inside Smithfield were still talking about it. A lot of the Black workers would ask me what I thought about it. When they realized I was in favor of organizing a union, we started having meetings at my house. My husband and I were strong supporters, and the other workers knew they could count on us. Our house was a safe place to gather. We could educate others there. I would say, at least give us the opportunity to see how a union could work. They had no experience with a union, no confidence in it, unlike those of us from other places. So we had to build that up.

There were a lot of different kinds of people in the plant. It was diverse. Men and women, whole families. Black people, white people, Native Americans, and Spanish-speaking people from all over. We weren't necessarily organized by race at work, but you could see the distinct groups of people in the cafeteria. The supervisors would try to create division around this. They would say things like, "The African Americans are like this, so we keep them here. And the Spanish people, you know they work really hard."

At the same time, they told other people that the Spanish-speaking people were there to steal their jobs. White people were mostly in maintenance at that time. Maintenance was very important to the company because, you know, they keep the line running. Maintenance workers sometimes had an easier time getting what they wanted from the company back then. Most of the African Americans were already in favor of the union, and I was helping them win support among more of the Spanish speakers. But fewer white people were with us at first. We knew we eventually needed everyone on board to win.

Of course, the company knew our chances of winning decreased the more divided we were. And they played on this. They brought us department-by-department into a room to watch a video about things that they said happened in the past, like strikes. They made it look like people had lost their jobs because of a union. I didn't understand why they were so worried about the union.

It's also hard for me to believe Smithfield did not know that some of the workers in the plant were undocumented. I wouldn't be surprised if they purposefully sought some of them out to work at the plant. If you can't present proof of Social Security, you're more vulnerable. And management knew it.

It wasn't long after we started getting more people excited about the union that ICE raided our plant and took twenty-six people. We never saw most of them again. The next day, you really knew how many immigrants worked at the plant because it was almost empty. People were scared to go to work. Many of them left town and never came back because ICE had also been knocking on doors in the community and taking people from their homes.

I couldn't eat for weeks after that. I was so sad. My husband and I would wake up in the night and just go over it again and again. What happened? People were always calling, looking for their family members. It created a lot of trauma.

In 2006, we were supposed to have another vote about whether to organize a union. But after the ICE raid it never happened. Smithfield took legal action to stop it. And people who had been ready to vote yes for a union were scared they would be next on ICE's list. On top of that, the company tried to blame those of us organizing a union for the raid! There were so many rumors.

We tried to get back to the business of organizing our coworkers again, starting almost from scratch. It was hard. And I had to change my own mentality to keep going back and talking to coworkers who had told me no. I knew I just had to keep going.

By that time I think my supervisors realized that I was able to talk to a lot of people at the plant—in English and in Spanish. And they knew I was for a union. They tried to pull me away from the union by offering me a position to talk to new hires. But I would have had to discourage them from talking to people about the union. They offered me a better-paying job, saying that I would be all set and that my husband would be all set. But I was like, what about the rest of the people that work on the floor? God only knows what I said. But they kept pushing. They were like, "The union only wants your money." And I started to smell a rat. Why are you so worried about someone else's money? I knew I had to go with my own truth, with what I know I had the right to do.

I was proud of myself for resisting that offer. I could have easily made a different choice, just for me. But that wouldn't have been fair. We had to stick together. So, yeah, I continued to fight for our union.

We were organizing with the United Food and Commercial Workers Local 1208 nonstop inside the plant. By that time it wasn't only me. It was my husband. It was other people, Spanish-speaking people, Black people. We even got white people, you know? It was a lot of people. We knew we couldn't do this by ourselves.

And outside, people pressured the company in different ways—at grocery stores and at corporate events. Different faith leaders and community groups supported us. Jesse Jackson came to the Yellow House, where we often held our meetings about the union. That was very exciting. They didn't mind that we showed up in our work clothes, covered in pigs' blood. People were coming from all over to support us.

And in the end we won the union. In December 2008, we won the vote by 2,041 to 1,879. Now we have a union. The company knows the rules. They have to respect us. I'm so proud of what we accomplished at Smithfield.

But I still tell people that it could be taken away at any point. They must still be active. Somebody fought hard for us to be here and have this union. It's our turn, you know? We must do it for the future employees, for our children. We all deserve to work in a place that respects us, where we have dignity. Some people have had bad experiences with unions, and I have to remind them that I am not the union. *We* are the union. And we can change things we don't like. Everyone has to do their part.

I still do my part. I walk the plant every day. It is so big! But I walk the length of it, trying to make sure Smithfield employees know they have a voice and that they can express themselves when they go to Human Resources with any issue. There are thousands of people in the plant. I can be there for hours walking sometimes. The people closest to the work really are the best to spot problems and propose solutions. So when I hear about something, I ask other workers if they're experiencing the same thing. Then we come up with a solution together with the company.

People now have the experience of what it means to come together and form a union. And we're all better for it.

Gender Discrimination and the Cycle of Inequality

In US society, patriarchy is just as pervasive as white supremacy—and it is just as powerful a tool in the hands of global capital.

The historical roots of patriarchy go very deep. In the early colonial period women from Europe who came to America as indentured servants had years added to their contract if they got pregnant. This incentivized the masters who owned the contracts to rape female workers in order to keep them longer as servants. In similar fashion enslaved Black women were raped and impregnated by plantation owners to force them to reproduce their "assets."

Laws validated this behavior. As Erik Loomis notes in *A History of America in Ten Strikes*, "In 1662, after a slave sued for freedom by claiming his father was White, Virginia decided that slave status was confirmed by the mother. This gave masters the right to rape their slaves and keep their own children as property. Forced sexual labor became central to a system that denied slaves basic human rights."[13]

Similar practices persist today. Despite the fact that slavery and sexual abuse have become less culturally acceptable, the bodies of women of color continue to be viewed by many as more accessible than their white counterparts. The trafficking of women to the global north from around the world is a phenomenon of both sexual and economic exploitation. Workers in low-status, low-pay industries like hospitality, housekeeping, and food service are also vulnerable to harassment and abuse on the job. The psychological impacts of this abuse are incalculable, even as it is part of the routine experience of millions of women. Here's just a single example, drawn from the testimony of a Black woman named Laurie Terrell in a report from the Restaurant Opportunities Center United (ROC United):

> I've been bit, I've been grabbed, I've been licked. You name it. . . . And you just learn to let it go. Then when you get older, when you start dating . . . you have a hard time distinguishing between good touches and bad touches in your subconscious. It's very, very damaging, especially when you learn how to wait tables before you've had any sexual experiences, and you have people manhandling you before you've ever even kissed a boy.[14]

The death of Sandra Bland in 2015 while jailed in Texas after a routine traffic stop illustrates the extreme, disturbingly frequent instances of violence on the bodies of Black women. Bland was thrown on the ground and harassed before the officer concluded she had in fact assaulted him. She was later found hanged in the cell where she was kept, despite no history of depression or suicidal tendencies.

Women are also subject to forms of economic exploitation that men rarely experience. For example, much of the domestic labor done by women remains unseen and unrewarded. Many women essentially work two full-time jobs, one of which—managing the home—goes completely unpaid. Adding insult to injury, the wages women earn in their paid occupations average 20 percent less than men make for the same work.[15] For women of color, this gap is higher. And similar dynamics persist among queer and gender nonconforming workers. A June 2020 ruling by the US Supreme Court acknowledged the discrimination that transgender employees suffer and ruled that such discrimination is barred by Title VII of the Civil Rights Act of 1964—an opinion that three of the court's most conservative justices strongly opposed.[16] The future will show whether this positive step will stand up to the assaults we can expect from right-wing legal operatives. It remains the case that fewer than half of the fifty states currently ban employment discrimination on the basis of gender identity or sexual orientation.

There is particularly pervasive discrimination against women as a side effect of their reproductive labor, including the opportunities and benefits child-bearing workers lose when they take parental leave or when they leave the labor force for an extended period of time due to caregiving responsibilities. In addition to missing out on opportunities for promotion, these workers suffer later in life because they've paid less into Social Security.

Women, particularly women of color, are easily exploited by the forces of global capitalism. Patriarchal attitudes encourage men (or those who identify as masculine) to consider themselves superior to women and all forms of femininity, and therefore to disregard the complaints of women and gender nonconforming people and dismiss them as potential leaders. This helps strengthen the hand of capital in its efforts to keep working people divided. This is why patriarchy, like white supremacy, must be centrally targeted by labor organizers and others who want to build a truly effective movement for economic democracy.

Sanchioni Butler. Portrait by Gwenn Seemel.

Profile of a Modern Worker:
Sanchioni Butler: This Is Our Women's Movement

Unlike the workers at Smithfield Packing in Tar Heel, the workers at the Nissan auto plant in Canton, Mississippi, have not successfully gotten the company to recognize their union.[17] UAW organizer Sanchioni Butler, a southern autoworker and one of the pioneering women in the industry, puts this and other struggles in the context of the battle against white supremacy and patriarchy.

My life changed in 1976.

I was in middle school when we moved from the city of Dallas to the suburbs. When I arrived, I found I was one of three Black children in the entire school. It was a tough time for me as a twelve-year-old girl. I was called the N-word. I was spat on. There were a group of kids who did not want me on the bus.

During those years I would spend summers in Louisiana with my grandmother and aunts who were all strong alpha women. We have a lot of strong women in our family, so I knew how to stand up and fight for what was right. Back at school, I tried to fight back against hate the best I knew how. I actually got into several physical altercations to prove I belonged at that school. But my parents got frustrated being called to the school all the time. They told me I needed to figure out how to get along with people that were different than me. They told me there were other ways.

My dad's union went on strike that same year, and I joined the picket line with him. For the first time I witnessed people standing together to make change in their workplace without a real knowledge of the depth of what that meant. I know people of color went through a lot in the 1960s. But for me, it was 1976 when my life was forever changed.

I soon found my voice through athletics. That's how I was able to fit in. My peers started cheering me on. They were still talking about me in ways that were uncomfortable, calling me "Black Magic," "Black Chocolate," and this and that. But the worst of the taunting went away when I started playing sports.

In fact, sports also got me out of high school. I went to college on a basketball scholarship. But after I got pregnant I had to look for work. My daughter was three in 1988 when I got hired at the Ford plant in Carrollton, Texas—the same plant where my dad had worked and gone on strike. The workers were predominantly men—mostly white men. I came in with a few other Black workers. We had all come through as kids in the summer program. That's how we got the job.

The work was tough, and they did not make it easy for us. They were especially tough on me. They would say, "Oh, you think you can do a man's job? Pick that up." And on top of that, I was sexually harassed. I was harassed by white men and Black men. I did not get a lot of help. But I had to stay there. I needed the job. I had a child to feed, and the job paid well and provided good medical benefits. So I endured it.

An opportunity came up after I'd been there for three years, a shot at a maintenance position. Maintenance is a prime job in any manufacturing facility. They made a lot of money, up to $35 an hour. To qualify for a job of this magnitude, you were required to take a test to get it, and I signed up. But it was unpopular and unheard-of for a woman to do this type of work. I had men from management come up to me and tell me to take my name off the list to take this test. And I had men from the union—the United Auto, Aerospace, and Agricultural Implement Workers of America, or UAW—come up to me and tell me to take my name off the list. They would say, "You can't take that test. It's not for you." I was getting threatened because this was a premier job and they did not want me to have it. They didn't give me the supplies or materials to study for the test. I had to go out and find the books on my own. The only person who encouraged me to take the test and get into the apprenticeship program was my dad. No one else. I had to fight just to take the test.

After years of discrimination the company started hiring more women. Needless to say, we stuck together—we were locked at the hip. I remember we had this crappy bathroom. By standing together and demanding it, we got them to put in a shower and a couch so we could have a place to sit down for a moment during our breaks and monthly cycles. We had all these little battles where we would take complaints to the union and the company. And when they would say no, we would rebel.

We got improvements by sticking together. When I fought to take that test and when we fought for a shower and couch in the women's bathroom, that was our women's movement.

Today, the UAW has women's committees. You hear about the women's liberation movement around the country. More than a hundred women serve in the US House of Representatives. But frankly, women's liberation for us was happening right there on the shop floor.

Fourteen years later my life changed again. The Carrollton, Texas, plant downsized, and I had an opportunity to relocate and work in Houston, Texas, or Memphis, Tennessee. I didn't want to relocate to Houston, so I made a bold decision to move to Memphis. It would be a huge culture shock, so different than Dallas. I had no family there—both of my parents were deceased by then. I had no friends there. I would have to start over.

For my first six months in Memphis, every Friday when I got off work at 2:30 p.m., I would drive six and a half hours back to Dallas. That got tiring fast.

And at some point, I knew I had to embrace this new place that I now called home. I remember my first visit to the National Civil Rights Museum at the Lorraine Motel in Memphis, where Dr. Martin Luther King Jr. was assassinated in 1968. I'd seen the pictures as a child, photos of men pointing in the direction of where the shots came from. But to see it in person was something else. I can recall Mahalia Jackson singing "Precious Lord" over the loudspeaker near the room where Dr. King had slept the night before his assassination, and I cried like a baby. It was like an out-of-body experience.

Dr. King had been in Memphis supporting sanitation workers who were simply asserting, "I am a man." And suddenly, I recalled my own experience—one of six Black kids graduating from DeSoto High School, class of 1983. I realized then that I had a calling in my life and serious work to do that would involve fighting for people who were disenfranchised, poor, and of color. And I knew it would be dangerous work.

I started organizing in September 2004. I knocked on the doors of workers in Columbus, Georgia, who had no union so I could talk to them about how they thought they could make their workplace better. I thought of similar people knocking on these same doors decades before, asking them to register to vote to make their lives better. I had the same fears. I even had someone pull a gun on me once in a small town just outside of Montgomery, Alabama. But I had to keep going. All workers' labor has value. All workers are worth listening to.

And so I would listen to people talk about how they wanted to improve their jobs and workplace. After all, the workers are the people best positioned to set rules for their workplace. We set rules almost everywhere else in our lives, why shouldn't we set them at work? We negotiate with lenders when we buy a home or a car. If you're about to make a major purchase or rent an apartment, you study the contract that you're about to sign regarding what the rules and regulations are on the property. Even when we die, someone is sitting at the table negotiating the terms of your burial and how to distribute the remainder of your money. We spend most of our time at work. Why not negotiate together with our employers?

We are up against large corporations that have a lot of money. I saw that when I was supporting workers at Nissan in Canton, Mississippi. Labor unions do not have the kind of money that companies have to bring in antiunion firms and fight against workers. We were fighting for one Mississippi, and they were trying to maintain two Mississippis—one for them and one for the rest for us. Supporting workers at Nissan was tough. Nationally the campaign was about the corporation as a whole. But we needed more focus on the shop floor. So many workers had been injured. Everyone had a horror story about them or someone else. Most of them didn't care how much some executive was spending on a yacht. They wanted to fix what was happening in their day-to-day lives.

I also saw how Nissan used their money to divide the workers. They would encourage white workers in the plant, who were in just as bad a shape as everyone
else, to still feel privileged over Black workers. And some people made it sound like
if they voted for the union, Black people were going to take over and overpower the
authorities. There was this idea that Black people were about to take something
from white workers. But many of them had their own "aha" moment after they
experienced an injury and saw how the company treated them just as badly as they
had treated Black workers who had been injured. It was then that white workers
were able to come down from that pedestal to see they were no different than their
coworkers. The lesson is that we may all come from different places but we share a
lot of the same experiences.

Still, many people in the South have negative associations with anything
called a union. They do not really know what it means and how it would work,
and we don't always do the best job at talking about it. They don't understand
that union workers have retirement protection, and I'm not just talking about
401(k)s—I'm talking about defined pensions. They don't always understand how
much better union wages are, or that we get leave time. And they also don't always see what we're doing in the community. Union workers collecting money
and toys for kids during the holidays, serving food at shelters—that's your local
union. But people don't always see that. They just see the word "union" and think
that the communists or the Black people are taking over.

So we have a lot of work to do as unions. We have a beautiful template. We
just need to bring that template into the twenty-first century.

I've learned that the messenger really matters. If you're making $30 an hour,
you're not from the area, and you're a man with a higher-than-mighty attitude,
knocking on the doors of women making $7–10 an hour, people will see right
through you. People know when you're fake. So, in the South, if we can't come
correct, then we can't come. Local people talking to other local people about
organizing—that's our best-kept secret. And that's what was behind the March
on Mississippi in the spring of 2017

The idea came up in a room of some of the Black pastors who were working
with us on the Nissan campaign. They were saying, "We need to take it to the
streets like we used to in the old days." Behind us was this picture of the long
march procession that happened after Medgar Evers was murdered in 1963. We
were in the same building, the office of the Mississippi NAACP, where the Mississippi Freedom Democratic Party returned from the Democratic National Convention in 1964 and planned their next actions. We planned the March on
Mississippi in 2017 in that space, and it materialized a few months later.

I remember one of the Nissan workers' eighty-seven-year-old father marching
with him. He kept trying to get his dad to get on the school bus to ride alongside

the march. But he refused, preferring to walk with everyone else just like he had done before. That moment was confirmation of everything that I felt during that time at the Lorraine Motel back in Memphis. It had come full circle for me.

We had not won everything then, and we did not win our effort to get a union at Nissan. And that's why we have to keep marching, keep fighting. People don't think that they're worthy. Some people are numb. I think it is conditioning. There is opportunity, but they don't think it's for them. They're encouraged not to rock the boat, not to say anything for fear of losing what little they currently have. And so we have to meet each other where we're at, and with a clear heart. Just identify one person at work or at your church or at the daycare where you take your kids. Building that support into our daily lives—that's the only way we can win.

Pushing Back: Multiracial Organizing in the Twentieth Century and Today

Working people are resilient. They altered the relations of power and reshaped the frameworks of collective bargaining in the United States in the twentieth century by building explicitly multiracial strategies against common exploiters.

In their long struggle to unionize workers at Ford Motor Company in the late 1930s and early 1940s, the UAW had been excluding Black workers from their organizing efforts, and many white workers did not believe Black workers should get equal pay for equal work.[18] The company had successfully thwarted unionization efforts by playing on these divisions, not only offering jobs to Black workers but also promoting them into higher-level positions—including within Ford's own security forces. In so doing, Henry Ford obscured his famously racist and anti-Semitic viewpoints with a new reputation that saw the company as a pathway—albeit a paternalistic one—out of poverty for Black workers, pitting them against the mostly white union.

Black workers who were supportive of the union fought back. They pushed the UAW to realize that in order to expand collective bargaining power for workers in the auto industry, they would have to confront white supremacy. Thus the UAW began exposing the discrimination Black workers still faced in Ford plants, including most of the Black workers in low-paying jobs. Pushed by the demands of Black workers, the union started to hire Black organizers and began engaging Black communities. They also renegotiated some of their existing collective bargaining agreements that had consistently disadvantaged Black workers in promotions, seniority, and higher-paying positions.

This comprehensive effort united the interests of Black and white workers in the auto industry, leading to increased bargaining power at Ford and throughout the sector for all workers. The efforts gave birth to a new local, UAW Local 600, which included Black workers. These workers' relationship to the union and to bargaining rights was based in campaigns that confronted discrimination. Local 600 became one of the most powerful locals in the union.

Leaders coming out of the local, having demonstrated their ability to win significant gains for workers and their families, established channels that would develop inspiring new leaders for future struggles around housing, public education, and voting rights. As Nelson Lichtenstein explains in his book *The Most Dangerous Man in Detroit*:

> With almost one hundred thousand Black workers organized in the Detroit area, African-American unionists from the Rouge and other UAW plants poured into the Detroit NAACP chapter, demanded the promotion of Black workers in metropolitan war plants, and mobilized thousands to defend Black occupancy of the Sojourner Truth Homes, a federally funded project that became a violent center of conflict between White neighborhoods and the housing-starved Black community.[19]

Today's workers are just as creative. They have not been waiting for a top-down team of experts to come up with the perfect strategy. Instead they have been experimenting with new models that the present generation can learn from as it attempts to rebalance the relations of power in our society—in the workplace and in our communities.

Several twenty-first-century movements have integrated the struggle against white supremacy with campaigns for workplace power with profound scalability. Here are just a few powerful examples.

In November 2014, protests in Washington, DC, that mobilized in response to the acquittal of Missouri-based Mike Brown's police murderer managed to shut down a local Walmart store—prompting several retail employees to leave their workstations and join in the chants.[20]

In July 2016, the SEIU made the courageous commitment to address anti-Black racism in solidarity with the Black Lives Matter movement as part of its Fight for Fifteen campaign for a living wage. That month the national convention of Fight for Fifteen workers took place in Richmond, Virginia, to highlight the need for racial justice against the backdrop of the former capital of the Confederacy. Two months later, Fight for Fifteen workers who went on strike in Charlotte, North Carolina, also protested the murder of Keith Lamont Scott, a Black father of seven children murdered by police near his home.

Both movements realized that they could not win without one another, and the leaders of the two movements incorporated this reality in their messages. Rasheen Aldridge, a former fast-food worker who led the Fight for Fifteen in

St. Louis, served on the Ferguson Commission established by former US attorney general Eric Holder to investigate the death of Mike Brown, became an elected Missouri legislator in 2019 and used his comments to the Jobs With Justice national conference in February 2016 to highlight the link between economic and racial democracy:

> In zip code 60105, the majority is African-American, and the median income is $15,000. In zip code 62105, the majority is White, and the median income is $90,000. The life expectancy between these two zip codes is a 15-year gap. These issues are connected. These issues matter. And we have to look at them like that. We cannot separate them anymore.[21]

In New York, individuals from both struggles converged again in April 2016 to protest the shooting of unarmed Akai Gurley, the father of a two-year-old daughter who was shot near her home. Dawn O'Neal, who traveled to New York from Atlanta to support both movements, explained her thinking to *ThinkProgress*: "When you think about the Fight for 15 and you think about Black Lives Matter, it intersects. . . . Police violence is usually, predominantly in communities that suffer economic violence. So it goes hand in hand."[22]

In similar fashion, Black Lives Matter Bay Area joined food service, homecare, and childcare workers in Oakland in their strike against the fast-food industry in November 2015, stating: "As an over-policed and underpaid community the Fight for Fifteen is personal for Black people. When we say Black Lives Matter, we are continuing a generations-long struggle for the dignity of Black people everywhere, from the courtroom to the workplace."[23]

The victories won by this collaborative movement go far beyond the fast-food industry. The fight for a $15 an hour minimum wage flooded cities and states nationwide, including Greensboro, North Carolina (Smiley's hometown).[24] The fight became a framework for workers of all races in low-wage service businesses, the public sector, and even in manufacturing, where what used to be good jobs are now low wage. Making race central to an organizing and collective bargaining strategy generated momentum and success far beyond any immediate union base, establishing a new floor for what an acceptable livable wage is in the United States.

The relationship between Black Lives Matter activists and the Fight for Fifteen campaign is not the only example of the integration of the fight against white supremacy with the battle for organizing and collective bargaining rights.

In May 2016, incarcerated workers throughout the country went on strike, starting with an initial call from workers in three prisons led by the Free Alabama Movement, and then spreading to workers in prisons across eleven states. In September 2016, when predominantly Black inmates in Alabama acted against inhumane conditions at the W. C. Holman Correctional Facility, including forced labor and violence, the prison guards, many of them white, also went on strike.

The Movement for Black Lives, a coalition of organizations supporting the upsurge, also released a policy platform outlining the right to organize and collectively bargain as essential to the freedom and security of Black people.[25] And in 2020, the movement was reenergized after the murder of George Floyd by police in Minneapolis, Minnesota. Derek Chauvin, the officer who murdered George Floyd, had eighteen previous complaints against him, but the Police Officers Federation of Minneapolis had helped prevent his removal from the force. The blatancy of this led the second wave of the movement to more aggressively challenge labor unions on their relationship with the police. Despite the historic record of police being used to break up labor disputes, their members are still a part of local, state, and national federations.

The events of 2020 led to some changes. The labor council in Seattle, Washington, gave the police union an ultimatum to address the disproportionate violence on Black lives or leave. They left. Union bus drivers in Minneapolis, many Black, refused to help transport police protestors to jail. And in several cities, union nurses supported protestors with masks and water. Nationally, the SEIU and the American Federation of Teachers (AFT) put out statements that were generally in support of the Movement for Black Lives' demands.[26]

In contrast, the AFL-CIO defended the membership of the International Union of Police Associations (IUPA) in the federation while calling for some general reforms that IUPA was still heavily offended by.[27] The tensions arising from the fact that much of organized labor is too often out of relationship with the majority of the US workforce were exposed by the 2020 uprisings for Black lives.

During the COVID-19 pandemic in 2020 and 2021, a disproportionate number of Black workers got sick and died from the virus. Many of these workers were deemed essential, yet their employers did not provide them with adequate protective equipment or comply with social distancing rules. Left exposed to the virus, they were infected. Essential workers staffing meat-processing plants, mostly immigrants from Latin America, were forced to continue working in unsafe conditions for the sake of delivering the United States' chicken and pork. In fact, the only time that the Trump administration activated the Defense of Production Act—a law that authorizes the president to expedite and expand the supply of key commodities and/or services in order to promote the national defense—was to keep meat-packing workers at work, not to produce more ventilators or tests that might have actually helped the country get through the pandemic. Once again, essential workers of color were hung out to dry.

The message is clear: labor leaders urgently need to expand organizing and collective bargaining in ways that address the needs of Black and Brown communities as a central part of their strategy—not just because it is morally right but also because failing to do so will render them irrelevant.

While we have focused primarily on US examples here, the international workers' struggle against global capitalism is part of the same intersectional effort. In order to combat global capital, unions and progressive organizations will have to unite across national borders, not just in moral solidarity but also through shared organizing and collective bargaining demands on multinational corporations and their government supporters. Such a multinational organizing campaign will require US workers, particularly white workers, to abandon the belief that workers in China, India, Mexico, or Tunisia somehow deserve less than them. This will require organizers to recognize the negative effect of white supremacy not only on the global south but also on workers in the global north, beginning with a deeper understanding of what various trade agreements actually do and the driving forces behind them.

The Asia Floor Wage Alliance (AFWA), which Jobs With Justice has proudly supported since its inception, has begun to build a campaign like this, establishing regional living-wage mechanisms that are translatable across countries and that target strategic transnational corporations.[28] The AFWA has also pressured a number of multinational companies into agreeing to a global convention to end gender-based violence at work.[29]

The Power of Centralizing Race and Gender to Win at the Bargaining Table

As we have explained, the history of the prevailing political economy throughout the world makes it natural that Black and immigrant workers in the southern region of the United States and people of the global south have some of the most creative approaches to transforming that economy and replacing it with a healthy democracy. This is just one of the important reasons why a reimagined and reinvigorated labor movement for the twenty-first century needs to embrace the goal not just of organizing *all* people, regardless of their race, ethnicity, gender, and other characteristics, but also of tapping the leadership skills and experience of all people. Economic democracy is for everyone—not just a few.

Clarifying workers' shared self-interests against common corporate exploiters is the only way to motivate white workers who have legitimate worries and fears to act in their shared interests with workers of color. Thus, the parents of children in rundown schools in a predominantly poor white community should align with the parents of children in similar schools in Black and Brown communities to confront the individuals who are responsible for underfunding, from local schoolboard members to the corporate actors who benefit from privatizing public schools. The same thinking can be applied to issues like housing, health care, public services, public utilities, and jobs. Lasting power and shared governance require us to adopt defeating white supremacy as a central strategy.

Similarly, efforts that centralize the struggle against patriarchy and gender-based violence have positioned many working people to negotiate directly with political and economic decision-makers when narrower workplace issues failed. For example, the #MeToo movement sparked shifts in workplace policy, such as banning nondisclosure agreements that cover sexual harassment as well as energizing campaigns aiming to raise the economic status of women workers.[30] In at least one case in India, a small caucus of women workers did a better job than their union of forcing a powerful multinational brand to the table by centering the discussion on the gender-based violence they experienced in supplier factories.[31] US unions, still overwhelmingly headed by white men, can learn a lesson from this example. Sometimes what gets the union to the table with some of the largest corporations is getting out of the way of women workers.[32]

The current economic, political, and social state of the world in 2020 looks like a catastrophe—police violence, a global pandemic, a Saharan dust cloud, a plague of locusts—all creating fissures within the corporate class and devastating blows to the economic sustainability of most working people. But crisis breeds creativity. As Arundhati Roy noted in the *Financial Times*, "unlike the flow of capital, this virus seeks proliferation, not profit, and has, therefore, inadvertently, to some extent, reversed the direction of the flow. It has mocked immigration controls, biometrics, digital surveillance and every other kind of data analytics, and struck hardest—thus far—in the richest, most powerful nations of the world, bringing the engine of capitalism to a juddering halt. Temporarily perhaps, but at least long enough for us to examine its parts, make an assessment and decide whether we want to help fix it, or look for a better engine."[33]

The crisis may offer an opportunity for unions and community organizations to build a new workers' movement, intentionally aligning the shared self-interests of white workers with Black workers, workers of color, and workers of all genders against systems of white supremacy, corporate control, and sexism.

This is not just a matter of doing what is right. It is also the only way to build lasting power for working people. Treating the battles against white supremacy and patriarchy as extra projects that can be compromised would be like making a boat lighter by removing the sails. Confronting the systems of white supremacy and patriarchy must remain a central element of our overall strategy to prevent the opposition from dividing workers and weakening our collective power.

BEYOND THE RED AND THE BLUE

A New Map for Twenty-First-Century Organizers

For Jacob Staggers, the evening of February 27, 2018, was a tense one. Staggers, a sixth-grade English teacher in Morgantown, West Virginia, joined educators in all fifty-five counties of the state in an almost unprecedented work stoppage. James C. Justice, the state's governor, had made a bid to end the work stoppages by offering a small raise for some state employees, including schoolteachers. Staggers and his colleagues were faced with a difficult choice.

This was no ordinary work stoppage. West Virginia teachers and educators had not walked off the job collectively in almost twenty years. As what is called a *right-to-work* state, West Virginia legally prohibits both striking and collective bargaining. Yet women and men throughout the entire state, from all kinds of backgrounds and political persuasions—including many from mostly white counties—had still decided to take the risk of collectively stopping work. They were tired of stagnating wages, both for them and other state employees. They had had enough of rollbacks to their health care coverage. They resented the state's demand that they share private information with the government using an intrusive smartphone app that only made the rollbacks worse. They were sick of school underfunding that ultimately hurt their students most. Finally, the idea of introducing charter schools into a state that had long uplifted its public schools pushed teachers to fight, not just for themselves but also for public education itself.

Feeling compelled to act collectively for the first time transformed many of these working women and men. Given this, they had no intention of going back to work without a real solution. In some counties, educators were already setting up long-term food pantries, online lesson plans, and other supports for students who would be missing school due to the educators' actions. Against this backdrop, the governor's February 27 proposal was simply not good enough. In addition to the targeted pay increase, calculated to divide the teachers from other state employees, it did nothing to respond to the issues around health care, including the invasive app that teachers were being asked to use. The governor's proposal fell short on all counts.

Jacob Staggers was tracking the situation with his county president and fellow cheerleading coach, Heather DeLuca-Nestor, who was texting him updates from the state capital in Charleston. It was an exhausting time for him. "I was spending a lot of time on the road and not getting a lot of sleep," he recalls:

> But I realized that I didn't want the work stoppage to end. At a particularly tense meeting that night, a lot of us met. And some were crying and asking why we were even meeting. "We got the raise, didn't we? Isn't that what we wanted?" But I told them that that's not what we went out for. It was because of our insurance, the charter school legislation, and other issues. Plus, we'd said we were going to do this for all state employees, and some of them weren't going to get anything from the governor's offer.[1]

Staggers's perspective carried the day. Ultimately the work stoppage continued, and through their actions West Virginia educators were able to win a 5 percent increase for *all* state workers. They were also able to stop—at least for the time being—the negative changes to their health care and the establishment of charter schools in the state.

The West Virginia teachers' work stoppage garnered headlines and TV coverage around the nation and the world. How had schoolteachers in one of the country's poorer and more politically conservative states managed to win such a resounding, unexpected victory—even in the absence of the legal right to strike or engage in collective bargaining? The answers to this question can offer important insights into strategies that organizers throughout the country need to consider as we design a labor movement suited for maximum effectiveness in the twenty-first century.

Organizing Workers without Legal Collective Bargaining Rights

As the story of the teachers' strike illustrates, many workers in West Virginia and other right-to-work states are demonstrating practices capable of engaging millions of working families who lack access to a union contract—and they are doing so without waiting to receive an official guarantee of protection. The West Virginia Education Association and West Virginia Federation of Teachers embodied what it meant to act like a union when they took mass action in support of people unable to access the protections of a union, in many cases winning important victories.

Another group of organizations that are operating in this fashion can be captured under the umbrella term *worker centers*. They have evolved in the last thirty years to meet the immediate needs of individuals who, for whatever reason, cannot form a union. And while they are not unions, they are about building the collective power of workers—unlike historic company-driven models of representation, such as Taylorism, which actively sought to mute workers' collective power.[2] The fact that many of these organizations support nonunion workers in what are now recognized as essential sectors illustrates just how sick our democracy has become: the most essential workers are those with the least power and access to democracy.

Jobs With Justice coalitions supported some of the earliest worker centers, some of which were launched by individuals seeking to join unions, others by people who simply needed help recovering stolen wages in order to get their lights turned back on. Over the years, many worker centers have organized by business or economic sector and worked with traditional unions to attempt to raise standards in an industry.

For example, in fall 2010, at the urging of a worker center called Domestic Workers United (DWU), the state of New York passed a bill of rights, the first of its kind, which essentially organized domestic workers, nannies, and other caregivers to negotiate with the state to include them in the basic labor protections afforded by law. DWU and similar organizations around the country went on to form the National Domestic Workers Alliance and later, the International Domestic Workers Federation, creating the potential for setting labor standards nationally through a federal domestic workers bill of rights as well as the establishment of a global framework for domestic work under the auspices of the International Labor Organization.

Another worker center, the Alliance of Guestworkers for Dignity, organized Indian metal workers to protect them from a company called Signal that was engaged in a number of exploitive practices. The Alliance of Guestworkers for Dignity later grew to become the National Guestworkers Alliance (NGA), which blazed a new path in 2012 when it helped eleven Louisiana workers under contract with a small company named C.J.'s Seafood to obtain a meeting with the ultimate beneficiary of their labor, the retail giant Walmart.[3] The NGA workers acted big, seeking to negotiate directly with the people at the far end of the food chain, and they won. We will delve more deeply into the strategy of negotiating with the ultimate profiteers of global capital in a later chapter.

Other worker centers are fighting to improve conditions in different sectors. The Restaurant Opportunities Center United has found new ways to negotiate with the food industry, taking on the issue of the so-called *tipped minimum wage*. Based on the idea that workers perform for tips instead of a baseline salary, the tipped minimum wage is actually one of the last relics of slavery. It originated after the Civil War when former plantation owners fought to ensure that former enslaved people would be dependent on charitable gifts from their employers rather than freely negotiated salaries.[4] Interventions by the National Day Laborer Organizing Network, which organizes many undocumented workers, have improved standards in the residential construction industry.[5] And the Coalition of Immokalee Workers and other farmworker organizations have leveraged consumer influence over multinational food brands to ensure safe, worker-defined standards for their members in agriculture.

A number of these worker centers went on to form the United Workers Congress (UWC), a federation-like coalition to address the interests of workers excluded from traditional union organizing, including many Black, Brown, formerly incarcerated, and immigrant workers. While the UWC no longer exists, its legacy continues in the successful organizing of both national worker center networks and strong regional worker centers throughout the country; in the deepened work of supply-chain and migration organizing of groups like Global Labor Justice; and in the campaigns centered around essential workers after the COVID-19 outbreak.

As you can see, the West Virginia teachers are far from the only workers in America who are taking on the powers-that-be without the protections most unions have. This is an important fact for would-be organizers to recognize. Power is not dependent on following traditionally prescribed paths. Instead, it grows from the collective action of people in shared economic relationships who are determined to work together to make their voices heard and to have their needs met from common decision-makers. Once those conditions are met, all kinds of victories are possible.

How Shared Worker Values Can Overcome Political Barriers

Many of the labor victories we have been describing have occurred in regions or sectors often deemed politically challenging by progressives—states like West

Virginia and Louisiana and sectors like agriculture, domestic work, and hospi-tality. How can this be?

Stepping back, it is not so difficult to reconcile. The work in West Virginia provides an excellent case study in how critical it is to see the whole person, not just the employee, when evolving our framework for organizing and collective bargaining. It shows what can happen when people unite around a set of shared values, even across seemingly deep ideological or political divides.

Comments by Amelia "Amie" Mullens, a West Virginia mom who teaches seventh and eighth grade science, go a long way toward explaining how this works. Asked to explain what motivated her and her fellow teachers to support the work stoppage, Mullens said, "If we couldn't take care of our own health care, how were we going to take care of the health of our students? And we really need to do that, because we have an opioid crisis here. My husband works as an emer-gency medical services worker and sees it firsthand. And we, as teachers, get notes from EMS that say HWC—handle with care—for students who may have been impacted by addiction. During the strike, we still had to be able to get to them. They may live over a holler and not be able to get to school. So we depended on local nurses, churches, and other nonprofits to help us. That's what we do as teachers."[6]

Mullens's explanation illustrates the compassion and commitment that mo-tivates workers like school teachers, not just in West Virginia but also in com-munities everywhere. But it does not explain a remarkable anomaly about the state's teacher stoppage. The first of the fifty-five West Virginia counties to call for and then implement the work stoppage were Logan, Mingo, and Wyoming Counties—all located in the southern part of the state, the epicenter of the mine wars after World War I, from which the miners who engaged in the Battle of Blair Mountain came.[7] Mullens lived and worked in Wyoming County during the time of the walkouts (see figure 7.1).

You might assume that these counties contain the most progressive activists in the state—the educators' movement avant-garde. Are these the counties where West Virginia's urban elite live?

The answer is a resounding no. If anything, voters in the southern end of West Virginia are more conservative than those in other parts of the state. Wyoming County, for example, is far from diverse (98 percent white), is relatively poor (a median household income of $36,000 versus $49,000 nationwide), and cast 83.6 percent of its votes for Donald Trump in 2016—the highest percentage of any county in the state.

As Amie Mullens puts it, "You can draw a line between the southern coun-ties and the rest of the state. We have a different mentality here. Down here, you

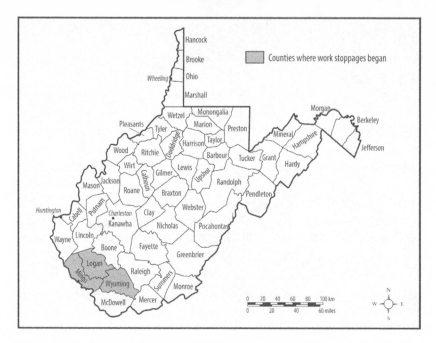

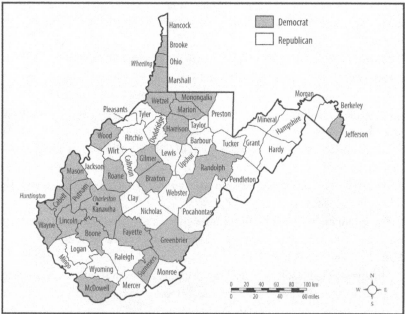

FIGURE 7.1. The two images sharpen how the electoral map alone does not project an accurate assessment of the willingness of people to act on progressive worker values. While the people in these counties do not identify overwhelmingly with Democrats, they do identify with the ideals of dignity and respect for working people, as previously framed by coal miners in the same region.

Sources: Senate election map comes from https://www.washingtonpost.com/election-results/west-virginia/?utm _term=.b1ece3f356f1. Map created by authors using www.mapchart.net.

don't mess with your people. And you're going to have people behind you if someone does. So, when the legislative attacks on teachers came, we decided we weren't going to wait. We took off in a school bus to Charleston to fight for our rights and the rights of our students. And it was such bad weather that the snowplow rode in front of the school buses to get us across county lines. We didn't let that stop us. That's the kind of support we had."[8]

Amie's experience helps clarify the willingness of working people to act collectively when motivated and inspired by a bold vision aligned with their shared values, including issues that go beyond their immediate wants and needs. Organizing people is not about their ideology. It is about appealing to the values that drive them.

Heather Deluca-Nestor and Allyson Perry. Portrait by Gwenn Seemel.

Profiles of Modern Workers:
Allyson Perry and Heather DeLuca-Nestor:
"Just Doing What We Had to Do"

Allyson Perry and Heather DeLuca-Nestor are two of the teachers who partici-
pated in the West Virginia work stoppage of 2018. At the time, both were presi-
dents of their county union locals—Allyson in Marion and Heather in Monongalia.
And both had stories to tell.

Allyson

I remember the night before the walkout in Marion County. I was staying late
in my classroom finishing up a lot of stuff because I wasn't sure when we were
going to be back. I remember leaving that school thinking that this was one of
the biggest things I've ever done in my entire life and that I had no idea what's
going to happen. We didn't have collective bargaining rights in West Virginia.
Who knew what the state leaders would do? But we still had power. I felt we were
on the cusp of something. It felt like being at the edge of a cliff and you're either
going to fly off or drop to your doom. I was nervous but I knew we had to do
this. I was ready. I'd been feeling the buildup for weeks. So, I wanted to hang
glide off the cliff, to soar. That's how I felt while I was waiting to leave work the
day before it all started.

Heather

I really didn't want to walk out at first. It had to be a last resort because, if you
lose, then what? You've exhausted all possibilities.

My dad was a teacher during the 1990 strike. My parents were divorced, but
I remember him going to my mom who was also a teacher and saying, "Don't
you cross that picket line, Cheryl." And she said, "Jerry, I can't afford not to." He
responded that he'd pay more in child support to make it work, and he said again,
"Don't you cross that picket line." And she didn't. They made it work.

The teachers did win an increase in pay along with a faculty senate that gave
them more of a voice. But that strike was not as successful as many had hoped,
and people still harbor bad feelings about it.

Allyson

I was in a graduate school program in Pennsylvania when I realized that I preferred teaching to research. I started substitute teaching. Everyone was a part of

the Pennsylvania State Education Association (PSEA), and I became president of the Southwestern Chapter of the PSEA student organization and attended various conferences. So when I came to West Virginia, I quickly joined the West Virginia Education Association (WVEA). It was kind of a no-brainer. That's what I knew.

Heather

To be a teacher you really have to love it. And there's a lot of work involved on top of being in the classroom. We coach sports teams. We support extracurricular clubs. We tutor students. The workday does not end when the bell rings at 3 p.m. When I go to the grocery store, the people I run into know that my identity is being a teacher, and that's what we talk about. And if you have your own kids, there you are sitting at gymnastics practice for three hours later in the day, trying to make sure their homework gets done and they eat. And some teachers still work other jobs to make ends meet.

People in other professions with comparable degrees make 21 percent more on average than teachers do.[9] I mean, that's the reality of the life that a teacher lives.

Knowing this, our union local supports students who are striving to become teachers. They can join the local as students. Then, when they graduate, they start paying dues and become full members. That's how I started out. And it isn't just about the union defending us when things go wrong. You get a mentor to guide you through the process, materials to help you unpack the standards that you have to go through. And our union does protect us, advocating for our students and our livelihoods. For me, it was the only option. Growing up with my parents, I knew I was always going to be a member of the teachers union.

Allyson

I'd seen my dad on the picket line growing up. He worked in a steel mill in Pennsylvania and so was part of a traditional union. My grandparents had worked there too as well as a few of my uncles. I only saw my dad on strike at the mill one time, for better health care and compensation. That was when I first experienced what it meant to fight for something you truly, wholeheartedly believe in—something that you would put it all on the line for, including your job.

When it came time for me to act with my union, my dad and I had a lot to talk about. West Virginia legislators were trying to limit our health care, making us pay more for less. And they were attempting to force us to use this app on our phones to track all sorts of personal information that could be used to cut benefits even more. And all of this was done while legislators tried to introduce charter schools into a state where we had not had them before. I knew I had my dad's support when we decided to walk out.

Heather

I had members come to me crying when they heard we might walk out. When we took a strike vote in Morgantown, one lady came to me in tears and said, "You know, at some point I have to ask myself, why am I still doing this? You know, is this the right thing to do?" As a leader and president of her local, I just had to listen. I had teachers in my local who were in different places. Some were like, "Let's walk out tomorrow!" And others were not supportive. I had to listen to all of them. Democracy is messy. But I wasn't scared. My dad reminded me from the get-go, "You do what you have to do, and I'll do what I have to do to make sure you're okay."

Allyson

Not everyone had my experience, and many of the teachers in my local were worried. People with young kids were worried about the state docking their pay. But at the end of the day, they knew what we were all up against. Teachers who cannot take care of themselves cannot take care of their students. And that's why most of us became teachers. So they were willing to stand with the majority. Only a few people declined to show up during the walkout. We were just doing what we had to do at the time. That's how important this was for us.

Heather

It was such a whirlwind. We had never really been in this situation before, not ever. We just had to put one foot in front of the other and do what we had to do to stop the attacks on public education. They were trying to cut back our health care, which is provided through the Public Employees' Insurance Agency. They were asking us to use this app called Go 365 that was invasive. It pretty much wanted you to share your whole life history down to your underwear size, and that really shook people. For years, public employees have taken hits to our health insurance, making up the difference with our own money. Funding for public education in West Virginia hasn't changed significantly in forty years, and now this?

Mitch Carmichael, the president of the state senate, and others had this task force that held twenty-one meetings all over the state to make recommendations about funding for public education—and particularly for our healthcare—to the legislature. WVEA president Dale Lee also served on the task force. So many people testified at meetings that went on for hours. And when it was all said and done, Carmichael said he didn't have enough data. How many people do you really need to tell you the same exact thing? That was when the dam broke. It was at that point I realized that I'm not giving up. I'm going to fight even harder. There's no way to get through to these people. Nothing I'm going to say or do, even putting proof right in front of them, is going to change their minds about what they're doing. We were done talking.

My church was somewhat divided. Some of the members were not supportive of what we were doing. It's not a large church, so it was tense for a moment. It was hard because I was close to many people there. Some of them used to watch my children. I felt judged, like I was being a bad mom for walking out with our union. So at first I kept very quiet.

At the same time, many of us were getting worried because some of our students wouldn't get enough food to eat during the work stoppage. One Sunday, Pastor Brad stood up and said that we as a church support people and organizations that are trying to fight for fair wages, and our doors are always open. He asked everyone in their hearts to seek understanding. I'll never forget him saying that. Afterward our church joined many others in opening our doors to help the teachers and families impacted by the walkout. Our church basement stored food for families to come and pick up if they needed it. And we let one of the schools set up shop in our parking lot.

Allyson

We mobilized to the state capital. We marched and spoke with every state legislator in Charleston. We had a constant presence and a lot of support. So many other labor organizations came out and stood alongside us. Elected officials, pastors, parents, and some of the high school kids came. Even the superintendents of each school system came out and spoke in support of us.

Ultimately we got the legislators to back down from changing our health care. And we won a 5 percent raise for all state employees in West Virginia. This was a big victory for the people of West Virginia. Had we not succeeded, the money the state would have saved by not giving us raises and cutting our health benefits would have headed to a bunch of big gas companies to do their worst with it.

Heather

We didn't realize how significant our victory was outside of West Virginia until later. We were just in our little bubble trying to protect public education. At some point I looked up to see four hundred pizzas roll into the capital building, sent by someone in California. And we were like, this is affecting other people. That is a moment I really remember.

I also remember sitting outside of the capital, shaking with my phone in my hand because I'd been asked to talk to CNN about what was happening and they were about to call me. I did not think I was ready for this. I felt unprepared, like I'm just a teacher, you know? Being in a classroom with twenty-seven kids is not the same as being on CNN Headline News to talk to that kind of audience. But I'm telling you now, the fact that I honestly believed in what we were doing made it easier for me. One of my colleagues reminded me that leaders aren't asked, they are chosen. So I stopped shaking and answered the phone.

Allyson

Obviously this was also a huge victory for us. It showed many of us what it meant to become more active in the democratic process. I've seen an increase in interest from members in my local about who to vote for politically, but maybe more important, an interest in being an active member of the union—just showing up to meetings and participating in union discussions and decisions at our delegate assembly. We have that assembly every year at WVEA, and it follows the democratic process. Any member who is an elected delegate can speak and be a part of making our legislative agenda for the year. I saw people go from seeing that as just another long faculty meeting to feeling energized by being clued into what's going on and having a say in the democratic process. After our victory in 2018, they became aware that they had leadership abilities they did not know they had. They had to see themselves as having that leadership capacity, whether as a building representative or a county president or in some state office. So, our success helped a lot of people recognize their own leadership potential.

Heather

To be quite honest, I never saw myself as a political person, at least not until I realized what that really meant. It's not that I didn't think politics was important. I just didn't think I had the time to be active in this way. But politics came to mean standing up for my life, my livelihood, my profession.

I remember another teacher had put up a snapshot on her social media feed about how the state was trying to lower Environmental Protection Act standards in the drinking water for West Virginia back to 1985 levels. I remember it because in my science class the students were discussing Earth's water. So I used the posting to spark conversation in my class. We are careful about not pushing our opinions on students. I don't want to tread on ideals that might be different than mine. I want them to be able to form their own opinions about things. In that discussion, I think we all came to agree—me included—that even if you think you're far removed from something, chances are it's happening right in your backyard. You know, if you're not at the table, then you're probably on the menu.

Allyson

What a lot of people don't understand about educators is that we are not just defending our jobs. We are defending the institutions that educate our children. Public schools were set up for a democratic republic, to make a democratic citizenry knowledgeable, and to ensure that by the end of their educational career they were good public citizens. So, the teachers unions are really wrapped up directly in the pillars of our republic. We were clear that our unions were defending public education. What was unclear was what the charter school coalitions were defending and what the state legislators were defending. If those groups aren't standing up for the democratic pillars of our republic, someone must do it, and that's us. Within a profession like ours, the union protects not only your job but also this thing that we all love and value—the institution of public education and its role in shaping our democracy. Whether you legally have collective bargaining rights or not is far from the issue when your purpose is to defend the institution.

Heather

I see a difference between some of the work we do and the general idea of the blue-collar union. We also protect our rights, yes. But it's about more than that. It's about defending the institution of public education. I guess you could call us the standard-bearers of public education and defending our children. We're not just fighting for ourselves alone. When steel workers go on strike, like some of my relatives back in Pittsburgh, they're not trying to defend the steel company. In fact, they're fighting against that company for fair compensation when it's in the company's interest to take advantage of them—to increase profits by paying employees less. But it's different for teachers and educators. We defend public schools, our employer. We fight to strengthen public education. Improving conditions for teachers makes public education better for everyone.

Allyson

If it were up to us we would increase state funding per pupil in public schools. We would have full-time school counselors whose sole job was to work with the children. We'd have social workers in every school because we all need help addressing this opioid crisis. And instead of bringing in charter schools, we would establish community schools with wraparound services with doctors and other programs children and their families need. We have empirical data that this model has worked in other places and similar data showing that charter schools do not. Again, we want what is best for our students, and it continues to be clear to us that this requires us to strengthen our public institutions.

Heather

There are people dying and these legislators sit up on a panel passing judgment. I'm not saying they're the enemy or bad people, but once they leave, Christmas is still coming to their family. The Easter Bunny is still coming to their families. Meanwhile, we're teaching while also providing students with pencils and making sure they have something to eat.

I'm just a normal person, and I get tired of it. Sometimes I want to be able to go into my classroom and just teach my kids. I don't want to have to continually fight tooth and nail for every scrap that the legislature decides to throw us. These kids are the future of West Virginia, and the legislature keeps taking funding away from our future. We've got kids living with their grandparents because their parents are absent or in jail or addicted to drugs.

I had a child coming to my class every day and sleeping through it. Around Christmas that year I finally just asked him if he had a bed. He kind of looked at me and was like, "yeah." And I said, "Do you have blankets and a pillow? I'm willing to buy you some if you don't have one, so you need to tell me." And he said he had them.

But now that student will come to me and say, "Mrs. Nestor, I'm hungry," knowing that I keep a little stash of food in my classroom. Those are the kinds of things teachers do every day. And that's far removed from how some of our legislators are acting, assuming that, "Well, the gas company is helping fund my campaign, so I'm not going to do anything." Our union helps us ensure that our values prevail, not those values. And that's why, despite being tired, I am still active in my union.

We may not have collective bargaining rights in West Virginia but our union is strong. We stand together. We recognize that we are a part of something greater than ourselves. We're part of an educational community. Some people are leaders in their schools, building representatives who everyone knows they can go to with questions. Others just listen.

That's what's great about our democratic process. You can debate and argue it and come up with some kind of consensus. Last year the consensus was, no, we're not going to go back to school. Next time may be different. The dissenters aren't bad on either side of the spectrum. I think that their positions are very valid. But you have to be a part of the process and recognize the structure that was set in place so that everyone has a voice—to prevent one group from becoming an oligarchy.

Allyson

I worry sometimes that people like to romanticize our grassroots movements as if there is no structure, like it's all just spontaneous. If you get rid of unions and try to imagine something that seems completely grassroots with no leadership at the top, it doesn't work in practice. Not everyone would have their say or ability to speak up. That's why we have unions, so we can have that democratic process in place. We have a framework where you run the gamut of members, those who want to go out tomorrow and those who are afraid to go on strike, people of all political persuasions, just like a voting public, right? You have conservative people and you have liberal people, but at the end of the day, because of our democratic process, we can make decisions. That's why we can have elected positions in a union that are going to speak on behalf of us based on our collective voice. We have representatives there at the negotiating table that hold everyone's best interest. That's why democratic processes and frameworks are important, and why the structures that our unions have in place are important.

I've heard unions called schools of democracy before. And that makes sense to me, because our unions create a place where we actively *do* democracy, even when it's messy.

Dismissed States: Sites of Tomorrow's Breakthroughs

West Virginia is just one example of a place where people who are usually labeled as conservative are organizing themselves and taking bold stands to defend their rights and to bring economic democracy to their communities. One way to understand how this is happening is to begin viewing our country through the lens of a new map.

Elections matter, and the red state–blue state divide that political pundits, television commentators, and politicians themselves like to focus on is a real one. But elections are not the only source of power in our country. Working people want more than competent elected officials. They seek the ability to govern in ways that maximize everyone's democratic participation and practice—at work and in their communities. To see how this dynamic plays out, we need a map that defines states not by the political leanings of their congressional delegations but by their relationship to twentieth-century democracy—both political and economic—and the protections it created for collective bargaining and workers' rights. Figure 7.2 offers such a map.

This new map categorizes states into several distinct categories.

First, there are the states that still have robust infrastructure and protections for working people's rights to vote and collectively bargain, based on twentieth-century laws and regulations. These states are shown in the lightest gray shading. States like New York, Massachusetts, and California still have robust union density. Their state political parties conduct contentious primary elections in which viable left-leaning candidates often participate. And these states boast a rich tradition of groups representing a popular majoritarian ideology that influences public opinion about the role of government, corporations, development, and workplace democracy. These states are not without problems. But working people can sometimes win using twentieth-century frameworks for democracy, particularly the protections of the NLRA.

States shown in the medium gray shading have some of the same characteristics, but they are in constant struggles against right-wing politicians and organizations to maintain them. For example, legislators in Missouri have been trying for years to pass a right-to-work law that would cripple unions. In 2017, they finally succeeded—but in 2018, through a ballot initiative, the voters of the state overturned the law.

In both the light gray and medium gray shaded states the working majority can continue to exercise power through the current channels and institutions. We can still win using existing rules to make our values real in the world. We can also experiment with new frameworks to expand how people collectively negotiate, including incorporating struggles from outside of the workplace into traditional collective bargaining.

The states shown with black shading have experienced a recent rapid erosion of protections for the voting and bargaining rights they enjoyed in the twentieth century. Individuals in these areas still have a communal memory of the power they used to have before the plants closed, the unions were busted, and the laws were changed. Members of these communities are often angry, skeptical about the old institutions that betrayed them, and hesitant about embracing untested strategies for regaining power.

As a result, organizers in these states find themselves having conversations like the one author Erica Smiley had with a laid-off manufacturing worker in

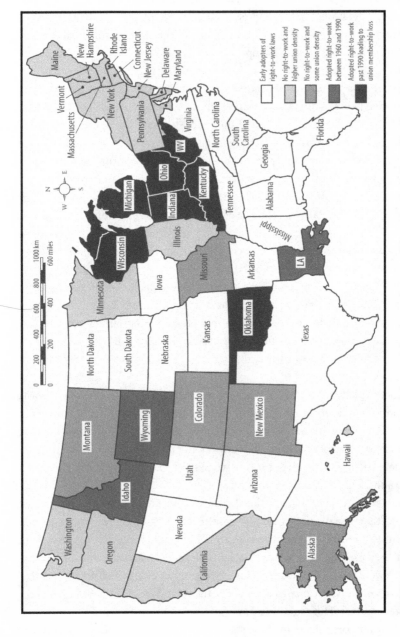

FIGURE 7.2. The map suggests a way of organizing in each part of the country tailored to that state/region's current relationship to political and economic democracy. Map created by authors using www.mapchart.net.

Michigan. When Smiley asked him what he thought about raising the minimum wage, he responded disgustedly, "I used to make $42 an hour. We don't need a minimum wage! We need our jobs back!"[10]

In the states with black shading working people can still sometimes win based on the twentieth-century rules, though the opportunities to do so are becoming scarce. Movement leaders must build campaigns that are sensitive to what working people have recently lost while helping them accept that the old system did not work. Such efforts can yield small victories to rebuild momentum and morale while also building organization, especially as communities in these regions recognize and relate to various traditional cultures of organizing. This is the necessary foundation for creating a new framework for organizing and collective bargaining.

The states with white and dark gray shading have been written off for generations by national progressive actors. These states have long lost most twentieth-century protections for workers—if they ever had them. Most working people in these states have little to lose. Perhaps partly as a result of this reality, these state activists who have come together to struggle against the existing power structure often demand far more than access to the twentieth-century framework of organizing, collective bargaining, and voting.

The southern states in particular are where some of today's most exciting and militant upsurges are happening. As the West Virginia teachers' story suggests, public-sector workers are among those becoming newly mobilized in these and other states. Several public-sector unions have reported significant growth of volunteer membership in states with extremely regressive labor laws, even in the face of looming threats to their right to organize in the form of US Supreme Court cases like *Friedrichs v. California Teachers Association* and *Janus v. AFSCME Council 31*.[11] Workers in these states often feel they have nothing to lose and everything to gain, which makes them psychologically ready to take bigger chances, reach for larger goals, and seek greater victories that go far beyond their immediate personal needs. In states like Georgia, workers are not only demanding the repeal of state right-to-work laws and protections for voting rights but also insisting that the people they represent who live, work, worship, and play in the state be able to have a collective democratic voice in how the state is run.

What is important for progressive organizers in these previously dismissed states is to support and reinforce local struggles in which working people are exposing the failings of the existing regimes and structures while also seeking to establish modern rules for governing, voting, organizing, and collective bargaining—essentially, the foundations of democracy. Coordinated victories in these states could change the national narrative, creating enormous new momentum behind the growth of working-class organizations.

Through the lens of this new map, the recent upsurge of activism among teachers and many others who reside outside the traditionally progressive states is not surprising at all. Thanks to working people, many areas ignored by the national political power brokers are becoming frontline sites for twenty-first-century movement-building. It is time to dedicate organizing resources to these regions, during both election years and off-years, in an effort to build political and economic power for the everyday people of these states. No working-class community should be left behind in defining the future of democracy.

Part 3

THE WAY WE WIN

You wanna fly, you got to give up the shit that weighs you down.

—Toni Morrison, *Song of Solomon*

Sarita Gupta. Portrait by Gwenn Seemel.

PROFILE OF THE AUTHOR

Sarita Gupta: Making Meaning of the World

My family immigrated to Rochester, New York, in 1975. My parents were first-generation Indian immigrants who helped establish various ethnic community groups that focused on celebrating our Indian culture and building community in a strange land. My parents were active in the Bengali Association of Greater Rochester and then cofounded the Indian Community Center. We grew up in a part of Rochester that was not diverse—it was majority white. My sister, brother, and I experienced a lot of racism as children. We were the "other," and most kids we grew up with had a hard time placing us in their worldview.

I was called everything from "Aunt Jemima" to "Pocahontas" to so much more that I can laugh at today but that deeply hurt me as a child. Kids would ask me, "What are you?" I would reply that I am Indian, which was met with kids circling me and mimicking their idea of a Native American chanting and singing. When I would explain that I was not a Native American but the other kind of Indian from India, they would either look at me like I was crazy since I mentioned a country they did not know of, or, for those who had, they would immediately equate me to the extreme poverty that they saw in Save the Children ads on TV. It was their only point of reference. I remember being surrounded in the lunchroom one day in second grade by kids who held their thermos cups and pretended to be beggars, asking for money and food. I got teased a lot, but nothing in comparison to the hate crimes my older sister experienced in middle school, or the regular fistfights my brother endured through much of his childhood.

I knew that I was a Brown kid and I was also very grounded in my identity as an Indian. But what perplexed me was the assumption of poverty and that I was worse off than the white kids whose parents' jobs were being threatened. In second grade I was confused by the assumptions of race and class. I clearly did not have that language as a seven-year-old, but again, I knew something was wrong.

We are always trying to make meaning of the world we live in. I have early memories of trying to do just that as I journeyed through my childhood as an immigrant in Rochester, New York. I grew up in Kodak City and lived through the early years of downsizing. I listened as my friends talked about their parents losing their jobs at Kodak and feeling a real uncertainty about their own futures. For many, their families had been working in the Kodak factories for generations and they believed they too would be working their someday. After all, these were good jobs with decent pay and benefits, and Kodak had a reputation for being a place that promoted economic mobility for working women and men. I remember sensing the powerlessness that people around me were feeling. Many of them had to settle for low-wage work that could barely pay the bills, with little or no benefits. This eroded the economic stability in the largely working-class community I grew up in. Families could no longer afford their "middle-class" lifestyles.

And I could not understand how people who worked there had, what seemed to me at that time, to be no say or agency in their future. What options did people have? Who was shaping the jobs that could replace these lost jobs? I was too young to ask sophisticated questions about corporate responsibility, economic development, and the future economy in Rochester. All I knew as a kid was that my community was changing and that something felt wrong about it, but I could not yet articulate what it was. And so a seed was planted.

Decades later, I continue to try to make meaning of how the city and community I grew up in has transformed. I now understand that Kodak was not unionized and, therefore, that the workers had limited voice and protections. They were always told that Kodak would take care of them. Kodak employees, much like other working people in the Rust Belt, lost good family sustaining jobs and faced a future of economic instability with no immediate prospects for economic mobility.

These two experiences and the underlying questions that they surfaced have been an important part of my journey as I explore questions of power and identity. I still remember my first memory of when I felt truly powerless and it radicalized me. Me and a few of my friends in high school went to a local Planned Parenthood to get birth control. As we pulled into the parking lot on a Saturday morning, the lot was full of people praying. I really did not understand what I was witnessing. We got out of the car and an older man approached me saying that he will write my license plate down and call my parents to let them know that I was at an abortion clinic. I was furious! Who was this guy? And why was he threatening me? Then a few people tried to block our entrance to the clinic.

We managed to get around them and make it inside, but not without fear for our safety.

This experience radicalized me. I had never felt so powerless than in that moment of trying to do the responsible thing, only to have these people judge me and threaten to punish me. I was scared for weeks that my parents were going to get a crazy call or letter that I would need to explain. And I feared for my friends who had much stricter parents on the issue of birth control. I knew I was a minor, but it still felt wrong to me that there could be a possibility that I would not have a say on issues about my own body. Don't I have the power and right to make decisions for myself?

In college I had the experience of exploring this question of power. I entered college the fall after the Los Angeles riots in 1992. There was immense racial tension on campus, as people were grappling with the complexity of all that had happened in LA. As a first-year student I was quickly recruited to build an Asian American student group that would work on issues of anti-Asian violence taking place across the country and to take part in a larger effort with other organizations to address issues around the lack of supports for women of color on campus (I went to a women's college) and how to manage the racial tensions people were experiencing. We organized a coalition of the women of color organizations on campus and designed a successful recruitment and retention campaign to win cultural space, ethnic studies program, more support for first-generation students, and an increase in recruitment and tenure of faculty of color.

It was amazing! It was my first experience with designing a set of demands and taking it directly to the president of our college. We organized a thoughtful campaign with tactical escalations that were rooted in a clear understanding of power. Ultimately, we did have to escalate with direct action, which resulted in meeting with the president, at which we shared our understanding of our power. This all resulted in our demands being met. This campaign taught me the art of organizing my peers, identifying the forms of power we had as students and consumers on campus, designing a campaign though which we could exercise our power, and winning through coalition building and collective action. I felt powerful!

Soon after this campus organizing success I became active with the US Student Association (USSA). USSA was an incredible training ground for me. I continued to learn about organizing and power from peers across the country, at small and large colleges and universities. During my tenure at USSA, the student movement was confronting a new assault on student power and voice in the form of attacks on student fee autonomy. A student activity fee is a fee charged to students at a college or university to support student organizations and activities. Over the last few decades, people have tried to legally challenge the idea that student fees can be used to subsidize "political groups." These attacks are taking away the ability for students to voice their opinions on how they want their student fees spent. For example, some student governments that are members of USSA run referendums on campus to raise money to support their membership at USSA. Their membership ensures that their voices are represented in federal policy-making on access to higher education issues. Opponents of student fee autonomy are essentially trying to limit the voice and agency of students. They are stripping away democracy on campuses.

Sound familiar? As I journeyed into the labor movement after USSA and learned about the attacks on collective bargaining rights, I came to appreciate the similarity of the attacks on workplace democracy to attacks on campus-based democracy. Instinctually I understood that the student and labor movements needed to work together to confront these attacks and strengthen democracy on both fronts. Historically, these connections have been drawn across various movements in history, the civil rights movement and labor for one. I asked myself, "who are we up against?" And in exploring that question it became clear that we must confront the greed of some corporations and some of the wealthy individuals in our society.

And much later in life, when I had the opportunity to visit the Narmada River Valley in India, I learned that there is a deep understanding of the attacks on basic rights and democracy in other parts of the world. The Adivasi (indigenous) communities I stayed with were clear about the attacks by corporations and governments on their voice and ability to live dignified lives.

My entry point into the labor movement was Jobs With Justice (JWJ). I was hired as a local JWJ director in Chicago. I got to work with an incredible set of local leaders who helped me learn what it takes to mobilize people, work at the intersections of issues, design campaigns, innovate new approaches, and build lasting relationships rooted in our values. I was in Chicago at the right time. There was an uptick in union organizing in the city. Most of these organizing efforts were focused on immigrant workers across various industries, including janitorial services, hotels, industrial laundries, and food production. This climate of active organizing created the conditions for JWJ to engage many people—students, faith and community leaders, academics, political leaders, and other influencers. And more important, it inspired us to create new structures to support organizing. Through these campaigns I came to appreciate the limitations of our current labor and immigration laws. I was able to leverage existing relationships and weave new ones to help us innovate new approaches.

Alongside these campaigns I worked with leaders at the Chicago Coalition for the Homeless, Chicago Interfaith Committee on Worker Issues, and the Center for Urban Economic Development at the University of Illinois at Chicago to open the first day labor center in the city. Up until that point there had not been a worker center in Chicago. This effort was born from research that quantified that about 100,000 Chicagoans were working as day laborers. We interviewed homeless men and women in shelters and learned that most of them worked as day laborers but never made enough money to be able to afford housing and food. This led us to begin an organizing effort in a neighborhood filled with temp agencies to learn more about the experiences of day laborers in the city, most of whom were Black, white, Latino and Polish immigrants. We learned that there was rampant wage theft, major health and safety issues, and much more. We opened the day labor center as a space for day laborers to come and share their stories, learn about the temp agency industry in Chicago, and develop strategies to address the problems.

This was my first foray into learning about the experiences of workers who fall outside of the traditional employer-employee relations that our current labor laws are based on. These are excluded workers with no real protections. We tried to create policy vehicles to set standards in this industry. Ultimately we were successful in passing a city ordinance and state legislation. And we were able to leverage JWJ's association with some local unions to establish strategic and supportive relationships. This was a time when many local unions did not look favorably at organizing this labor force. For many, day laborers were the strike breakers in campaigns—they were the "scabs." The dominant narrative was that these people were undermining union work in various sectors, including construction.

The day labor center offered a new pathway to organize these workers and begin to regulate the temporary agencies in the city. We learned a lot from peer worker centers across the country and the National Day Laborer Organizing Network. I credit this local experience with my appetite to learn and be in relationship to new worker organizing taking place outside of traditional unions. Most of these efforts are being led by local worker centers and national worker center networks. Since then I have worked on campaigns with domestic workers, guest workers, and restaurant worker groups and have learned to develop strategies that are relevant for workers who are excluded from collective bargaining rights either explicitly or implicitly. I have learned about informal sector organizing in the global south through partnerships with social movements. In fact, the Asia Floor Wage campaign that JWJ helped to develop and launch with worker organizations and unions in Asia is an attempt at developing new bargaining pathways for garment workers throughout the region. I was fortunate to take part in key strategy meetings at which new bargaining theories were being developed and, since then, tried.

My experiences with the organizing efforts in the United States and globally have helped expand my thinking on bargaining rights. I am aware of the infrastructure and capacities we need to build and/or strengthen as well as the shift in cultural values that we need to create the narrative and political environment that makes the evolution of bargaining rights possible.

We are always trying to make meaning of the world we live in. I deeply believe that people should have the ability to shape their futures. They should be able to govern every aspect of their lives. As an organizer, I know that an evolution of bargaining rights is a critical vehicle through which more working people can collectively exercise their voice and agency to shape their lives, communities, and workplaces. We need them to be in the driver's seat of shaping the economy and our democracy into the future. I know that practicing democracy is messy and hard, but I also know that it is empowering and effective in making sure we are addressing needs for the common good.

As a parent I feel a responsibility to teach my daughter to value her voice and to see power in the collective. Whether it is having her and her fellow Girl Scouts identify, debate, and vote on which country they will learn about for World Thinking Day; or make choices as a soccer or basketball player that benefit the collective versus only her; or to vote in her school elections to select the leaders she believes can address important issues, I am clear that I need to intentionally model and practice everyday democracy for my daughter, to seed the demand and practice within her to be able to govern over every aspect of her life. She needs to have the tools to make meaning of the world we live in. And she needs to be ready to struggle to make sure our vision of people being able to live a dignified life in a healthy democracy is not only possible but also inevitable.

BARGAINING WITH THE REAL DECISION-MAKERS

The Ultimate Profiteers of Global Capitalism

Several decades ago, a person could walk into a large retailer, hotel, hospital, manufacturer, or restaurant and assume correctly that most, if not all, of the people working there were employees of the company or brand displayed on the building outside. Under that framework, the rules of twentieth-century collective bargaining made sense. It assumed that direct employees could negotiate with their direct employers, often represented by on-site executives and managers accountable to the brand.

Today, that has changed. A person may walk into the same building they did thirty years ago, a building with the same logo on the outside and many of the same people working inside. But the underlying reality has shifted. As explained by David Weil, formerly the administrator for the Wage and Hour Division of the Department of Labor under President Obama,

> When most people walk into a Hilton or Marriott, they see the marquee and the brand on the staff uniforms and their hotel room amenities, and they come to the logical conclusion that everyone who works there is a Hilton or Marriott employee. . . . [But] often, most of the work has been parceled out among multiple players. Management service providers may manage the hotel property for a group of investors, who do not represent the brand itself, but could be any number of entities (i.e. private equity) who are smaller players in the hotel industry. That hotel management company will then typically break up the day-to-day work of the hotel among another host of players: the front

office work to one company, landscaping to another, restaurant activity to another (hotel restaurants may further "farm out" work to still other food service entities). Though we often think of hotel cleaning staff as providing a service core to the hotel's business, those services are often carried out by multiple agencies, including temporary agencies or labor brokers. This is emblematic of a fissured workplace: a constellation of different companies delivering what the consumer may think of as simply "the Marriott experience."[1]

Trying to empower the voices of working people in this type of workplace can be confusing. Traditional collective bargaining strategies are often stymied by a lack of clarity over who the actual boss is. Who do workers negotiate with? Who can actually make changes? Their direct employer—often a franchisee or subcontractor—may not actually have the power to adjust the exploitive business model, even if they are willing to negotiate with a union of their employees.

In this new workplace, in addition to negotiating with the employer they know, workers need to target the individuals and organizations that own the enterprises and thus hold significant positions of power in our economy. These individuals are often multiple steps away from a *direct* employer. This requires a shift in our thinking and behavior. We need to realize that those in power are not simply vague "systems" to analyze or generic "corporations" to be angry at. They are people making decisions that ultimately benefit a small select few at the top to the detriment of everyone else.

In the new world of global capital there simply is no winning plan to build a shared prosperity without confronting these individual owners and their corporate power directly. We refer to them as the *ultimate profiteers*.

How Global Supply Chains Have Reduced Corporate Accountability

Consider the case of the textile industry. Historically, textile manufacturers like Cannon Mills in Kannapolis, North Carolina, set the terms of production and business practices and thus established the delicate balance between the cost of resources (for example, cotton), the cost of labor (wages and benefits), and the price of the end product (in the case of Cannon Mills, all-purpose fabrics used to make sheets and towels) in ways that maximized the profits of company executives and investors. But with the growing influence of a booming retail industry with the capacity to buy products from around the globe, the ability of local manufacturers to have control over their business practices has shifted away from them and to these new multinational retail brands. In a detailed case study on workers' organizing efforts at Cannon Mills, Lane Windham writes:

> Though the apparel and textile sectors had long been interdependent, starting in the mid-1980s what had been separate operations were more tightly linked into global supply chains. Now large retailers, not manufacturers, would increasingly determine what products would be produced, what raw materials would be used, and how and when the goods would be transported.[2]

This change in power dynamics led to new arrangements that disadvantage workers. Thus, even when local textile manufacturers shared specific interests with the unions of textile workers, the companies found themselves pushed toward choosing to align with their class interests within the retail industry, to their own detriment and their employees'. As Windham explains, "When textile employers fought their workers' efforts to form unions and prevented the unions from growing, they weakened the textile labor-management alliance, which had served as a counterweight to these retail interests."[3]

As a child in North Carolina, Smiley visited robust textile mills and expos where you could pick up free socks after watching a machine make them in front of your eyes. Today, most US textile plants—in North Carolina and elsewhere— are now museums, outlet malls, or gone altogether. As scholar Beverly Silver states, "Once the labor movement made a show of force, capitalists responded with a spatial-fix strategy that accelerated the diffusion of production to new sites."[4] *Spatial fix*—distinguished from *technological fix* and *product fix*—refers to an industry's decision to avoid labor militancy and power by relocating sites of production.

Those still working in the textile industry today experience a situation where their direct employer is not fully in control of the terms of production. Yet many workers in this situation have often continued to utilize twentieth-century practices and laws to form unions and negotiate with employers—even when those employers cannot deliver on improved wages and conditions because they are dependent on multinational brands who can order from anywhere and set prices based on their ability to relocate production from one supplier to another overnight.

Transnational Collective Bargaining with Transnational Corporations

Some unions and other organizations have realized the futility of trying to organize and collectively bargain solely at the factory level. To obtain collective power to govern themselves and their industry, they needed a framework through which to engage the person who profits most from their labor.

Enter the Asia Floor Wage Alliance (AFWA), an organization that provides a great illustration of the new practices and approaches modern-day garment workers are taking to address twenty-first-century employment relations. With Asia boasting the highest density of garment suppliers in the world, the AFWA is a strategic network of garment-sector unions and other worker organizations from countries across the continent, seeded with support from Jobs With Justice in the United States and India's New Trade Union Initiative. These organizations seek to create a framework for transnational wage parity that would end the ability of companies to simply abscond from any country (spatial fixes) in which workers begin to gain power. This transnational collaborative effort among unions and worker-based organizations in Asia allows garment workers to negotiate with their direct employers in textile and apparel factories, and undermines the ability of multinational corporations to pit one country's workers against another in search of the lowest price.

Here's an example of how AFWA works. Across Asia, the minimum wage varies as governments try to compete for business. Garment suppliers are loath to pay more than any given national minimum wage—kept extremely low to attract business—given the price pressures from large multinational brands such as H&M, Walmart, and Gap, Inc. So, in 2005, the AFWA assessed what a living wage would be across Asia, using the costs of food (based on recommendations for caloric intake from the United Nations) and other necessities in each country to establish a universal formula for calculating the livable wage in any Asian country.[5] This calculation established a shared cross-border floor wage, allowing working people in the garment sector to make consistent wage demands and negotiate with large garment suppliers and multinational brands.

Recognizing suppliers' position within the overall apparel economy, the unions within the AFWA then began pushing the garment suppliers to pay the minimum wage—fighting to increase it when politically possible—while negotiating other local conditions that they have control over. In addition, they simultaneously pushed the multinational brands to pay suppliers enough to pay more, targeting a wage that matches the floor wage calculated for that country. So, if the garment suppliers pay the country's minimum wage, AFWA calls on the multinational brands to make an additional wage contribution to make up the difference between the minimum wage and the floor wage that AFWA has calculated for the relevant country.

This approach gets to the heart of how twenty-first-century bargaining in supply chains needs to work. It allows garment workers to negotiate with their direct employers in the factories, their governments setting the minimum wage, and the ultimate profiteers, all within a transnational collaboration among unions.

In a global economy, with global corporations, AWFA unions are logically attempting to form a global bargaining unit with an equal role in governing the industry rather than allowing suppliers and the global retail brands to pit working people from one country against those from other countries. Furthermore, targeting the large retailers enables working people in the global south to expand the social consciousness of consumers in the United States and Europe, encouraging them to join in solidarity with retail workers in the global north in pressuring the multinational brands to come to the bargaining table. The AFWA continues to thrive even in the harsh circumstances presented by the COVID-19 pandemic and the ongoing shifts in global capital.

Bettie Douglas. Portrait by Gwenn Seemel.

Profile of a Modern Worker:
Bettie Douglas: We All Need a Piece
of the Pie

One of the global industries dominated by multinational corporations is the fast-food business. Some of those who oppose workers' rights say that fast-food companies shouldn't have to respect those rights because almost all the people who work at places like McDonald's are well-to-do teenagers working for spare change. The story of Bettie Douglas, a Black grandmother working at a McDonald's in St Louis, Missouri, who reminded both authors of their own mothers, gives the lie to this excuse—and it also illustrates why targeting the ultimate profiteer rather than local franchise owners is such an important strategy.

Children are taught from an early age whether or not they have a voice and should use it. My mother and father taught me and my siblings to speak up when I was little. They taught us to stand up for what we believe, anything we truly believe in, no matter what. Actually, with ten siblings I learned to speak up early. I was in the middle, you see. So they always knew that I would speak out, I don't care what. I was going to speak out for what I felt was right. They were going to hear my part just like I was going to hear theirs. All of us have something to add. All of us have value.

But it was all based in love and our relationships with each other. When we got up out of bed and went downstairs, whoever you saw you had to say, "Good morning!" And most times, you had to say it with a hug. It's just a habit now. I speak to everyone I work with at McDonald's. And I hug them too. My coworkers and I show each other a lot of love. We support each other. I know we all have something to contribute. God put us all on this Earth with some kind of gift, and we're each trying to find the space to work that gift—at work and in our lives. Given the opportunity, Lord only knows what we might be able to do.

My parents also taught us to be resilient. My dad in particular had a lot of responsibility thrust on him at an early age. His father wasn't in the home, and he had to take care of his mother. He only had a second- or third-grade education. My mother taught him to read and write. I didn't always understand why he was so tough on us. But now I get it, because when I'm at work and dealing with the snippy things my managers are saying, I think of some of the things he used to say like, "Is that the best you can do?" He taught me to be like a duck. I let it all roll right off my back.

They also taught me the value of work. We believe in working. I've been working since I was twelve years old, starting at the businesses my parents had and then moving into retail and other jobs. I'm sixty-one years old now, so I've been working for a long time. Even when I feel I'm not being treated fairly, I could be as mad as a bear, when I walk in the door I'm going to do the best job that I can. If I know I've given it my all, it's hard to shake me. I got suspended for giving out a cup. Of course, that's not the real reason I was suspended, but that's what they said. But I knew I'd always done my job well. And I told the franchise owner, "I've been with you for thirteen years!" And even he had to admit that every time he saw me I was mopping or wiping tables or helping a customer. Clearly I was doing a good job. They weren't mad at me for doing a good job. They were mad because I was trying to organize my coworkers into fighting for union rights with the Fight for Fifteen.

Honestly I was scared at first. I had a lot on me, still do. I was taking care of my parents, who have both now passed away. I have three sons, one of whom has autism. Another just survived surgery to remove a tumor. They're older now, but it has still been hard. I'm thinking that I can't lose my job. The bills are all still due. My washing machine needs to be fixed. My refrigerator is broken. We're buying food every day because we can't keep it cold. We had to go without heat during the winter at one point because my furnace was broken and I couldn't afford to fix it. And the bill collectors want all of my tax money. I figured God would see me through it. He doesn't put anything on me that I can't handle.

Well, it must have been God that kept the organizers coming back over and over again to talk to me. I certainly didn't give them good reason to keep talking to me. I kept telling them from the drive-through window that I did not want to lose my job. No, not today! I was scared. But I was thinking about what they were saying.

I thought about how it takes me longer to get to work and get home than the actual time I spend on the job. With the buses I have to catch to get to McDonald's, it takes me four hours to get there—no matter what the weather is each day. I can't afford a car. I walk seven blocks from my house to the bus stop. Even if I am only scheduled to work for four hours, it still takes me another four hours to get home. That would be difficult for a young person, and I'm in my sixties.

I also thought about the machinery at the store, which was raggedy. My co-workers and I have to work on the equipment to get it functioning again. I'm not a mechanic, but I often have to act like one at McDonald's. I've had to pull stuff out of the toilet to unclog it. I'm not a plumber, but I often have to act like one at McDonald's. It's all a part of doing my job well. But I shouldn't have to do that.

I was really scared. But then I thought about what my family had been through before. I had a cousin who was roped up by white people and then dragged by a car. He was my dad's first cousin. He was dating a white woman and people didn't like that. My dad used to tell us the story, and I knew it had really impacted him.

He said his cousin was dragged all through the town where they grew up, his brain matter leaving a trail. His body was torn up so bad that there was no body to bury. My family has gone through so much for me to be here, not having to worry about that kind of attack. And to see that we're now at risk of losing all that they fought for, how could I stay quiet? If they could survive that, and speak out against it so that my children didn't have to face that ever again, could I really keep my head down and not speak up at McDonald's? I think it was then that I realized that I had to make a different choice. I knew I couldn't just be scared. I had to get out there and do the best that I could. Even if I messed up, I had to try. It was the least I could do. I felt something rising up in me, telling me I had to speak up. Awaken the sleeping giant! I had to become a monster for good. Soon after, some of my coworkers walked out and the news cameras came to our store. One reporter walked right up to my window and it just happened. I was tired of riding the bus for eight hours and not getting paid enough. I was just tired. And you know, when you're sick and tired, you're sick and tired. And I was truly sick and tired. I had a whole lot to say.

Well, our managers didn't like what we were doing. But I had to do it. I had to at least try, to know I did my best for me and my family. Closed mouths don't get fed. And we were hungry. We had to fight to survive. They said we were crazy, that we would never get $15 an hour. But never tell me never, honey. Now I had something to prove. And we did. We won an increase from the city of St. Louis to $10 an hour.

And let me say, nothing motivates you like success. My managers have tried to bring me down from this high. They've told new employees not to talk to me or talk to those of us who are trying to organize a union. I haven't been promoted since I started fighting for better pay and conditions. They cut my hours back to just five hours a day. They really tried to break me down. At the peak of it all, they suspended me. They suspended me for handing out a cup to a customer. We hand out cups all the time. That's not why they suspended me. They were trying to keep me from organizing, and they wanted others to see that if they organized, they would be punished. It was about retaliation. But it's no matter. Like a duck, I let that roll right off me. That little five-day suspension didn't get me down. To tell you the truth, I needed the break. Like I said, I was tired. And because of working with the Fight for Fifteen, us employees told the NLRB we knew it was about retaliation. And after that my managers bumped me up to forty hours a week! So that moment was kind of a win-win for me.

Still, I wouldn't mind more honesty on the job. I'm not saying I need to push my way into every manager meeting, but I want them to listen to the problems we're having. Let us come to the table. Let's talk about it. It could be a win-win for all of us. We'll get to make enough to sustain our families, and they'll be able to solve problems a lot better with those of us directly in contact with them. Actually, when I spoke to the franchise owner, he acknowledged that not much goes on in the store that I don't know about. And I realized that it wasn't just a decision he could make. We had to get his boss to the table. We had to try to engage the executives at the top of the McDonald's corporation.

During that meeting with the franchise owner, I could tell he and all of my other supervisors were trying to intimidate me from talking to company executives. These are the big boys! And I finally had the opportunity to speak to them directly. I was so nervous. But my mother used to say to us, "You have just as much right as anybody else. And if you feel something, there's nothing wrong with expressing it. You don't have to have all the answers, and you may not always be right. But if you don't stand for something, you'll fall for anything."

That was one thing that stuck in my mind the first time I had to testify in front of a large audience that included McDonald's executives. I thought about my parents.

And then I thought again about all the things my family had to do for me to be here. If I don't stand up, how can I sit back and complain about something? I had to get my feet in the fight. You can't cry over spilled milk. You have to get out there and try to wipe that milk up! You can't make change with your mouth closed. And I thought about how tired I was and how President Trump was giving all these tax breaks to the rich, and the only break we were getting was a broken check. I really don't like bullies. And this all gave me courage. Nothing beats a failure but a try. And despite being nervous and stuttering, I testified to my experiences at McDonald's and shared what I thought would make things better for all of us. I learned that when you do that, express your true feelings from the heart, it lifts you. It transforms you. It transformed me. I learned in that moment that in order to make change in the world, we ourselves also have to change. We transform into monsters for good. I sure did.

My experiences since then have been good. And we're still fighting. Through the process of joining together with my coworkers I learned how we can combat and even prevent retaliation when we're united more than when we're acting alone. You've got to unite and come together. There are more poor people than there are rich. There are more people out here suffering. We want the executives to see our faces. We want to talk to them and tell them what we're really feeling. We want them to come to the table with us. If I'm all the way at one McDonald's store and you're always in your office headquarters and we never get to deal with each other directly, then we're going to assume all kinds of things about each other. But if we sit and talk face to face, we can see where each other is coming from. We can know what type of person you are, and you can know us. We can't hold anything against you that you might not know anything about. But when we know that you know better, oh, it's on baby. There's no excuse!

It's not fair for a small number of people to bully us into thinking that it's ok for some people to do well and for others to suffer. All of us should have a piece of the pie. Anyone who works and who is trying to improve the lives of their families should be able to, you know? But a lot of these corporate executives want to hold us back. They don't want to share in the wealth. They act greedy. They'll let us smell the pie but not let us taste it. And that's not right.

This organizing work has taken me to all kinds of places—Canada, Brazil, Great Britain. When you open up, let go, and let God in, the sky is the limit. I'm as poor as a church mouse. But look at the places I have been. Look at the things we have done together. I am so blessed. I know we got this, and if I need to be in the dark a little bit well I've got some candles and batteries to keep me going. We do what we have to do. When you're clear about your purpose, even with the bad you find life to be wonderful.

And we're still fighting. I stay humble and remember what we're really fighting for. We aren't just fighting for ourselves. We need to solve the problems at our store and then address some of the larger issues we're all facing. I've got grandchildren now. I see so many children suffering by not getting a good education or a decent school lunch. Children need to be taught and guided. I have so much hope, though. I have one grandson who reminds me of me. I can't tell him nothing because I always know where he's coming from. He recently saw me organizing with the Fight for Fifteen and said, "I am very proud of you." That gives me the initiative to keep going.

I try to pass on the things I have learned to the next generation, to make it easier because life is hard. Children are taught from an early age whether or not they have a voice and should use it. And I want my children and grandchildren to hear me using mine.

Challenges of Collective Bargaining with Transnational Corporations

Of course, global brands will not come to the table just because they are asked. A glance back at the history of the labor movement suggests what needs to happen. Originally, working people formed local guilds and regional unions, then transformed those locals into amalgamated unions targeting growing national industries. Today, the same institutions must reorganize again in order to gain the leverage needed to force the global brands into active and equal negotiations with workers. Having national unions in international solidarity with each other is good, but it is no longer enough. The new shape of global capital necessitates intensive collaboration around bargaining demands and organizing goals across national borders.

One attempt at such collaboration occurred in the global arena through the creation of the Accord on Fire and Building Safety in Bangladesh, one of the world's poorest countries, where atrocious violations of basic worker safety principles are commonplace.[6] The accord is described as an "independent, legally binding agreement between brands and trade unions to work toward a safe and healthy garment and textile industry in Bangladesh. The Accord was created to enable a working environment in which no worker needs to fear fires, building collapses, or other accidents that could be prevented with reasonable health and safety measures."[7] It was crafted by trade unions, community groups in Bangladesh, and international human rights and labor rights advocates—including the AFWA, in negotiation with multinational companies producing clothes in Bangladesh, the garment factory owners, and the national government.

Unfortunately, some United States–based retail giants like Walmart that sell Bangladesh-made garments have still refused to sign on to the Accord.[8] And there is a distinct difference in compliance between factories where workers have unions who collectively bargain with factory owners and factories where workers are not organized into a union.[9] Clearly there are still big challenges ahead for those who hope to expand collective bargaining to global supply chains.

AFWA is not the only organization pioneering this new approach. Labor leaders in many parts of the world are making similar attempts to add new leverage to traditional bargaining. But it is hard to overstate the difficulty of organizing workers located in so many countries. Consider, for example, the mixed record on this front of global union federations (GUFs).

GUFs are international collaborations of unions around the world active in a particular sector. Some GUFs were started as early as 1896, while others were launched very recently.[10] For example, IndustriALL is a GUF founded in Copenhagen in 2012 that represents more than fifty million working people in more than 140 countries, working across the supply chains in mining, energy, and manufacturing.

In recent years GUFs have worked to construct global framework agreements (GFAs) among multinational corporations, the GUFs themselves, and the relevant unions in the countries of interest. GFAs generally incorporate the core international labor conventions set by the International Labor Organization (ILO), which ban forced labor, guarantee freedom of association, protect the right to organize and engage in collective bargaining, ban discrimination, and ban child labor. An example of such GFAs includes the agreement between the Union Network International (UNI Global Union), the North America—based United Food and Commercial Workers (UFCW) union, and the clothing retailer H&M. A similar agreement was signed between the GUF IndustriALL and the Inditex Group, the parent company of Zara.

Unfortunately, these agreements often lack real enforceability. The UFCW was able to support H&M workers in New York but had a lot of difficulty in other places despite the agreement. Even when multinational corporations that operate within the United States agree to GFAs, the US subsidiaries of those corporations often opt not to recognize the agreements and continue with their union-busting tactics, in many cases with the support of state and federal government. For example, though IndustriALL publicly accused Volkswagen of violating the terms of a GFA it had signed by refusing to bargain with a group of workers at its Chattanooga, Tennessee, auto plant, Volkswagen has still not recognized their union, the UAW.

It is also important to note that the GFA process has been very Eurocentric, with the overwhelming majority of agreements having been signed by companies based in Europe.[11]

All these factors have led GFAs to have less effect on US labor practices than many worker advocates had hoped. One study found that US subsidiaries and US unions both argue that GFAs do not apply to the United States, with unions arguing that the differences in labor law between the US and Europe render GFAs unenforceable here.[12]

For GFAs to become relevant to US bargaining, GUFs must negotiate GFAs with a specific intention to make them binding to subsidiaries, contractors, and suppliers, broadly defined, and enforceable either by the NLRB or US courts. If that proves too daunting, GFA violations should at least lead to consequences for labor relations between European unions or the US workforce and the multinational corporation. And all of this says nothing about the needs of workers outside of the global north, which are often ignored in GFAs. Of course, this is what makes the strategies of the AFWA so promising. They seek to move beyond dialogue into a sharper understanding of the relations of power, which will make it possible to truly hold companies throughout a supply chain accountable for their behavior.

Financialization Redefines the Real Boss

Just as the growth of multinational retail brands transformed the textile industry, the expanding power of finance capital is quickly overpowering retail. As more hedge funds and investors buy majority shares in publicly traded corporations, the willingness of those companies to protect workers and their communities erodes. These financial entities seek to buy up companies and turn them around for a quick profit, even at the expense of shutting the companies down altogether.

John Stumpf, former chairman and CEO of Wells Fargo, is an example of an ultimate profiteer who came directly from the financial sector.[13] In that role he had direct control over the working conditions of hundreds of thousands of individuals employed by Wells Fargo, most of whom were frontline nonunionized workers earning little more than the minimum wage and receiving few benefits. He also had control over the tens of thousands of subcontracted workers that Wells Fargo uses throughout its system, such as security guards, custodial workers, and so on.

Wells Fargo holds or services the mortgages of millions of homeowners and their families, which means Stumpf ultimately had control over foreclosures that leave thousands of people homeless. Hundreds of thousands of students owe Wells Fargo billions in student debt; tens of thousands of small business owners are dependent on the bank for lines of credit; and millions of credit card holders are Wells Fargo customers. Furthermore, across the country, state and local governments, school districts, and other public entities rely on Wells Fargo for cashflow loans, bond financing, and banking services. That means that Stumpf also wielded control over the children who attend public schools, the commuters who ride public transit, and the patients who use Medicaid to get access to healthcare.

Wells Fargo also has a huge investment-management business that manages the retirement savings of millions of people, which gave Stumpf hundreds of billions of dollars to invest in other companies. For example, Wells Fargo is a major financial backer of Corrections Corporation of America (CCA), the largest private prison company in the world, which makes a huge amount of its income by jailing immigrant detainees. Those investments gave Stumpf tremendous power over those corporations and companies.

Stumpf also sat on the board of other companies like Chevron and Target. Thus, he was responsible for these companies' management and deserved to be held accountable for polluting communities and exploiting workers worldwide. Finally, Stumpf also used the wealth and power of the bank to push his political agenda through groups like the American Legislative Exchange Council (ALEC).

Only small portions of the people who were impacted by John Stumpf's decisions actually brought their fights to his doorstep. But there were literally millions of people suffering because of the unfair practices and influence that he wielded. If we unite, we stand a much greater chance of forcing people like John Stumpf and other ultimate profiteers to deal with us—people like Stephen A.

Schwarzman of Blackstone, Sam Zell of Equity Group Investments, and Stephen Feinberg of Cerberus. For years, these executives have wielded unregulated power in all aspects of our lives, from employment to housing to education and beyond. Their unfettered reign must be challenged by workers who demand the power to bargain with the ultimate profiteers.

Taking on the Untouchably Rich, and Winning

In 2019, workers at the Toys "R" Us retail chain proved that it is not impossible to win a fight against a large retail brand backed by finance capital. The company went bankrupt, satisfying only their commitments to investors while leaving employees in the lurch with unpaid wages. The workers were told that they had no leverage because they had no access to the company's customers or shareholders. In response, they targeted private equity firms that have been making billions from leveraged buyouts and bankruptcies, many of which owned shares in Toys "R" Us. After the workers pressured hedge funds and other large investors— including New Jersey's Public Investment Fund—the company was forced to make its employees whole for gambling with the economy.[14] More than thirty thousand laid-off workers won $20 million in severance payments, a significant victory given that the company had not committed any funds to cover the losses for workers.[15] Financialization of the economy requires that workers continue to find new approaches to negotiating with the ultimate profiteers, as this victory demonstrates.

Migrant Workers versus the One Percent

Organizing along commodity supply chains is not the only approach to targeting multinational companies. Some workers have started to organize and attempt to collectively bargain throughout migration corridors—industrywide patterns of moving people between two or more regions for work, perhaps timed with a specific growing season or retail peak.

Migrants, often coming from the global south to the global north to work, face hard conditions and limited protections due to their precarious immigration status most often controlled by their employer. Company bosses can threaten to shift work between migrants from one community and migrants from another community, or between migrants and native-born workers, as a means of suppressing wages and heightening workers' economic insecurity. But when working people collaborate across these divisions, setting standards within a migration corridor is possible.

One example of what can be done is represented by the workers leading Familias Unidas por la Justicia (Families United for Justice). For years, Driscoll's, a major company in the US berry market, had used supplier Sakuma Brothers in Washington State to employ immigrants and long-term residents from southern Mexico to pick berries and live in company-provided housing during the harvest season.[16] The immigrants were largely indigenous people with first languages other than Spanish.

In 2013, berry pickers at Sakuma Brothers began protesting low pay and bad working conditions. When the company fired the protest leaders, many other workers began a strike against the company. They eventually organized into Familias Unidas por la Justicia to bargain on their behalf. Sakuma Brothers retaliated by greatly expanding their request for H-2A guest worker visas, asking the Department of Labor for 479 visas when, previously, they had used fewer than 80. To justify this request, Sakuma claimed it was unable to find workers in the United States. H-2A visas are supposed to be reserved for seasonal work in cases where employers cannot find a local workforce to fill necessary positions. But they are often used to hire and exploit vulnerable workers because undocumented workers and guest workers are not consistently protected by existing US labor law.[17] At the same time, Sakuma told the people who had engaged in a strike against them that they were terminated, a permitted act because the farmworkers were not covered by the NLRA.

Next the workers unleashed a bigger weapon against Sakuma. First, each one of them wrote a letter to the US Department of Labor refuting Sakuma's claim that it was unable to find workers in the United States by saying that they themselves were willing to work at Sakuma. Second, they organized a boycott against Driscoll's, the ultimate profiteer. The upside of not being covered by the NLRA was that there was nothing to prevent them from organizing a secondary boycott of Driscoll's to win concessions from Sakuma—a powerful tactic otherwise banned by the law. The boycott against Driscoll's won support from other unions, including the longshoreman's union, which one day refused to load any Driscoll's berries onto ships. In addition, the union organized student protests and consumer boycotts of Driscoll's. Another key step that they took, which is particularly important for workers today, especially in a global industry such as agriculture, was that the workers reached out to their counterparts in Mexico, their country of origin, to ask them to join in the action against Driscoll's. The workers in both countries set up a binational front to launch a strike *and* a boycott.

All of this pressure brought Sakuma to the table. Despite the lack of legal protection for the workers, Sakuma agreed to negotiate with the workers' newly formed independent union in 2016, and in 2017 they agreed to a collective bargaining agreement.

The union has not stopped there. It now has plans to start up a union co-op farm, which would allow the union to set labor standards for themselves rather than negotiate with growers to obtain fair working conditions, ideally introducing competition within the sector that could raise standards.

The National Guestworker Alliance used a similar approach in 2012. Workers, many targeted from the same community in Mexico, were recruited to work in the United States in food-processing plants under temporary H-2B guest worker visas. These workers were often recruited annually to the same company, in this case C.J.'s Seafood. They lived on-site at the shrimp-processing plant in Breaux Bridge, Louisiana. The managers often locked them into the boiler room, forcing them to work long hours, causing some to faint, and keeping them from using the bathroom. They received pay that was much lower than the amount required by law, and when they complained, supervisors threatened their families.[18] It was a combination of abuses rarely seen in the United States since the end of sharecropping.

The National Guestworker Alliance's strategy to target the ultimate benefactors of their labor is a powerful example of bargaining with the ultimate profiteer—in this case, the Walton family.

Founded by family patriarch Sam Walton in 1962, Walmart today directly employs 2.3 million workers.[19] It also has tentacles throughout the economy. Consider one Walton in particular, Greg Penner, Walmart's chairman, son-in-law of Sam Robson "Rob" Walton, and grandson-in-law of founder Sam Walton. Penner has his own investment firm, sits on the boards of Walmart and Hyatt Hotels, and funds anti-public-school initiatives through a set of nonprofit organizations. Charting out all the workers he touches, whether or not they are directly employed by one of these companies, we find Walmart "associates" and the Louisiana seafood workers whose employers supplied almost exclusively to Walmart. The list also includes subcontracted workers at the Hyatt in Los Angeles, workers at the Hyatt in San Francisco, and temporary construction workers building new Hyatt hotels. It includes the janitors in the Silicon Valley building of Penner's investment firm and the educators at the charter schools benefiting from donations from his Charter School Growth Fund. These workers and many, many others make up the army of people whose labor ultimately benefits Greg Penner (see figure 8.1).[20]

So, when guest workers at Walmart's supplier in Breaux Bridge, Louisiana, faced abuses, their power analysis pushed them to go around their apparent "boss" and instead target Greg Penner and his team of Walmart executives. They organized at great risk to their safety, engaging other guest workers and Walmart

The Waltons are worth $103 billion.

Walton Family $103 B

Companies they run or direct are worth $215 billion.

| Walmart $193 B assets | Hyatt $8 B assets | Arvest Bank $13 B assets | eHarmony | Greener capital >$1 B | Community Publishers |

They pour $E million into anti-99% causes, groups, and political races...

| Charter Fund, Inc. | Stand for Children | KIPP Foundation | US Chamber | ALEC |
| Business Roundtable | Retail Ind. Leaders Assn. | US-China Business Council | Conservation Int'l | |

Together these companies directly employ 2.2 million workers.

| Walmart 2.2 M workers | Hyatt 50,000 workers | Arvest Bank 5,000 workers |
| eHarmony | Greener Capital | Community Publishers |

To buy these politicians and public officials.

President — Congress — Federal Regulators — Governors
State Legislators — State Regulators — Mayors — Local Lawmakers

They control D million more workers through subcontracting, supply chain operations, and other relationships.

Walmart Suppliers — Walmart warehouse workers — Hyatt subcont & franchise 90,000

The Waltons and their companies impact the daily lives of all 300 million people in America and can unite us in common struggle.

| F million workers | G million women workers | H million lowwage workers | J mil. public program recipients | 183 million credit cardholders | 112 million people of color impacted by racial injustice | 12 million undocumented immigrants | K million directly impacted by enviro. damage |

FIGURE 8.1. The figure shows a flowchart of working people who, whether they realize it or not, are directly impacted by decisions made by the Walton family via employment, debt, or some other economic relationship. Chart taken from Lerner and Soni, "Bargaining with the Top One-Tenth of the One Percent."

associates alike. And when the *New York Times* published an editorial about Walmart titled "Forced Labor on American Shores," it changed the scale and scope of the fight demanding justice for Walmart workers. The approach taken by the Louisiana workers forced Walmart to the bargaining table.

More action is necessary to push Walmart and other companies to take full responsibility for the workforce throughout their supply chain, labor migration chains, and other employees that are directly impacted by their policies and practices. But the successes achieved by the National Guestworker Alliance demonstrate what is possible when following this strategic framework.

Cynthia Murray. Portrait by Gwenn Seemel.

Profile of a Modern Worker:
Cynthia Murray: "I Stay for the Fight"

Associates working within the Walmart stores are now extending their fight for fair treatment beyond their local management to the ultimate profiteers who drive the corporation's policies. Cynthia Murray, a tenacious older white woman organizing with what was known at the time as the Organization United for Respect at Walmart (OUR Walmart), now simply United for Respect, put it best when she said, "With a company like Walmart, you can't just go store to store. We had to get to the top of the company."

I grew up in Pittsburgh, Pennsylvania. My father was a single parent, and he was a Teamster. He drove a tractor trailer for a living. My father was active in the union, and as kids we used to set up the union hall when they had their meetings. I remember he told us that if there's a picket line you don't ever cross it. "If you're not going to pick up a picket sign and join them, you walk away, you never cross it." My father used to stand the four of us in a line and say, "Never tell on each other. You either stick together or you fall together."

My father took care of four kids and his mother, who took care of us. There were six of us in the family and he was the single earner. My grandmother was a very strong individual to take care of four children at age sixty-nine. She instilled in us the compassion of being able to take care of one another and loving each other. She taught me that you've got to hold onto your faith regardless if times are rough. Now, in my life experience, I can see how generation after generation repeats history. When my grandson was born, he and my daughter lived with me. We all took care of him. So many families today have to come back together, to support each other to be able to live, which means our economy is not the way it should be in the United States.

I worked in the canteen at US Steel for a short period of time before they closed. And then I ran two bar clubs. It supported what I needed for my two kids. Back then, that area was booming. It had anything and everything you needed. Once the steel mill closed, there was a lack of jobs. By then I had met my husband and we agreed to move to Maryland. I wanted my children to be able to have a better life.

When I got here, I drove a truck for the *Washington Post*—picking up bundles of papers and dropping them off at sites. I injured my back there. It took a long time for me to recuperate. But when I did, I couldn't move my legs the way I needed to drive a truck. So, that's how I ended up going to work at Walmart.

I have worked at Walmart for nineteen years, and I still don't make $15 an hour. That's sad. Now I stay for the fight!

It all got started for me in 2007 with the Wake-Up Walmart campaign effort run by the United Food and Commercial Workers Union (UFCW). There were a few of us from my store who got involved. I spoke out about the Fair Share Care Act. I never thought about being on television or anything else. I remember that my sister-in-law's sister was in the hospital and she saw me and said, "Oh my God, Cynthia's on the news." So, after standing up and speaking out in front of everyone, my store manager singled me out at work the next day as "the one who's been talking." I participated in the campaign until the UFCW decided to shift strategies.

I knew there had to be something for me and others at Walmart. We realized how disrespected we were. Management at Walmart was bragging about paying workers like me nothing. You don't think that's wrong in the United States? I was yelled at in front of customers, and I could not take time off to care for my daughter when she was sick with cancer. My father taught me that a good employer is one that will treat you with respect, and respect is free. So, I never understood how you can treat workers like they are less than nothing.

We could not stay silent. So, at first we tried to unionize. I had been handing out union cards to my coworkers. One of the workers gave my store manager the union card, and he put it above the time clock behind a piece of glass. This was supposed to be a lesson for us, right? I started jumping up and down. I was mad as hell. I felt betrayed. How could someone give that union card to that asshole? I told the manager that the card belonged to me and that I wanted it back. I remember he was standing in the doorway. I had tears of anger in my eyes. When I looked at the faces, he said to me, "Look at these people, they need something, and it's not a union." I was so mad.

When I got home, I called Dan, the organizer at the union, and told him that this union stuff ain't working but that we needed something for us workers. I grew up in a union household; I believe in unions. But it's not the right thing for us, especially up against a major company like Walmart. We talked about building an organization instead. I took a sign-up sheet to work the next day, and eight workers signed on immediately. This was how we began to build OUR Walmart, the Organization United for Respect.

I have been to many actions at Walmart's home office and shareholder meetings, and I have met with top management. It can be scary to do that. I think that's the first emotion that I felt, but then I got grounded in my belief that what I'm doing is right. I don't even know how to explain the different mixed emotions I have felt when taking part in an action. Like my grandmother taught us, I believe in standing in my faith. And I know this is what I gotta do. It just has to be done for all of us. It's about us, not just about me.

One of the first issues I organized on was scheduling and having enough hours of work. At one point, workers in my store were getting schedules with only two days of work per week available to them. How could you feed anybody, how could you pay any bills with that kind of schedule? This wasn't just happening to new workers, this was happening to workers who had been there for twenty-plus years. So, in my store we kept approaching the manager about this and asking for more hours. We kept organizing actions in the store until he finally said he would meet with us. For example, we just started clapping once until he would meet with us. It was so amazing because every worker in the store was involved. The store manager told us that they had schedules with nobody assigned to certain days and hours. So he said that anybody who wanted more hours could go meet with personnel. Well, half the group left after that because they thought they would be fired if they showed up to the personnel office. There was a lot of fear. But me and others went as a group. And we were told that they had open shifts and they would start posting the shifts so that people could sign up for what they wanted and needed. He agreed to post open available shifts three weeks out and agreed that people could sign up for as many days of work as was available, even if the work was not in their assigned department. Workers did not care if they were working in other departments, they just wanted as close to forty hours a week as possible.

This was our first win in my store. And soon after, Walmart implemented this scheduling process and technology to make it possible in every store. With a company like Walmart, you can't just go store to store. We had to get to the top of the company.

I remember at one of our actions we met with Doug McMillion, a Walmart executive. He says he came from the bottom up. Well, we wanted him to hear from us what it is like to work for this company. We made him listen to one of the worker's story—her story of losing her baby while working. She had told the manager that she did not want to pull a pallet jack because of her pregnancy. The manager threatened to fire her if she did not. She lost her baby. He had to listen to her tell that story to his face. And that was the first time that I could see that he was human, and he realized we were humans too. We were able to say, "You may make the money 'cause you're a CEO, but what about us? We're the ones who make that money so that you can sit back and do whatever you want."

I heard so many stories of struggle from Walmart workers. Stories about having to spend your time at a food bank on your day off. Or stories about being able to pay rent, but not being paid enough to pay the groceries to feed their kids that night. How do they face their kids? These stories are what made me want to build an organization for every worker in the country. After our first win with scheduling we organized on issues like raising the minimum wage and pregnancy discrimination. We knew we had to listen and understand what workers really needed. Some workers were parents and needed childcare, others needed care for their parents, and much more. These issues were part of our true lives. We've been underpaid and disrespected for so long now that it's time for them to give back to their workers and stop draining us.

We all want to be respected. For me, respect means dignity. We want to have dignity in the workplace. Come on, we're humans. We want to be treated in a fair way. My father said, if you work hard, you should be paid for that. You shouldn't be beaten down, it doesn't have to be that way. We should be able to walk onto our job and do that job with dignity and be able to hold our head up when someone tries to make us feel like our job is worthless. Like when people say, "Oh, you're just a Walmart worker." Why does that make me less of a human? Or if you work at McDonald's. A McDonald's worker is feeding you or your kid a sandwich this morning, so why are you treating them with disrespect? Why treat anybody any less of a person? Why shouldn't we just have to work one job to take care of our kids?

Walmart has a diverse workforce. There are many people working for Walmart in management positions who do discriminate against others. I see people of color treated sometimes less human and I think it's because they think, "Who cares? Who's going to stick up for us?" That's what really pisses me off. We are all human no matter our color.

You see, back in Pittsburgh I grew up in an Italian community within a larger Black, white, and Jewish community. We were treated poorly; we were one of the underdogs of the races. We had a lot of struggles with racism. But my father always taught me, "It's not the color of your skin. It's in here. It's in your heart. It's the person in there. That's the person you should be seeing. If I cut you, you bleed just like if I cut a person of another color."

I remember my father falling in love with this Black lady. She lived in the projects and I remember my father would take us over to play with her kids. One day, someone in the community hung a rat on her door. My father saw it and said we can't go back over there because we don't want something to happen to her and her kids. So, he would bring them over to our house.

Given the hate and racism we see today, I think white workers like me have to stand with our brothers and sisters of color. I think we have to sing from the mountaintop that we're not going to accept this. It's unacceptable. My grandson is biracial and my husband is Black. We can't let race divide us. This is a time when we have to stand together. Some may call us the entitled race. We're not.

Workers need a predictable schedule, a decent wage, and decent health care. We need to be supported, not constantly threatened to be fired. Women need to be paid the same wages as men. And our seniority should be recognized. We need family medical leave. My daughter, who is in cancer remission, is sometimes sick. I want to be able to take care of her, even if that means I miss a day of work. I should not have to pick between work and my child in this way.

I believe that we need to put workers on the boards of all companies, not just Toys "R" Us. We need to stop CEOs from raking these companies out of everything they've got, shutting the companies down with no care for the workers, and taking all of the money.

I also believe that if workers could have a voice and power in the workplace, it would change their lifestyles for the better. We won our scheduling and wage victories because we spoke up and took action. There is so much we still need to change. We're not going to just stop with Walmart workers.

I took my grandson with me to Walmart home office actions when he was young. I took him because he's the generation that's got to continue to fight for respect. If we don't teach our kids and grandkids, then who will? This fight has to be about each and every one of us making it better for the next generation.

Targeting the One Percent: Why It Works

A bargaining effort aimed at the ultimate profiteer provides a framework for a multifaceted campaign to address the myriad problems caused by the consolidation of wealth by the superrich—the powerful elite group often referred to as the 1 percent. This tiny club of individuals accounts for nearly 40 percent of political spending and thus disproportionately influences our government.[21] In addition, the 1 percent are also responsible, as individuals and through the corporations they control, for huge donations to right-wing lobbying groups, think tanks, and other organizations that aim to protect property and profits over the basic needs of people—for example, ALEC, which drafts probusiness, antiworker, anti-majority-rule bills for state legislators to introduce and support.

Additionally, targeting the billionaires who are the ultimate profiteers of their exploitation helps once-disunited workers to realize that they have many interests in common. This is why longshore workers, over-the-road truckers, warehouse workers, manufacturing workers, janitors, and delivery workers are now joining together to confront Amazon CEO Jeff Bezos, demanding better working conditions for those whose labor feeds the company's profits—including all the workers throughout the company's supply and distribution chain who nominally work for other companies and who have recently recognized their power in the economy as essential workers.

There are other approaches to bargaining with the ultimate profiteer beyond supply and migration chains. Working people are now banding together not just based on traditional definitions of who is an employer and who is an employee but also in ways that respond to how work is currently organized. For example, temp agency workers across sectors and geographies are banding together to assert their collective power.

These organizing practices are allowing workers in states without access to twentieth-century-protections (the mostly southern states shaded white or dark gray in the map we presented in chapter 7) to engage those who have such protections (in the light and medium gray shaded states in chapter 7). This is why workers even in states like Louisiana—not exactly hotbeds for traditional union membership—are now finding ways to demand and obtain a seat at the power table.

COMMUNITY-DRIVEN BARGAINING

Negotiating beyond the Workplace

In the spring of 2012, Mark Butler, then Georgia labor commissioner, cut off access to unemployment benefits for contracted school workers in the state, the majority of whom were Black women. These jobs—cafeteria workers, bus drivers, school support staff, and even some charter schoolteachers—had once been considered good jobs. In fact, it was public-sector jobs like these that created pathways out of poverty for many Black families over the last century. But by 2012 after years of intentional fissuring, these same jobs had been contracted out to companies like Sodexho and Aramark, limiting the state's responsibility for these workers and introducing a level of flexibility that helped a set of corporations but ultimately devastated workers. Butler's action sent thousands of school workers, again primarily Black women, into crisis.

Unemployment insurance was designed specifically to limit the hardship created when someone lost their job through no fault of their own. This is the law and the accepted norm, even in the United States where the social welfare system is relatively weak. Certainly, workers in the construction trades who are known to be out of work intermittently given the nature of the work would (and have) justifiably raised hell if unemployment benefits were taken away from them. And the state most likely would have listened to this predominantly white male workforce. But the school workers of Atlanta were mostly Black, and they were women. They were easier to exploit.

School workers enlisted the support of Atlanta Jobs With Justice and others to reverse Butler's decision. They established a community-based hub for organizing, the Justice for School Workers Committee, that functioned across several existing unions, included nonunion workers, and positioned workers to counter future attacks while setting an agenda to redefine the value and standards of school worker jobs in Atlanta and surrounding counties. They fought a battle with the Georgia Department of Labor and the Georgia General Assembly to prevent the cuts from being permanent and to restore the benefits. Instead of developing a short-term campaign that focused on the need for unemployment benefits as services, the coalition took a very different worker-centered approach—framing the loss of unemployment benefits as stolen wages.

By framing the issue not simply as an attack on the social safety net but also as an issue of wages and income, the community-based coalition was able to win $8 million in previously denied unemployment benefits paid directly back to the workers. Some of these workers were able to go on to win collectively bargained agreements the traditional way with the companies they worked for. Others are still organizing, trying to identify opportunities to collectively confront the powers that be in Georgia's public- and private-education sector.[1]

What Is Community-Driven Bargaining?

Workers are whole people whose daily interactions and struggles with the economy go far beyond the workplace. Therefore, while a union contract at work is an important step toward economic democracy, working people must also be able to collectively negotiate economic relationships far beyond their worksites, in all aspects of their lives. This is what *community-driven bargaining* is all about.

Through community-driven bargaining, working people organized around a specific economic relationship are at the table with decision-makers and are driving the process as a "bargaining unit." In previously discussed models of expanded forms of bargaining, community interests may be represented at the table but they are not driving what is ultimately a process between a union of employees and an employer. In community-driven bargaining strategies, organizations representing tenants, community and neighborhood residents, debt holders, and consumers sit across from landlords and building owners, government agencies, developers, and others. The result is still a legally enforceable agreement.

Here are some of the kinds of economic relationships that community-driven bargaining is designed to address.

Renters versus corporate landlords. Ever heard of a rent strike? Large property owners count on rents, tax subsidies, and in some instances a more speculative property value to borrow against to increase their profit margins. To get their attention, working people may collectively withhold rent payments or prevent subsidies so that properties are not profitable unless the owners agree to come to the table with tenants. This approach may require massive numbers of individuals to take shared action, but in other cases it may be effective when just a few strategically positioned tenants (such as high-priced business rentals) band together to withhold payments.

While the first image that comes to the minds of many people when they think of a landlord is a local on-site supervisor, a large number of rental properties are owned by Wall Street corporations led by executives who have never stepped foot in the buildings they control. Their number one motivation is making money, with little concern for the communities that live in their properties.

Consider Sam Zell, the head of companies that own over 150,000 rental properties, including apartments, manufactured homes, and RV parks. In 2019, Zell was ranked number 119 on the Forbes 400 list of the world's wealthiest people, with an estimated $5.5 billion in personal wealth. When the COVID-19 pandemic hit, one of his companies, Equity Group Investments (then reported as Equity Residential), announced a temporary freeze on evictions, but it simultaneously increased rents.[2] Even when confronted with the knowledge that many tenants had been laid off and would not be able to pay, representatives of many corporate landlords like Zell still refused to forgive rent payments altogether. Instead, industry groups including the National Apartments Association called on Congress to use the tax dollars of many of those same tenants to pay landlords for the rents they were losing.[3] And they were successful. After a series of congressional stimulus packages, corporate landlords joined the elite group of executives who profited off the COVID-19 pandemic.

Consider the private equity company Cerberus Capital, which in addition to owning several grocery store chains and health facilities also owns FirstKey Homes, which boasts over twenty thousand properties in the United States. For the owners of Cerberus, the pandemic was more of a blessing than a curse. One report explained, "Steve Feinberg, the billionaire co-founder and CEO of private equity giant Cerberus Capital, has seen his wealth increase $276 million since March 18, from $1.5 billion to $1.776 billion. Cerberus owns a number of companies with frontline essential workers, including Albertsons Companies—a grocery store chain—and Steward Health Care."[4]

Exploitation like this makes the rent strike a necessary part of a community's toolkit. But rent strikes have their risks. Like striking workers, rent strikers may fear reprisals such as increasing rents and eviction. Some cities have passed theoretical rights for tenants, including rent stabilization, building codes, housing codes, and the right for tenants to withhold rent if an apartment or building needs repairs. But as with non-union worksites, these rights have often been difficult to enforce without organization. In fact, the knowledge of such provisions is held more by lawyers and government officials than by tenants who are likely to be low-income, have limited English proficiency, work multiple jobs, juggle childcare, and do not have the time or financial resources to take on building owners and their attorneys.

To address this, many residents have joined together to assert their rights as renters, offering members a range of supports. The Crown Heights Tenant Union (CHTU), consisting of tenants residing in a number of buildings in Brooklyn, New York, joined together to negotiate with the corporate landlords that would allow them to more easily exercise their housing rights and have a process to raise and address grievances.[5] They have formed locals similar to unions, in this case organized by building complex. And to get corporate landlords to negotiate, they are prepared to withhold their participation in the economic relationship through a rent strike.

Deloris Wright, a CHTU member, talks about why the organization has been important for her:

> With the Tenants Union we have been able to negotiate with landlords and building owners. We form committees of people to join our neighbors in housing court when they are summoned so they don't have to navigate the system by themselves. Some of them have lived in their apartments for over forty years, and that is often who landlords are trying to remove.[6]

The ultimate goal of the tenants' union organizers is not only to sign collective bargaining agreements but also to use such agreements in the fight against neighborhood gentrification, displacement and other attacks on affordable housing. The CHTU is seeking to get building owners to agree that in the case where they offer buyouts to renters to get them to leave their apartments and then increase the rent, the buyout must be worth at least five years' rent for the tenant's apartment after renovation at the current market rate.[7]

This model is alive in other cities, including Boston, where City Life/Vida Urbana, a Boston-area housing organization, says that its goal for renters is to "build strong tenants associations that work together to bargain collectively with corporate landlords and to demand policy change."[8] The Autonomous Tenants Union of Chicago says on social media that it provides members with a "collective bargaining strategy, which include but are not limited to, collective delivery of demand letter, call-in campaigns, caravans, collective protests, and/or collective demonstrations."[9] There is also at least one statewide tenants union in Washington State that not only has won benefits directly from landlords but also has won a number of legislative victories in Seattle, including a *just cause* ordinance requiring landlords to demonstrate justification before terminating a lease and a right for tenants to organize without fear of retaliation or eviction by the landlord.[10] (Unions fight for similar provisions in the employment relationship, pushing employers to provide just cause when attempting to terminate an employee.) While the Seattle victory was not a product of collective bargaining, it does highlight the similarities between tenant organizing and workplace organizing and their shared impact on the whole lives of working people.[11]

Debtors versus big banks. Another group with enormous power to impact the lives of working women and men are the stakeholders of finance capital—the banks, hedge funds, mortgage holders, and creditors that hold our debt. While the system of finance capital is complicated and dynamic, there are still economic relationships to organize and negotiate over. There are many movements demanding that the government tax Wall Street or break up the banks—and these are great fights! But we could also take a bargaining approach, withholding participation in the economic relationship with a bank until a power-sharing agreement is reached.

For example, taxpayers could insist that government refuse to give aid to a bank—say, through a bailout—until the taxpayers themselves are given the ability to elect representatives to sit on the corporate board. Or perhaps a group of homeowners who carry mortgages with a particular bank could collectively re-negotiate the loans or interest rates based on changing housing values caused by Wall Street. This is what it might look like to bargain with the ultimate profiteer of our collective debts outside of an employment relationship.

Strategies like these are now being explored by homeowners seeking to negotiate with the banks or hedge funds holding their mortgages and who manipulate the value of their houses. Student debtors have also joined together in various ways to seek to negotiate with the financial institutions holding their loans, including projects like the Debt-Free Future Campaign, the Debt-Free Collective and, borrowing from the labor movement's most potent powers, Strike Debt. Debtors in general are seeking to come out of isolation and band together to understand and attack the structures that put them in such a precarious situation.[12] None of the strategies prescribed here are easy, but they are necessary to ensure debtors are able to equally negotiate standards and practices in finance capital.

Consumers versus corporations. Historically, consumer activists have understood that collective action is a necessary element of democratic politics and a way to combat powerful economic entities. Groups like the National Consumers League provide government, businesses, and other organizations with the consumer's perspective on concerns including child labor, privacy, food safety, and medication information. We can thank consumer activists from years ago for the labels on food packaging that we take for granted today. They understood the importance of knowing what ingredients were being used in food to ensure healthy products and to hold corporations accountable to a set of standards in food quality. There are countless other examples of consumer actions that have benefited working people in a myriad ways.[13]

Throughout US history, activists have also sought to employ consumer power to address a wide variety of causes, from the abolition of slavery to unfair labor practices and civil rights. In recent history, improvements in working conditions at some apparel and footwear factories overseas occurred in response to a highly vocal antisweatshop movement that leveraged institutional consumer power. Pressure from groups leveraging the consumer power of the global north, like the United Students Against Sweatshops (USAS), the International Labor Rights Forum (ILRF), Global Labor Justice (GLJ), the National Labor Committee in the United States, and the Clean Clothes Campaign in Europe led some factories that make goods for industry giants like Nike and Gap, Inc., to crack down on child labor, the use of dangerous chemicals, and the practice of requiring employees to work eighty-hour weeks in their suppliers throughout the global south.

But how do consumers withhold their participation in the economic relationship? Well-organized boycotts allow consumers to disrupt the economic drivers of their corporate targets to get them to the table. To be effective, a large percentage of consumers must come together to no longer purchase a product/service, including large-scale bulk consumers like hospitals, grocery stores, and other businesses. One of the most successful boycotts in US history was the Delano grape strike and boycott in the 1960s, which resulted in a significant victory for the United Farm Workers, including the signing of the union's first contract with the growers. Of course, this is not a perfect example because it landed an agreement with workers, not consumers.

The legendary 1955 boycott of the Montgomery, Alabama, bus system by Black riders demanding racial integration is perhaps a sharper example since it won changes specific to the demands of riders. Unions of transit riders around the country continue this tradition today, often working in solidarity with unions of transit workers to prevent the all-too-common tactics that divide workers and riders by pitting demands for fair wages against resistance to fare increases.

However, unless operating within an extremely tight product market (such as the Montgomery bus system), consumer boycotts can be incredibly difficult to pull off. And even when successful, boycotts rarely end up in collective bargaining. But they could. Why shouldn't consumers participate in negotiations with a company alongside workers and other stakeholders? Imagine transit riders negotiating directly alongside transit workers with similar proposals around wages and fares. Imagine Amazon Prime members negotiating with the company alongside warehouse, tech, and delivery workers around the company's behavior in their county or state. Imagine what possibilities would open up if consumers began more aggressively negotiating enforceable agreements with corporations.

Do Not Settle for Improved Policies— Help to Govern

Many community organizations and advocacy groups focus almost exclusively on electing people who share their values, passing legislation, and to some degree using the courts and various lobbying practices to enforce those new policies. This is important work. But it uses only a portion of our movement's power. Why take the rest of that power off the table?

Community-driven bargaining uses the economic relationships of any constituency to exert leverage on the corporate executives who are the direct cause of their grievances. At its best such bargaining can enable working people to play a permanent, direct role in governing the institutions that impact them rather than merely winning occasional concessions or policy improvements.

One model of community-driven bargaining centers on the creation and administration of a trust board that governs a public fund advancing community interests. In this model, representatives from the community, a particular workforce, the government, and the private sector elect representatives to sit on the board. The approach derives from the Community Change Housing Trust Funds, which involves housing advocates and low-income residents in decisions about affordable housing. These funds aggregate streams of public and private revenue for affordable housing, which a board oversees, negotiating over the funds. A board holds regular meetings, often open to the public. Through their representatives on the board, community members thus have decision-making power in determining fund spending.[14]

The bad business fee, a policy approach conceptualized by Jobs With Justice, National People's Action (now People's Action), and SEIU, attempted to consolidate the voices of impacted workers and community members in ongoing negotiations over their economic sustainability.[15]

The bad business fee targets large high-profit, low-wage employers based on the gap between their current wage levels and what worker and industry standards determine to be sustainable. Based on the cost to taxpayers and the community of public assistance programs, created by the need to essentially subsidize the wages and benefits that are not being provided by these companies, workers set a fee that low-wage employers would then pay. This could also be generated by closing corporate tax subsidies to reextract wealth from the top profiteers of an area, but the latter would not necessarily lead to an enforceable agreement. From the money generated from a fee, a fund would be created specifically for the purposes of supporting the outlined needs of those working for low-wage employers. Unlike revenue from the sister strategy of levying a tax on Wall Street and large corporations, funds from a bad business fee are *not* allocated to a state's general budget but rather to a dedicated funding stream for the sole purpose of offsetting the local costs that poverty wages exact on workers and society.

Maybe most important, a democratically elected committee or council of workers—including those who would benefit from the fee as well as those who might implement programs that would be funded by it—is created to oversee the fee. Ideally, this group is democratically elected by workers in related industries, is accountable to them, and has full decision-making authority—although even the establishment of an advisory committee can increase workers' voice in setting better standards in chronically low-wage sectors. In an ideal scenario this approach would expand workers' ability to negotiate with employers over their workplace conditions and benefits.

In 2015, Jobs With Justice joined a local coalition of care workers in Connecticut along with childcare and senior-care consumers, including SEIU and Connecticut Citizen Action, to establish the Connecticut Campaign for Worthy Wages. The campaign aimed to encourage policymakers to consider a "McWalmart Fee" that would have redirected the hefty price tag of public-care services to large low-wage corporations that operate in the area. They defined this as companies who employed more than five hundred people in the state of Connecticut, and the fee was calculated for every work hour that anyone was paid less than $15. Many of Connecticut's largest low-wage employers mirror the national list, with Walmart and McDonald's right at the top. But other less famous companies would have also been impacted, including Stop and Shop and Cigna.[16]

It was estimated at the time that low-wage work was costing Connecticut approximately $486 million in public-assistance-related expenses a year. Connecticut care workers had actively fought to fund state programs like Medicaid, the Children's Health Insurance Program (CHIP), and Temporary Assistance for Needy Families (TANF) and improve overall standards.[17] But with no consistent revenue stream, they were vulnerable to the state budget's ebbs and flows, often in competition with other important communities over pennies in the budget process. In 2015 alone, Connecticut governor Dan Malloy implemented midyear budget cuts in childcare, education, and health care, impacting workers from the care sector and many others.

The McWalmart Fee aimed to fix this, generating revenue for the senior-care and childcare services needed by many McDonald's, Walmart, and other low-wage workers. While the Connecticut fee did not pass, it represented a game-changing fight that exposed the true benefactors of austerity.

Note that a company that wants to avoid paying a bad business fees can do so simply by working with their own employees to improve wages and standards. In fact, one Connecticut-based company demonstrated some leadership by doing just this. The insurance giant Aetna, based in Hartford, announced that it would raise its own starting wage to $16 an hour.[18] Aetna also announced that it would reduce out-of-pocket health-care expenses for its lowest-paid employees. The presence of a bad business fee could encourage more companies to make similar choices.

Workers organized at their worksites are not the only ones who have attempted such an approach. In 2016, community leaders who were a part of the Illinois and Indiana Regional Organizing Network (IIRON) in Cook County, Illinois, crafted the Responsible Business Act, which would have allowed a fund similar to what would have been created by Connecticut's legislation to be spread out over several programs to support housing assistance, unreimbursed health-care costs, and even grants to nonprofits providing direct support to workers in low-wage sectors, such as heating and nutrition assistance. Under this model, people in low-wage jobs would be organized as members of a local community group, and in the process would be given both a powerful voice over how fees would be allocated as well as some resources to better monitor the program which, in itself, builds organization. Despite popular support, they too lost. Legislators prioritized proposals to increase the minimum wage instead, which was still helpful to many area workers.

Caring Across Generations—a national campaign launched by Jobs With Justice and the National Domestic Workers Alliance—employed this strategy in the home health-care sector. In 2016, Caring Across Generations partnered with the Maine People's Alliance to seek passage of a universal home care ballot measure to establish universal access to home care supports and services for more than ten thousand seniors and Mainers with disabilities. Their proposal would have created a dedicated funding stream, likely through a tax on income from wealthy individuals that was not subject to Medicare and Social Security taxes. Instead of directing existing government agencies to oversee enrollment targets, set standards that employers of care workers must meet, and otherwise oversee implementation, the campaign would have given the decision-making power to a new governing board comprised of stakeholders elected by workers, employers, and the government. Unfortunately, the political Right understood this was a direct threat to their power and used misleading tactics to confuse voters about the costs this would inflict on them via taxes. The measure did not pass.

However, the National Domestic Workers Alliance (NDWA) did not let this setback stop them from trying similar approaches elsewhere. They crafted a domestic workers bill of rights that essentially legislates the standards domestic workers would like to see in their worksites, which are people's individual homes. Like the nineteenth-century washerwomen of Atlanta, these workers have gone to governments in states like New York, Illinois, and California to lay out the ground rules that should govern the industry.

Building on a 2018 victory in Seattle, in which they established the Seattle Domestic Worker Standards Board, domestic workers are now pursuing federal legislation that will include the standards won in states and cities and the creation of a standards board. According to the City of Seattle, "The Domestic Workers Standards Board provides a place for domestic workers, employers, private households, worker organizations, and the public to consider and suggest ways to improve the working conditions of domestic workers. The Board makes these suggestions to the Office of Labor Standards, Mayor, and City Council. Examples may include new laws or programs, and changes to the City's outreach and enforcement efforts."[19] The proposed standards board could provide a new framework for collective bargaining and demonstrate a path for workers to build and exercise power in a fragmented industry, a game-changer for domestic workers and workers with similar challenges in other sectors.

When they are able to negotiate together with one employer, or some combination of employers, groups like NDWA will likely insist on the same standards. Such was the case in the 2021 agreement the NDWA signed with Handy, an app-based company for domestic cleaners that—perhaps accidentally—amalgamated previously isolated domestic workers into a common platform. "After two years of negotiation, advocates for domestic workers won an agreement that includes $15-an-hour minimum pay, paid time off—paid for by the company (20 days per year for those who work 40 hours a week)—occupational accident insurance, and a formal process to address workplace concerns, with anti-retaliation protections. But most importantly, these conditions are legally enforceable through a private agreement—worker advocates literally wrote protections into a private contract with input directly from domestic workers, something they could not count on politicians to do."[20]

In each of the approaches noted, the campaigns positioned working people in direct, decision-making position to hold their employers and other economic actors accountable. If successful, strategies like this would yield on-going authority, beyond a one-time agreement, including the potential to attach enforceable provisions to the funding in the future, such as a minimum wage rate for state-funded care providers. And in the spirit of expanding democracy and shared governance, such boards often institutionalize the practice of opening their proceedings for public input, creating additional opportunities for organizing more people into democratic processes.

Imagine how this approach might be expanded to other forms of community engagement—for example, with local school systems, immigration authorities, and others.

Deloris Wright. Portrait by Gwenn Seemel.

Profile of a Modern Worker:
Deloris Wright: "Tell Dem Slavery Done"

Deloris Wright has helped to provide a voice and a measure of power to some of the most unheard, individuals in US society—domestic workers. Through her organizing work, she is making life better not just for herself, her family, and her colleagues but also for people throughout society who need a place to stand from which they too can assert their right to be heard.

Life in Jamaica was very different than it is here, in some good ways and some not so good. As a child I watched my great-aunt fix porridge and breadfruit for passers-by on our street in Jamaica and felt good about sharing with people who had less. That's what you did. I joined my grandmother in the coffee plantation fields of Jamaica, reading letters to the farmworkers who did not know how to read. They got letters from their wives and their kids and other relatives who were living abroad or in other parts of the country. I would read them, and they would tell me what to write back.

But the economy in Jamaica wasn't always good. And my little girl was smart. The teachers said she had so much potential. Even though I was working full time as a store clerk, I found myself worried about how I would pay for her schooling if she passed the common entrance exams. If she was going to have a fair chance at getting a good education and be able to provide for herself in the future, we had to leave. And so I came to this country to help her, sending money back—school fees, books, clothes—and preparing the way for her to join me, which she did when she was grown. Here she graduated from college, and she lives in Washington, DC, where she makes her own life.

When I first got to New York in 1987, a friend of mine was returning to Jamaica and asked me to take over her job as a live-in caregiver for a family. I stayed for two years. I was glad to have work, but I was also deeply homesick. It was hard being a live-in domestic worker. I missed my family. I couldn't get the food I was used to. When I think about my life and my daughter's life now, it was worth the sacrifices I made in the beginning. Still, it was hard.

I got used to it after that first job, and I started doing live-out work. While I was able to get a position as a domestic worker with employers who treated me with respect, I saw many others who weren't as blessed as I was. I would meet up with other nannies out in the park, talking about what they were going through. One woman was making less than minimum wage. Some couldn't afford to buy lunch. And yet their employers wouldn't let them take so much as a slice of bread from their homes. They could prepare food, but they couldn't eat it. Some families would throw food away before they let their nanny eat it. One day, I remember three of us sharing one lunch—literally getting three plates and splitting up the food so we could all eat. I could afford lunch, but I didn't feel right seeing others like me go hungry.

I realized I had to do something. My great-aunt was a domestic back in Jamaica. I remember her washing and ironing the clothes of white people. I thought things were different now. For me to leave that and then see the same thing here in the United States, I knew I could not stay quiet. I heard another nanny say that there was this woman—Ai-jen—walking around the neighborhood with flyers, and I went looking for her. It took a while for me to build up the courage to go to my first Domestic Workers United (DWU) meeting, but once I did I never stopped. I started handing out flyers to the nannies I knew.

I realized that many of the skills I had in Jamaica were also needed here in my new home. I was always good at helping others interpret the world so they could make decisions about what they wanted to do. In addition to reading letters in the coffee fields, I remember as a child helping one of our neighbors who was partially blind. I would make it easier for him to get around on his own. In Brooklyn I saw that most of the flyers were in English, and some of the domestic workers I knew mostly spoke Spanish. So, I arranged to have bilingual signs made up, English on one side and Spanish on the other, which I would show to the Spanish speakers and ask the ones who spoke some English to translate for the others.

We all began to come together more to talk about how we wanted to be treated. We did not want to be invisible anymore, and we wanted the dignity that other people got from their employment. Farmworkers and domestic workers had been excluded from previous labor laws passed during the Jim Crow era in the United States, and we were ready to crack that ceiling. Together we started to assemble the first Domestic Workers Bill of Rights—a package of laws allowing domestic workers a fair wage and access to overtime pay, time off, and the protection of other labor laws.[21]

Many of us would wrap up work with our employers and then go to the DWU office. And we started to organize trips to Albany, New York, to negotiate with state lawmakers around the bill. We refused to be hidden. We wanted to be recognized as people who did work, and to be treated like everyone else. We are the ones who do what makes all other work possible.

Some legislators were so tired of us showing up. But we did it anyway, to "tell dem slavery done." That was our slogan. We are humans, and we are tired of some of our employers treating their dogs better than us.

It took us six-and-a-half years, multiple trips to Albany, hounding legislators, and a long hard fight, but we persisted and finally won! Not everything we asked for ended up in the final law, but we won so much. And it really hit me the day we went to see the governor sign the bill. I looked up, and I saw the name on the building was "The Dwyer Cultural Center." Dwyer was my grandmother's last name. And when I saw that, I knew she must be proud of me.

After that, some employers began calling us at DWU to ask for guidance. We were telling them how to be compliant with the law, and basically how to treat us like employees for the first time. Sometimes it wasn't their fault—they just didn't know. But now the law could spell it out. This was a big improvement, especially for the women who were always scared to negotiate with their employers over their rights and conditions. This changed everything!

By this time I had moved into an apartment in Crown Heights where I still live today. But the neighborhood has been changing. Rent costs were through the roof. One man at my church said his tenant paid six months' rent at a time, and here many of my neighbors struggled to even get one month's rent together. It was more crowded, and more white people were moving in. I didn't mind that at first, but then I realized that some of my neighbors were being manipulated into moving out so that landlords could increase the rent. Landlords would give them cash to leave. Many of these people were seniors, and you're asking them to just up and move to East New York? The new people didn't have to move to East New York, so why did we have to leave? Naturally, I couldn't sit by and watch. I knew what could happen if we joined together and asserted our dignity together. I'd already done it before. I knew what was possible.

Yet again, it was a flyer that led me in the right direction. I ran into someone named Joel who was passing out flyers at the Utica subway stop. It was for the first congress of the new Crown Heights Tenant Union. I called three of my neighbors to go with me, and we joined right away. We were organized into locals, and our local included our three buildings. I learned that things were worse than I had imagined. Some people didn't even know who their landlord was. They would pay rent to an LLC or some other vague company name. With the Tenants Union, we have been able to negotiate with landlords and building owners. We form committees of people to join our neighbors in housing court when they are summoned so they don't have to navigate the system by themselves. Some of them have lived in their apartments for over forty years, and that is often who landlords are trying to remove. I was a part of a group that helped one of our neighbors understand and respond to a letter they received that threatened eviction. It was just like I used to do in the coffee fields of Jamaica. I know it will take us a while to challenge some of the larger building owners, but it feels good to win these small victories, to be there for each other.

I've now been in my apartment for over thirty years. And I've been working for the same family for over twenty-one years. I've watched both children grow and am now caring for their grandfather. I love being a caretaker. And I can hold my head up high knowing that the people I work for and the people I rent from respect me. This is what democracy is supposed to be. It means that we can all speak and be heard, that there is transparency and a right/wrong way of doing things. Even when I am scared, I do it anyway because we have to keep "telling dem slavery done."

The Other CBA—Community Benefits Agreements

Community benefits agreements (CBAs) are a family of approaches that came into play within the last twenty years and soon became a key tool in the arsenal of working people, led in large part by the Partnerships for Working Families network (now PowerSwitch Action). CBAs are agreements between a developer or other company, a coalition of community partners, and most often a government agency to address the needs of those living in an area that has experienced or could soon experience new large-scale development of nearby land and facilities. Developing any property requires licenses, investments, and other permissions, and working people can leverage this process to ensure that the project does not harm their economic well-being.

The original impetus for these agreements was the gentrification and corresponding displacement of low-income residents that surfaced when cities that had been losing population and wealth for decades began to revitalize their image in the 1990s, often with the help of large-scale public investments in development projects.[22] The problem was that when private companies invested in urban areas, particularly poor areas and areas with significant populations of Black and Brown families, the costs of rent and housing increased. Rather than benefiting the existing population, who were often displaced instead, this kind of urban development benefited large property owners who often did not live in the community, real estate speculators, and later people with higher incomes who moved into the new housing. Thus, it was necessary for neighborhood organizations and worker advocates to convince elected leaders that simply supporting private urban development alone was not enough to help their communities.

The community-defined benefits covered in a CBA can be as broad or as narrow as the negotiators are able to agree on. From the perspective of the people who are or would be working in and around the development project, agreements might include a promise to hire some percentage of local residents, payment of prevailing and living wages, local sourcing for products and supplies, employer neutrality regarding union organizing drives, and targeted hiring to ensure that jobs go to the underemployed communities that need them.

Additionally, specific benefits are often defined in direct relationship to the neighborhoods surrounding the project. In Milwaukee, for example, community leaders sought requirements for developers to provide affordable housing to ensure that existing residents did not become priced out of their neighborhood by the development.[23] The Northwest Bronx Community and Clergy Coalition worked with others in New York to negotiate an agreement with the developers of the Kingsbridge Armory to guarantee funding for community organizations who would essentially monitor the long-term effect of the development on the neighborhood and campaign for improvements and adjustments as needed.[24] Other groups have included in their CBAs environmental justice initiatives, requirements that developers build recreational facilities such as parks and playgrounds that benefit the community, and funding for job-training programs for local residents.[25]

Unions also engage in negotiations over community benefits in various ways. First, unions are often part of the coalition negotiating a community benefits agreement. Unions played a key role in guaranteeing one of the original agreements that was negotiated with the developer of the Staples Center project in Los Angeles, winning provisions that, in addition to community goals, made it easier for workers to form unions.[26] Unions often add more power to enforce the agreements along with community partners, having the institutional capacity to monitor a CBAs implementation.[27] Unions have also included negotiations for CBAs as part of their collective bargaining agreements with employers alongside traditional collective bargaining agreements.

For instance, the California High-Speed Rail Authority signed a CBA that required 30 percent of the work on the project be performed by people from economically depressed areas along with a requirement that 10 percent of the work be performed by someone who is disadvantaged because he or she is a veteran, is homeless, is a custodial single parent, has a criminal record, or meets other criteria. The contract provides that although the project will normally hire workers through union hiring halls, if the union is unable to produce workers meeting the disadvantaged worker hiring standards, the contractors can hire such workers from any source.[28] Such agreements may also incentivize less-diverse unions to ensure their memberships are inclusive of Black and Brown communities.

The Workers Defense Project (WDP) in Austin, Texas, supports individuals across several sectors in organizing for better wages, standards, and conditions using a community-led bargaining approach. WDP successfully got the city to establish economic development incentives based on worker safety and health—a critical concern of the many immigrant workers in the construction industry.

In 2012, Austin withheld permits for several large building projects until companies signed Better Builders agreements developed by community leaders at

WDP.[29] These agreements specified terms and conditions for each worksite and empowered WDP monitors to enforce the agreements via safety walk-throughs. For example, Apple and WDP negotiated an agreement covering Apple's $300 million building project in North Austin. The agreement required a minimum wage of $12 an hour and specified that all workers on site must be certified with basic OSHA-10 safety training, provided with all necessary personal protective equipment free of charge, and covered by workers' compensation.

Trammel Crow Green Water Master Developer, LLC, also signed a Better Builder agreement, pledging to comply with prevailing wage and OSHA requirements and all applicable state and federal laws relating to construction and to work with the WDP on enforcement of these standards.

The City of Austin's use of its zoning power and development incentives in support of WDP's Better Builders Program is what made the Apple and Trammel Crow agreements feasible. The requirement that developers hire third-party monitors creates an opportunity for WDP to build organization from its enforcement work.[30]

While community benefits agreements have traditionally been negotiated with developers or companies that are moving into an area, there is no reason they need to be so limited. CBAs could be negotiated with any entity that affects the community, such as existing retailers, banks, any other type of company, or the government. Since these entities rely on the community for some portion of their power and wealth, the community could act on that economic relationship to bring them to the bargaining table. Again, imagine Amazon Prime members in a particular community attempting to win a CBA with Amazon to provide free same-day delivery in their neighborhood that has been denied this service to date, all without negatively impacting Amazon workers.

Additionally, these agreements could be made even more effective if combined with some form of long-term oversight led by community leaders. It is not enough for the initial agreement to be legally enforceable. It must also provide the community bargaining unit with ongoing governing capabilities and the opportunity to renegotiate and adjust based on changing conditions.

As with all strategies, working people should be wary of the ways in which companies will try to use these frameworks to limit the participation of impacted communities. Partnership for Working Families has identified problematic or even sham community benefits agreements. In one example, developers hand-picked the community organizations with which they negotiated the agreement rather than letting people who were actually impacted choose their own representatives. In another, the developers only signed a sort of gentleman's agreement that did not include enforceable commitments.[31] Such problematic agreements were then used as public relations devices to convince elected officials, the media, the community in which the development was sited, and the general public that the developer had community support and was a responsible business. The point is that the negotiations must include authentic stakeholders from both sides in order to effectively expand economic democracy for working people in their role as community members.

Community Pathways to Workplace Bargaining

The following examples are not necessarily acts of expanded bargaining in their own right but rather important potential on-ramps in that direction.

Coenforcement. As we know, laws—while theoretically enforceable—are often easily overturned, repealed, watered down, or blatantly ignored. And while labor and employment laws on the books may technically grant working people more protection, those who have a union worksite are in the best position to maintain standards. Therefore, organization is key to enforcement, to holding employers and other economic stakeholders accountable, and to keeping working people's concerns and voices heard long after the political climate shifts.

In a union worksite, this problem is solved through a grievance process. Worker leaders collaborate with union representatives to file complaints directly with their employer. But when a union is not present, as in most worksites, a different infrastructure must be in place as a bare minimum enforcement mechanism for the standards imposed by a new law. One such structure is coenforcement.

Coenforcement is an approach in which worker organizations broaden the scope of bargaining by negotiating with government or private actors to play a formal role in enforcing labor and employment laws. Through coenforcement, working people have a forum for building collective power via community-based organizations. The model arose because companies can engage in massive violations of the laws protecting working people and get away with it because government officials at the federal, state, and local levels do not have the resources to force compliance.[32] And the courts are often inaccessible to working people, who may not have the money or the time to get caught up in a legal process.[33] Worse, many modern workers are tricked into signing nondisclosure agreements (NDAs) when they first get a job, making it illegal for them to take legal action if something goes wrong.[34] This crisis is even worse for people of color, women, gender non-conforming workers, young people, and immigrants, who may be less likely to come forward for a variety of reasons, including justified concerns about their safety.[35]

Government officials have always informally relied on individual workers to flag problematic employers by filing complaints against them, a daunting task. In response to widespread corporate lawlessness and as a method of building collective power, worker organizations have sought a greater role in the enforcement of workplace standards—or to create them where sufficient statutory standards do not exist. In using this strategy, they can target the worst actors and not simply depend on disparate complaints to come in.

Janice Fine, one of the leading experts on coenforcement, documented how the Coalition of Immokalee Workers (CIW) was able to negotiate an enforceable set of standards for tomato farmworkers even though these workers are excluded from the protections of both the National Labor Relations Act and the Fair Labor Standards Act.[36] CIW publicized the fact that growers who sold their tomatoes to top restaurant chains such as Taco Bell, McDonald's, and Burger King were abusing their farmworkers with brutal hours, extremely low pay, and even slave labor. Through a corporate campaign and consumer boycott of Taco Bell and related restaurants owned by Yum Foods, CIW was able to win an agreement creating the very type of enforceable standards that did not exist in federal law, such as wage and hour protections.[37] The agreement also gave CIW the power to investigate growers, and those found to be out of compliance could no longer sell to Yum Foods.

CIW faced a backlash from Burger King and from the tomato-growing industry, which threatened to fine growers who cooperated with CIW.[38] But the collective power CIW built was strong enough that it eventually forced Burger King to enter into the agreement as well, taking away the leverage the tomato-grower group had to threaten fines.[39] Today, CIW continues to enforce the agreement as well as work to expand justice for farmworkers with campaigns involving Publix Super Markets, Wendy's, and other large produce buyers.

Another example of coenforcement involves more formal cooperation between government regulators and worker advocates. In both San Francisco and Seattle, municipal agencies that enforce labor standards have allocated resources to worker organizations to help them enforce labor laws. San Francisco was the first to launch an Office of Labor Standards and Enforcement; Seattle then followed suit. After advocacy by worker organizations, the Seattle Office of Labor Standards awarded more than $3 million in grants to worker, community, and civil rights organizations and partnerships to help enforce the statutes for which the agency is responsible, including Seattle's minimum wage law, paid sick leave, scheduling ordinances, and other laws. The organizations focused their advocacy on communities that are unlikely to complain to government officials, including people of color, immigrants, and returning citizens. The organizations agreed to do door-to-door outreach, host trainings for working people and other organizations, collect complaints, participate in complaint resolution, and make referrals in cases of unresolvable alleged labor-law violations.[40]

In 2014, Jobs With Justice San Francisco led a successful campaign to have the city enact one of the first set of laws in the nation ensuring more predictable and fair workplace schedules for nearly forty thousand people who work in formula retail and restaurants in the city. The campaign ignited several similar municipal and state efforts, including the recent fair workweek win in Oregon.[41]

Those who have a union worksite are in the best position to maintain standards won by the San Francisco legislation. For instance, the victory helped employees at Macy's get back to the table with the company to renegotiate a better contract given the new leverage gained from the policy. But beyond these individuals, the coalition had to navigate how to maximize the policy's implementation to create new channels for organizing.

Luckily, the Office of Labor Standards and Enforcement, the San Francisco agency charged with enforcing the scheduling statutes, values coenforcement practices. This agency granted $250,000 to local worker-led organizations to organize the people affected by the San Francisco ordinance so to increase compliance with the law and make sure that workers' rights are respected. Doing so allows retail workers who pushed for the law to now monitor implementation store-by-store, legitimized by the local government, setting them up to organize and talk to others in those same stores—ultimately outlining shared interests and goals among not just those working at large *formula* retailers but also those employed by all retail workers in the city (around 100,000) that could lead to a more collective engagement of the retail industry in San Francisco.[42]

Ultimately, coenforcement allows community-based organizations to directly organize working people through outreach and education grants, allowing them to understand the problems that working people face. This allows workers themselves to have a better understanding of issues in need of reform and the best allocation of government enforcement resources. And in some instances, the outreach can improve the landscape for more formal organization building.

Procurement strategies. When state, local, and federal governments ask the private sector to bid on projects, they have the right to require contractors to meet a set of socially responsible goals in addition to providing the service or constructing the project requested. Procurement-based strategies center on the premise that it is a fundamental requirement of democratic governance that communities, workers' rights groups, and unions—rather than the richest corporations—should be the ones in control of how government spends the money entrusted to it.

There is a long history of using government procurement to lift economic standards, beginning with prevailing wage laws that were passed in several states in the nineteenth century and culminating on the federal level with worker advocates pushing Congress to enact the Davis-Bacon Act of 1931, which required contractors and subcontractors on public works projects that received federal funds to pay the people who worked on the project the local prevailing wage. One purpose of these laws was to ensure that government funds were not given to companies whose business models relied on undercutting competitors by paying low wages to their workers or otherwise skirting the law.

Government procurement later moved beyond ensuring economic justice and into the realm of social justice when labor and civil rights leaders, such as Brotherhood of Sleeping Car Porters' founder A. Philip Randolph, pushed President Franklin Roosevelt to ban companies that discriminated based on race from receiving defense contracts. Randolph threatened a march on Washington to pressure the government at a time when the United States was increasingly under pressure in World War II, calling off the march only when Roosevelt signed an agreement to ban discrimination by defense contractors.[43]

Today, procurement-based campaigning is a keystone approach whenever public assistance—whether in the form of direct payment, tax abatements, zoning variances, or other assistance—is used on a corporate project. These strategies are employed when significant public resources are used to fund major building projects like stadiums, highways, expanded transit systems, and large corporate headquarters.

The procurement process often provides the leverage needed to make many of the other bargaining strategies described in this book work.

Jobs to Move America (JMA) is an organization that has sharpened procurement strategies within transit manufacturing. Cities spend more than $5 billion a year on buses and train cars. Much of this money currently either goes to overseas manufacturers or to manufacturers that create temporary jobs for specific projects. The JMA model of "inclusive public procurement" calls on local and state governments to leverage their transit procurement money to help communities that are underserved by public transit by building clean, nonpolluting, and efficient public transportation options while at the same time creating good permanent jobs for these same communities. The model calls on procurement agencies to require bidders on transit projects to include the US Employment Plan (USEP) as a mandatory part of their bids.[44] In accepting the USEP, the bidders agree to project the number of local jobs they will create as a result of being awarded the contract, the projected salaries of those jobs, and the outreach they will do to ensure that disadvantaged groups obtain a percentage of the jobs. The request for proposals in such a case will explicitly say that the procurement agency is less interested in the lowest bid than in evaluating the entire project, with special emphasis on the USEP submitted by bidders. The request for proposals also specifies that the winning bidder will be subject to oversight to enforce the promises made in the USEP.

The JMA theory is that winning bidders will do more than simply fill out forms predicting employment; they will act by working with unions, seeking out community leaders and organizations to recruit disadvantaged workers, negotiating a community benefits agreement, and allowing related workers and community organizations to audit them to ensure compliance with the USEP the bidder submitted.

JMA does not suggest that procurement agencies directly include these additional issues in its request for proposals. That is because federal law—which applies to almost all public transportation projects because such projects invariably receive federal funding via the US Department of Transportation—requires state and local agencies not to add restrictions that limit competition between bidders.[45] Therefore, state and local government cannot add requirements such as local hiring or creation of a certain number of local jobs or negotiation of a community benefits agreement as a *prerequisite* to bidding on a contract. Nonetheless, proposals that include such provisions can be deemed more attractive.

The Department of Transportation under President Obama interpreted the open-competition requirement to allow state and local procurement authorities to require that bidders submit a USEP, since that requirement itself does not shut out any bidders. However, the Department of Transportation did not reaffirm this position under Donald Trump.

The JMA strategy was successfully used in both Chicago and Los Angeles, leading to the creation of family-supporting jobs in transit manufacturing for those communities. At a time when other government funding may be shrinking, both parties have infrastructure spending programs, so it is *possible* that additional transit funding will come from the federal government, giving additional options to put the JMA strategy into effect.

However, even when generously interpreted, federal regulations do not allow state and local procurement authorities to disqualify bids from bad employers solely based on a contractor's USEP submission. Therefore, even if a low-road employer were to submit a USEP that clearly notes how the contractor is not emphasizing fair wages, local hiring, or any of the other worker and community benefits they are required to speak to in their bids, the state and local procurement authorities would not be able to deny them the contract based on this alone. If more emphasis is given to the cheapest bidder, for example, then a bad employer could still be awarded a contract.

Similar limitations persist outside of transit manufacturing. One of the more notorious cases of a government contractor acting badly and still winning federal contracts is Avondale Shipyards in New Orleans in the early 1990s. Avondale both received federal contracts and billed taxpayers to fund its antiunion campaign when workers sought to form a union, committing hundreds of unfair labor practices in the process. So, while the NLRB was prosecuting the company, Avondale was still billing the government for its own legal services to support its battle against the workers.[46] Some of that changed under the Obama administration, as laws previously proposed under the Clinton administration but stymied under the Bush administration were finally put into place.

Some efforts to reform federal acquisitions regulation have attempted to change low-bid contracting both before and after contractors get beyond the initial litmus test of being "responsible." These include awarding points to contractors who model other behaviors deemed positive for taxpayers, such as giving credit for having good employment practices across its existing workforce.[47] But these rules remain vulnerable to the seesaw of politics—enforceable and even erasable based on who is in federal office.

In summary, procurement strategies enable working people, through their unions or community-based organizations, to have a seat at the table with both government and government contractors. The contract between the government and the contractor is enforceable by the government, though it is not enforceable by anyone else unless stipulated. Thus, a successful procurement-based strategy that seeks to include working people in a position to enforce the agreements they win would have to include writing in worker-led enforcement mechanisms and oversight into the procurement contract. Such an approach could create conditions through which workers can build collective power, provide a pathway to organization and collective bargaining, and ensure long-term benefits to others in the community through such programs as providing incentives for local hiring.[48]

Applying Collective Bargaining Outside of an Economic Relationship

Collective bargaining can be applied to many different contexts outside the economy. In 2017, Rhode Island Jobs With Justice successfully passed a Community Safety Act modeled after similar legislation passed in New York four years before, aiming to end policing practices that discriminated against Black and Brown youth.

Inspired by the victory, Central Indiana Jobs With Justice began to experiment with the idea of a community safety agreement, an enforceable agreement negotiated directly between a specific community of young people, their tax-paying parents, and the local police. A joint board would have then allowed all parties to enforce the agreement together. Police are often opposed to this kind of coenforcement for a variety of reasons, not the least of which includes their own systemic bias against communities of color. While the effort to create such a community safety agreement has yet to succeed, the idea illustrates how applying a bargaining framework can be a powerful tool in a community relationship not directly based in economic interests. Current debates about reforming the police while shifting funding from violent law enforcement capacities to human needs such as health care, education, and mental health treatment offer a powerful opportunity to apply the collective bargaining model to community issues.

Like the strategies noted in other chapters, these community-driven bargaining efforts model how working people are coming together to govern themselves in all aspects of their economic lives. Whether or not they are protected by twentieth-century laws, they are defining their own bargaining units from the perspective of what they seek to govern over. They are clear about the need to collectively negotiate in their worksites—including those sites that are less formal, such as those of domestic workers—as well as in collaboration with others who share an economic identity with them beyond work. And in so doing, they are fighting to expand systems of economic democracy—maximizing the decision-making power of the majority in all arenas.

BUILDING LONG-TERM LABOR-COMMUNITY POWER

Bargaining for the Common Good

Imagine the hypothetical community of Metropolis. A large chemical plant is located there that provides a high percentage of the community's jobs. The plant was recently bought by a set of fund managers working on behalf of several banks that are known to own abandoned buildings and other blighted property in town. While the executives who manage the plant deny any involvement, the plant has been cited by several state and federal agencies for polluting the local waterways, including the sources of the community's tap water, which has been linked to an increase in digestive problems in area children—including yours!

Now imagine that your spouse and several neighbors work at the plant and are part of a union local that is about to negotiate a new contract with the company. You all agree that one of the primary issues that should be covered in the contract negotiations is to get the plant to find a safer way to dispose of its chemical waste that does not harm the community's children.

But is that allowed?

As we noted in chapter 1, the NLRA lays out three kinds of subjects for bargaining: mandatory, permissive/voluntary, and illegal.[1] The examples provided by the NLRB almost exclusively focus on worksite-specific topics.[2] However, this was not always the practice. Historically, union workers have often fought to have a say over an employer's business practices and governance, attempting to negotiate over far more than wages and worksite conditions.

For example, in the 1945 strike at General Motors (GM), the UAW demanded that the company raise their wages by 30 percent *without raising the price of cars*.[3] In doing so, they directly challenged the collective bargaining paradigm that aimed to limit negotiations to terms and conditions of employment. The economy of World War II provided a political context supporting these demands. However, after the war, labor unions lost the federal government as an ally, and companies were able to refuse to negotiate over any topic not explicitly stated as mandatory in the law. Not surprisingly, as became the practice in most industries post World War II, GM refused to negotiate with workers on any of its business practices outside of wages and working conditions. The UAW ultimately accepted a contract that addressed only those issues.[4]

This trend in bargaining persists today. So, while many unions in Germany, South Africa, and countries throughout South America have a role in governing a company's business practices in addition to negotiating a fair wage, US unions have long been squeezed into a narrow negotiation position that precludes such a role. Unions in those other places have successfully pushed their governments to provide stronger social safety nets that include many of the benefits US unions bargain over—health care, retirement, sick time, sick leave, and more. This freed those unions in Europe and elsewhere to negotiate for all workers as a sector and take bolder action without fear of having to bargain away a critical benefit for workers and their families. While much of this is now under attack from the European Right and multinational corporations, European workers still have a stronger foundation to build from than their US counterparts.

Many unions in the United States have been attempting to overcome these challenges through various forms of *social movement unionism*. Over several generations, community organizations and unions in coalition with others have fought for quality public schools, hospitals, mass transit, affordable housing, and the regulation of health and the environment to create a civil society that serves all of us. These institutions are in jeopardy after years of attack from the financial sector and global capital, which lusts hungrily after the opportunity to profit off these sectors. The same forces that seek to defund government and privatize services are dismantling the social safety net, destroying good jobs (particularly in the public sector), and driving ever-increasing wealth inequality. Communities of color are particularly impacted, but damage to the public sector also hurts working-class white communities who are equally dependent on Medicaid, Social Security, public schools, and public hospitals. In fact, white workers make up the majority of families who benefit from most of these services.[5]

To navigate this environment, some unions who have largely followed the traditional models for bargaining are now moving to broaden the scope of what is negotiated to include the community interests where workers' families live. These leaders recognize that an employer's impact goes well beyond the worksite, and they are organizing to pressure executives and administrators to negotiate over those issues.

In the words of Allyson Perry, president of the West Virginia Educators Association's Marion County local, "Within a profession like ours, the union not only protects your job but also this thing that we all love and value—the institution of public education and its role in shaping our democracy. Whether you legally have collective bargaining rights or not is far from the issue when your purpose is to defend the institution."[6]

To bring these interests to the table, unions of working people are developing partnerships with the communities they serve and live in. They are striving to create a shared understanding of how their employers affect the community and engage community members in the process of addressing these impacts. During collective bargaining, workers are bringing community interests to the table and seeking permission to bring community members to sit in on bargaining sessions with them. Workers are also running campaigns that shift the context of organizing, striving to put pressure on employers to agree to these new forms of broader community-centered collective bargaining.

The Seven Pillars of Bargaining for the Common Good

One popular approach to using the collective bargaining process as a site of struggle to negotiate over issues beyond the worksite is known as *bargaining for the common good*. This approach is rooted in the reality that unions and community-based organizations are actually engaged in the same struggle. At its core this approach recognizes the role of corporations in driving the austerity agenda, particularly in the public sector, noting that the government representatives sitting across from public-sector employees are not necessarily holding all the decision-making power. Going after the corporate targets who are not necessarily at the bargaining table is central to winning when bargaining for the common good.

The Kalmanovitz Initiative at Georgetown University, the Center for Innovation in Worker Organization at Rutgers University, and the Action Center on Race and the Economy (ACRE) support union locals that are seeking to bargain for the common good and are willing to explore new forms of bargaining that can challenge the predatory impact of financialization on workers and their communities. They recommend incorporating seven key elements in the process.[7]

- *Expand the scope of bargaining beyond wages and benefits*: Identify issues that resonate with members, partners, and allies and that impact our communities.

- *Put forth demands that address structural issues*: Do not just focus on symptoms of the problems.
- *Go on offense*. Identify, expose, and challenge the real villains—the financial and corporate actors who profit from and increasingly drive policies and actions.
- *Engage community allies as partners in issue development and the bargaining campaign*: Bring in community partners on the ground floor and ask them what they need out of the bargaining campaign.
- *Center racial justice in your demands:* Address the role that employers play in creating and exacerbating structural racism in our communities.
- *Strengthen internal organizing, membership, and member engagement*: Deeply engage the memberships of both unions and community organizations, and create opportunities for deep relationship-building and joint-visioning between the members of the different organizations
- *Leverage capital:* Develop strategies that leverage the financial power of workers' pension funds and endowments in order to win common good demands.

A campaign to promote community-centered bargaining should not end once the union settles its contract. Bargaining for the common good is about building long-term community-labor power, not about giving unions some good publicity during a contract fight. The boss does not automatically become a good actor once the contract is settled, and the community's demands do not become any less important.

Bargaining for the common good presents a union's contract negotiations as a site of struggle in ongoing efforts for social change in which community organizations, religious leaders, and students often engage. This is particularly true when the common good is defined to put racial justice at the forefront. For the leaders of Jobs With Justice, this approach has been an inspiring evolution of traditional labor-community coalitions that have been rooted in the values and practice of solidarity. This strategy has centered the opportunity for relationships based on long-term solidarity to create partnerships that are rooted in a shared vision and a set of interests that benefit everyone.

Bargaining for the Common Good in the Public Sector

Bargaining for the common good has been most often associated with public-sector unions because these employees are engaged in the provision of actual public goods—for example, teachers providing an education to a community's children and bus drivers providing the means for people to travel to and from work.[8]

It is also particularly important for unions of public employees to reach out to the communities they work and live in. These unions have been under strong attack from the right wing, partly because union representation has remained much stronger in the public sector than in the private sector.[9] Beginning in Wisconsin after the election of Scott Walker and then continuing in other states after they came under full Republican control, large numbers of public-sector workers have lost the legal right to organize, collectively bargain, fund their unions, and much more.[10] In addition, in the *Janus v. AFSCME Council 31* case, decided on January 27, 2018, the US Supreme Court overturned the ability of such unions to collect fees from all the public employees that benefit from the work of the union.[11]

Bargaining for the common good provides a built-in way for public employees to strengthen their unions by determining what the community most needs as it relates to the services they provide and including them in the bargaining process to the greatest extent possible. This in turn encourages stronger community support for employees' demands. This approach also ensures that both unions and communities can challenge the negative effects of financialization.

Teachers and school workers have waged some of the best-known versions of this strategy. One of the most discussed examples is the experience of the Chicago Teachers Union during its 2012 strike and later again in 2019. The union argued for proven educational reforms to dramatically improve the education of more than 400,000 students in a district of 675 schools, through increased funding, stronger curricula for students, better support infrastructure for parents and the surrounding community, higher-quality facilities, and equitable treatment of students, particularly those tracked and segregated.

Through bargaining, the Chicago Teachers Union uncovered a large gamble the Chicago Public Schools had taken to fund schools through the use of complex and obscure financial instruments known as interest rate swaps. No other school district in the country relied on this type of financial product to fund schools. According to the *Chicago Tribune*, this gamble ultimately forced the schools to pay back $100 million more (adjusted for inflation) than if they had chosen a traditional fixed-rate borrowing product. This needless expense competed with the money needed to fund schools in real time, causing the closure of some Chicago schools. The Chicago Teachers Union continues to negotiate with the school system, the City of Chicago, and the banks profiting from the toxic interest rate swaps. The union demanded that the city stop closing schools and renegotiate the terms of school funding to ensure that children and their schools receive the resources needed for a good education.[12]

In 2013, educators in St. Paul, Minnesota, went a step further, convening parents and other community advocates to outline a shared agenda before beginning their contract negotiations. In addition to the shared needs of educators at the workplace, the union took a bold bargaining-for-the-common-good approach by recognizing the role of finance capital and big banks in making life hard for students and their families. They inserted into their negotiations the request for the school district to cease all business with banks that foreclose on families with school-aged children during the school year, essentially seeking to leverage government contracts with banks in order to stop banks from taking actions that were harming kids' educations.

Here is how Mary Cathryn Ricker of the American Federation of Teachers (AFT) who hails from the Twin Cities in Minnesota, explained the strategy:

> "Us" had become the rank-and-file members who no longer felt the negotiations were being conducted behind their backs. Now, local shop stewards were being treated as leaders in the process instead of just following orders. "Us" had become a neighborhood group that had been organizing independently but were now our partners. "Us" became parents who attended negotiations and shared their hopes and dreams for their children in our public schools at the bargaining table.[13]

When the employers tried to shut down negotiations, the St. Paul Federation of Teachers held firm and organized actions to change the employer's position, including going door-to-door to explain what was happening and how they— parents and kids of these same schools—were being shut out of negotiations. The union also mobilized public demonstrations and rallies to show strength and support, organized school walk-ins (in a blizzard!), and voted to authorize a strike that was ultimately averted when the school system came back to the table.[14]

The Fix LA campaign is another example of how bargaining for the common good is not only morally right but also leads to bigger wins for working people when there is a clear understanding of the role of Wall Street. As described by Marilyn Schneiderman and Secky Fascione:

> Prior to going into bargaining with Los Angeles in 2014, the Service Employees International Union (SEIU) Local 721 and AFSCME locals joined with community allies to craft demands that would push back against an austerity agenda that was hurting both municipal workers and the people they served. Under the banner "Fix LA," city workers and community and racial justice groups documented how exorbitant

Wall Street fees were draining the municipal budget and starving critical city services.

When the campaign demanded that the city bargain with Wall Street, it achieved a significant victory:

> The campaign won a commitment from the city of Los Angeles to hire five thousand workers from disadvantaged communities into a range of jobs in Public Works, General Services, Recreation and Parks, the Airport, and a city-financed revenue commission to identify alternatives to high-fee Wall Street loans, closing a variety of local tax loopholes to raise revenue and avoid dependence on predatory Wall Street loans. The campaign's narrative and power successfully fought off concession demands from the city.[15]

Los Angeles workers employed this strategy again in 2019 when the United Teachers of Los Angeles (UTLA) went out on strike. UTLA president Alex Caputo-Pearl said, "UTLA is part of a growing national movement that is centered on the idea of bargaining for the common good. By the time we get to the bargaining table, we're taking demands and proposals that have come out of months of working with community organizations, youth, and parents, and that bring to light things that are not typical, mandatory subjects of bargaining."

This bargaining approach can also provide a powerful method of dealing with issues of racial injustice. For instance, AFSCME Local 3299 made racial justice a central part of its bargaining with the University of California (UC) system, demanding that the system's administration create local-hire and job-training programs to increase jobs for low-income people of color living in communities near the universities. Local 3299 also demanded that the UC system make a greater commitment not to collaborate with ICE agents unless they produced a valid warrant, and the UC system agreed not to impose additional requirements for work authorization, including not participating in any federal worker registry.[16] In all these ways the union went beyond the traditional jurisdiction of bargaining and expanded it to include the conditions of their entire community and their broader workplace.[17]

In yet another example, Portland, Oregon, service workers—including librarians, social workers, and guards—organized with AFSCME Local 328 to ask for translation and interpretation services for the people accessing the services they provided, prayer spaces, gender-neutral bathrooms, multilingual safety training, the establishment of a community-employment committee to work on recruitment, and retention and career development of underrepresented communities, among other things.[18]

As a strategy, bargaining for the common good has also created a platform for addressing other community issues. For example, Oregon's State Employees Union used this strategy when they demanded the state make mass transit passes available for purchase at pretax rates for employees *and* residents.[19] And in the small city of Pottstown, Pennsylvania, nurses and hospital personnel attempted to include expanded pediatric care, especially for children without insurance, after the facility owners had eliminated it.

Some unions have even begun addressing the existential threat of climate change in bargaining, seeking policies that change practices to slow down and/or adapt to shifting climate patterns. The Florida Public Services Union, SEIU Local 8, demanded that the state stop providing subsidies to companies that rely on fossil fuels as a core component of their business model. A similar union in California insisted that their city government issue a report clarifying the impacts of any potential city contracts on the economy and the environment before signing. And the Oklahoma Education Association demanded the state institute a higher tax on oil production, gas production, and motor fuels in order to fund public education.[20]

Bargaining for the Common Good in the Private Sector

The idea of bargaining for the common good has also made inroads in the private sector. Here are few notable examples.

UNITE HERE Local 2 is a union that represents hospital workers in San Francisco. The union has seen a steady erosion of jobs for Black workers in its hotels at the same time that gentrification is forcing Black families out of the community. To address this two-pronged crisis, a decade ago the union won language in their collective bargaining agreement to increase hiring of Black workers in San Francisco hotels. The local has also helped create a nonprofit called Equality and Inclusion in Hospitality, Inc., that recruits, trains, and places workers of color from ballparks into higher-paid hotel jobs. Parallel to this effort, community organizations such as Causa Justa/Just Cause and several others are continuing the fight for affordable housing in the city, ensuring that workers from a variety of racial backgrounds can actually live a reasonably commutable distance away from their jobs.[21]

An alliance including Jobs With Justice of San Francisco, the National Union of Healthcare Workers, and the California Nurses Association forced Sutter Health into an agreement that stipulated that, as a condition of getting city approval to build a new hospital (California Pacific Medical Center), they had to agree to hire at least 40 percent of the hospital's entry-level employees through a local community workforce program. This was in addition to a set of community-centered demands that focused on accessibility for patients at the hospital. Parallel language was included in a community benefits–style agreement as well as the collective bargaining agreements of the nurses.

The Health Professionals and Allied Employees union locals in New Jersey negotiated with Christ Hospital and Bayonne Medical Center to keep dialysis and pediatric units in-house instead of outsourcing them to for-profit institutions. They also requested that the hospital not sell the medical debt accrued by patients off to third-party debt collection agencies notorious for harassing people for the cost of their care.[22]

Some of the most exciting examples of private-sector bargaining for the common good come from the finance sector. The Communications Workers of America, the Committee for Better Banks, and other organizations have begun laying the groundwork for improving pay and benefits for the country's more than one million bank workers. In doing so, the coalition has positioned itself as a defender of consumers and an opponent of banks' most notorious predatory practices, including an end to sales goals and metrics that forced bank workers to sell predatory financial products as a condition of employment. In 2016, acting on their shared values with bank customers, Wells Fargo workers connected to this campaign acted as whistleblowers, exposing the bank's cheating scandals.[23] In 2019, Tim Sloan, the CEO of Wells Fargo, was forced to resign after congressional hearings where he was confronted by Wells Fargo workers who blew the whistle on Wells Fargo's reinstitution of toxic sales goals.[24]

Employees of Santander, a multinational bank based in Spain that is known for its subprime auto lending in the United States, have exposed similar practices. And due to the organizing activities of bank workers, Bank of America increased the minimum pay for its employees to $20/hour in April 2019, thereby meeting one of the demands of CWA and the Committee for Better Banks.[25] By taking a bargaining-for-the-common-good approach, bank workers are demonstrating how they can change their industry—and finance capital as a whole—from the bottom up.[26]

In all of these examples, union workers are taking on a broader set of issues in the bargaining process, galvanizing more community support for their workplace demands while also building increased power for the communities they operate within.

In addition to putting specific community-based remedies into a collective bargaining agreement, workers can propose that the company and community groups set up separate governing bodies to work for the public interest beyond the life of the workplace-specific contract, thus developing different types of en-forceable agreements and expanding economic democracy.

None of the strategies we have described in this chapter are easy. Each requires targeted, intentional organizing to mobilize and then leverage the various forces of power people have, both as workers and as service recipients, consumers, cli-ents, and taxpayers in their communities. The necessary relationships are not built overnight but instead demand long intentional strategies to authentically organize around shared interests.

Still, bargaining for the common good can help both unions and community groups move beyond reactive and defensive battles toward aligned and proactive approaches that challenge the financialization of the economy. This strategy has been embraced in the light and medium gray shaded states where traditional bargaining still prevails. And many workers in states filled with white and dark gray shading also see its potential—including the benefits that workers in more union-dense states can negotiate in support of those with fewer legal protec-tions. Maybe most important, this approach brings to greater numbers of ordi-nary people the opportunity to participate in processes that lead to them governing themselves and their conditions, thus helping to expand the practice of eco-nomic democracy—one of the crucial goals of the twenty-first century.

WHO BENEFITS?

Technology, Work, and a Future Not Yet Written

On January 13, 2019, Smiley participated in a panel discussion entitled "Black People vs Robots" organized by Data for Black Lives, an organization focused on the use of data in ways that affect Black communities.[1] She laughed at the image the title evoked—square cardboard-box robots chasing Black people out of buildings. But behind the catchy title was a truly important topic—the challenges of automation and its disproportionate impact on communities of color.

Technological change has been a constant thread in the history of human development. But to hear any cable news network talk about it, you would think it was a new development unique to the last twenty years. What is more, most people seem to assume that automation and the shifts it is producing in how work is organized will bring dire consequences for working people. As scholars Martin Carnoy and Derek Shearer put it, "At times, technology appears to *control* our society, to have an independent existence and to dictate society's living patterns."[2]

This sounds like a very up-to-date diagnosis, does it not? But Carnoy and Shearer wrote this in their book *Economic Democracy: The Challenge of the 1980s*, first published in 1981. And they went on to explain that this fear of technology is actually misguided, writing:

> But this is a popular misconception fostered by those who actually control technology—the large corporations. . . . The daily lives of all of us are affected by "scientific progress"—by the development of new products such as the automobile, the computer, and the television set to name

a few of the more dramatic examples. A price is frequently paid for this progress: a social cost that corporate capitalism passes along to society itself. With automobiles came greater mobility, but pollution and traffic jams also resulted; with computers came instant calculation and better planning for enterprises, but invasion of privacy, centralized credit, and other dossier systems also became more feasible; with television came instantaneous global communication and in-home mass entertainment, but the decline of social interaction outside the home and invasion of the home by commercial advertising accompanied the new technology.[3]

Carnoy and Shearer, writing almost four decades ago, were right, and their message is still relevant today. The fact is that computerization and artificial intelligence do not represent the gravest threat to our future. The greatest threat is the concentration of wealth and power by those who do not want a future where working people have an equal and democratic role in governing.

So, when we think about new technology and the changing nature of work, the important question to ask is simply, "Who benefits?" Do the applications of new technology and shifts in the organization of work speed up the concentration of wealth into the hands of a tiny select few while exploiting working people and/or destroying the climate? Or do they allow working people to benefit through increased resources, more time for recreation, and nonlabor activities while providing sustainable practices that allow human life to survive and adapt to growing shifts in the climate?

Again, automation will create wealth. Will that wealth be used to create more productive jobs and useful things? Will it be invested to build a society with opportunity and economic mobility? Or will it be used merely to generate more wealth for those who already own a dominant share of the world's resources? Who will see a bump in their paycheck? And who will lose a job?

Fundamentally, it is not the future of work that causes concern but the future of working people within it. Technological change holds important implications for workers and the labor movement. Yet too many current discussions accept as inevitable a future in which jobs will be scarce and a firmly entrenched wealthy elite will set our priorities. Such conversations narrow the range of social vision to the question of how to ensure that the citizens of the future simply get enough to survive.

What is more, these discussions tend to be dominated by the thinking of the very CEOs, financiers, and consultants who are engineering changes in the workplace. And even as they tighten their grip, these architects of inequality seek to control the alternatives we envision for our future. In recent years, they have promoted fevered "future of work" scenarios that imagine the disappearance of jobs before sweeping waves of automation and artificial intelligence, hyping up visions of the future of work that place capital's needs at the center. They suggest the inevitability of even greater levels of inequality. But is what they envision really inevitable?

These discussions of the future distract us all from the real relations of power at play. They move us too quickly into policy debates that do not address these dynamics or the economic and political trends that have hurt working people.

Let us take the early policy debates around universal basic income (UBI) as an example. Some saw the idea that government should guarantee UBI to people victimized by technological unemployment as a humane solution. But absent from this original policy proposal was the idea of granting working people the ability to negotiate their own conditions. And done poorly, a UBI could actually let large corporations off the hook by putting the burden on the state and the taxpayers instead of those with the most extreme wealth in the country. Alarmed at the prospect of such an explosion of government spending, some swung to a different solution, advocating steps to stop new technology at all costs and leading with slogans like the Luddite "Smash the Machines" and the more modern "Stop the Robots."

Arguments like these were mere distractions unconnected from the lived experience of real workers. Fortunately, in recent years the debate has become more nuanced, recognizing some of the deeper underlying realities that need to be addressed.

Rampant automation and job loss are not the problem. By 2019, the United States had added fourteen million jobs after the Great Recession. The challenge is that many of those jobs were not good jobs, and many working people could not qualify for the few good jobs that were being created. We are experiencing employment polarization. On the one hand, there is a set of highly paid, highly educated professionals doing interesting work; on the other hand, there is a large number of people in low-paid jobs whose primary responsibility is to see to the comfort of the affluent.

Ultimately, new technology itself is not good or bad. What shapes the impact of technological developments is in fact the values of the people inventing, proposing, and implementing them. When working people can insert themselves directly into the processes of designing, adopting, and governing new technologies and shifting the organization of work, the result will be overwhelmingly positive for much larger groups of people.

Automation and the Future of Jobs

Automation has become an umbrella term for those projecting the inevitable loss of jobs from new technology and is thus a fear tactic used against working people to prevent them from organizing unions. But this is not a new trend. Scholars like historian Donna Murch have explained the role played by the introduction of mechanical cotton pickers in the Great Migration, in which six million Black people left the rural South for urban areas in the West and North.[4] Murch argues that while a complex set of factors, including the push of Southern racism and the pull of wartime jobs, touched off the migration, agricultural automation accelerated it. As Black workers began to leave, big farmers turned to machines to fill their labor shortage. Few descendants of enslaved Black workers are sad about the development of the cotton gin and other tools that decreased the agricultural industry's reliance on enslaved individuals toiling on large plantations. However, many descendants of those same individuals are still waiting for their forty acres and a mule—that is, their piece of the profits generated by their labor and the increased productivity generated by new technology.

Automation has long been introduced in ways that perpetuate inequality and racism. Stephen Pitts, while a professor at the University of California–Berkeley noted the effect of automation in the 1950s and 1960s on manufacturing and its specific impact on Black workers. "What manufacturing outfits survived," Pitts writes, "began to relocate operations out of the urban core. So, at the exact moment that the civil-rights movement was opening up industrial unions and jobs, many factories were closing in the places where Black people were forced to live. In the San Francisco Bay Area, for example, that meant factories closing in Oakland only to reopen in the (nearly) all-White suburbs to the south."[5]

But despite the many horror stories, all forms of automation are not inherently bad. Increasing productivity through automation and new technologies can be beneficial. And workers who had bargaining power from the 1940s to the 1970s, when the growth of productivity was fast, enjoyed increases in wages and in work benefits such as paid time off and retirement income. Automation has helped to improve some jobs and eliminated some dangerous ones.

In recent decades, workers who have managed to maintain the power to engage in mass action to level the playing field when negotiating with employers have successfully bargained around new technology, turning it into a source of increased benefits for workers.

According to Carl Rosen of the United Electrical, Radio and Machine Workers of America (UE), workers at Allen-Bradley Automation in Milwaukee, Wisconsin, were able to negotiate benefits as the company was adapting to new technologies between 1998 and 2010. One of the core issues won at the bargaining table was increased opportunity for workers with seniority to be trained for any new jobs created in the plant due to new technologies. Another was the creation of apprenticeship programs in higher-skilled trades, which were made available to people whose jobs were being eliminated. This was particularly important for women, who tended to have lower-skilled jobs with less pay and who were at risk of having their jobs eliminated. Through bargaining the union was able to make sure these women got trained for pathways to high-skilled jobs. Ultimately this helped to diversify higher-skilled jobs for more women and people of color. The union was also able to create balance between the elimination of jobs and the creation of new jobs. When the company announced plans to close the plant due to technological change, the union negotiated the pace of job elimination to ensure people could retire rather than simply lose their source of income. By the time the plant closed in 2010, all the workers received full pensions.

In this case, management at Allen-Bradley Automation bargained in good faith and valued the input of the union. Unfortunately, only a tiny portion of workers have been able to turn automation into a success for workers—in large part because they do not have the ability to organize and collectively bargain as the Allen-Bradley workers did. Not surprising, most of the workers that do have some control over the introduction of new technology live and work in states that are still able to access twentieth-century forms of bargaining and political power. Whether automation will benefit or hurt workers depends on whether workers develop the economic power to negotiate over it in other parts of the country.

Jeff Crosby. Portrait by Gwenn Seemel.

Profile of a Modern Worker: Jeff Crosby: "We Have to Build the Power We Need"

Unlike Allen-Bradley, General Electric forgot the value of negotiating with its own employees in ways that could benefit both the company and the workforce. Jeff Crosby, a veteran labor activist and a sophisticated organizer, recounts how GE opened its Factory of the Future, rejecting union proposals aimed at enhancing worker skills. The failure of the Factory of the Future illustrates how self-destructive it is for corporations to ignore human rights and workers' interests in pursuit of short-term gains.

I worked at the General Electric (GE) plant in Lynn, Massachusetts, for thirty-three years. I was twenty-eight when I started in 1979. It was my first regular union job. My wife and I wanted to start a family, so I just wanted to get an actual job with a stable income. I could plan a life. There was a grinder's job open, which is what I was doing at the time at another plant, although I was doing tool-cutter grinding. This was a different kind of grinding. I was sent to the foreman who asked, "Do you know how to work to tenths?" I had no idea what he meant. So, I said, you mean tenths of an inch? And he started laughing. He actually meant ten thousandth of an inch, which you can't even see. I mean, that's how you know you're working with aircraft engines. It's really precise.

I had no idea what I was doing. But I got in there and I showed up every day and worked really hard. As long as you were making an effort, the older folks would take care of you and help you out. So, you know, I kind of got carried until I knew what I was doing.

At the beginning, I was just keeping my mouth shut and learning the job. I worked third shift for two years, 11 p.m. to 7 a.m., trying to figure out how to sleep. And then we had two kids. And so I was trying to deal with small children while shifts were changing and Margie, my wife, was working full time at the post office. We were pretty busy.

Thinking back on how I got there, when I was ten or eleven years old, I spent a couple of years in Pakistan. My dad was a World War II vet. After the war, he stayed in the Reserves and taught at the US Air Force Academy in Colorado Springs for a few weeks each summer. Then he was asked to go to Pakistan for two years as they were setting up their air force academy. We were in the Northwest Frontier near the Khyber Pass on the Afghanistan border. There were no other Americans in the town except for one missionary couple.

I was exposed to drastic poverty. There was one time we stopped to see these nomadic people of a different ethnic group. I don't know who they were. We stopped our Volkswagen bus and my dad got out to take some pictures and this guy yelled out *doe annas,* which was like four cents. I think it was the smallest monetary measure at the time. My dad said "sure" to the guy. And people started coming out. I mean, my memory is it was hundreds of people asking for money, for four cents.

I went to a missionary school, and we were the only government kids. The school had me all day long. I was reading the Bible at 7 a.m. I remember they asked me if I wanted to go to Heaven and rest in the bosom of Jesus for the rest of my life or go to everlasting Hell. I was like, simple choice, and these were nice people. So, I got deeply religious after that.

You see the world a little bit differently after you've lived in a developing country. Plus, it was right in the middle of the Cold War. It was coming back from that experience having been exposed to drastic poverty in Pakistan and running into people who hated us there that changed me. I was eleven and I remember being impressed by the hypocrisy of this country that said it was a Christian country. At the time, I was pretty devout. Civil rights struggles were on the TV every day. It was the fall of 1962, and I started seeing Black people get blasted off the steps of white churches with fire hoses. I remember Dr. King at some point saying that 10 a.m. on a Sunday morning is the most segregated hour in the United States. So, I kind of drifted away from religion and started focusing on political activism.

In high school, I got active in the Student Nonviolent Coordinating Committee (SNCC), not doing anything dramatic, just stuffing envelopes or whatever was needed in a church basement in Cambridge, Massachusetts. My wife Margie and I met as kids, and she was also involved with SNCC. We both signed up for civil rights school, and we went to Bricks, North Carolina, with a racially mixed group of Black and white kids from Newton and Roxbury, Massachusetts. Bricks is in rural North Carolina and was a place for training by Black organizations.

One day we went into the nearby town. It was like the whole town just stopped and everybody knew who we were—we stood out. There was so much hatred, it was palpable. And some of the kids just started crying. Then I just realized, my God, there is a whole other world here. We interviewed sharecroppers, because back then it was still mostly sharecropping, and that had an impact on me. SNCC just blew my mind—these kids were so brave, and they were getting killed.

I got increasingly politicized. The maids in McComb, Mississippi, were getting paid sixty-six cents an hour. There was a protest at the Ramada Inn in Lynn, Massachusetts, to support the maids, which I went to. In high school I helped form what we called the Human Rights Club. We did stuff like Draft resistance. I took part in Vietnam Summer, knocking on doors and neighborhoods and talking to people about the war. And I went to the demonstration called From

Dissent to Resistance in DC. We marched on the Pentagon. That was the first time I ever saw the Eighty-Second Airborne with fixed bayonets deployed against the US population. I mean, I don't remember seeing any violence or anything, but I saw that and it had an impact on me.

I worked in a local roofing factory in Watertown, Massachusetts, in the summers and on college vacations. It was a brutal job, catching the hot shingles as they came off a huge tar-and-slate stamping machine. It was nonstop and it paid cash by the day. I was young and it didn't bother me much. The workers had been promised things like a fifteen-minute break every hour and a new pair of gloves every week, since the slate on the shingles ate through your gloves and skin. The promises were given to defeat a UAW union drive, but after the union was defeated the promises became memories.

I went to college at the University of Wisconsin–Madison. The antiwar demonstrators were getting tear-gassed and the campus was shut down a number of times. It's hard to overstate the constant level of activity and tension on the campus. I was mainly organizing against the war and for civil rights. It's all I did every day. I would only occasionally go to class, so I didn't exactly have a stellar academic career. But I studied a lot, just not very systematically. I realized that I didn't really think I needed to go to school. I was going to learn everything on my own and learn everything in the streets.

I dropped out of school and began to work. I cleaned out laundromats, worked on the docks as a longshoreman in Milwaukee for a while, and then worked on the railroad for a summer. Working on the docks and on the railroad was hard work. They were both unionized jobs although I did not get into the union on the docks because I did not get enough hours of work to qualify. They both paid well. At that time, those were the best jobs I'd ever worked.

By the time I got back to Massachusetts I knew I was looking for a union job. I got active in the union early. I knew GE had a great union—the International Union of Electrical Workers (IUE) Local 201—with a long history. I knew how important it was because of the experience I had growing up.

My plant in Lynn has a really long history, as does the city. I'd come to meet all these people whose family were shoe workers. There was a large shoe strike in 1860. It was the biggest strike in the country at the time. These were folks whose family or grandparents were in the American Revolution, and they saw that wealth was developing and really resented it. It was also the beginning of the end of artisan work, you know, where people were working in the home. In the factories, work was being sped up due to changes in the mode of production. I started realizing that as shoe factories were dying out, there was close to an eighty-year period where people migrated into GE and brought that militancy of the strike with them. Local 201 was always one of the most militant locals in the GE chain.

One of the first things I did in the union at GE was form a new technology committee.

When I was a kid there was the threat of transistor radios, and that they were going to revolutionize everything and put everybody out of work or everyone was going to work only twenty hours a week, which oddly never happened. Jobs change. Without power, it doesn't matter what we think and what we know; no one's asking us. So, I formed the new technology committee so we could insert ourselves into the discussion.

Before I got involved, there were fights in the 1960s over what type of technology was going to happen and if the tech was going to automate metalworking as much as possible. There were two different types of automation, one of which would have left more control in the hands of the workers. The other was the numerically controlled stuff, which management eventually chose. Numerically controlled machines would mean more control by employers over the workforce, which was really about control for GE. There were fights over unskilled and semi-skilled work and pay rates. There were fights over piece-rate work. The union went on strike at the turn of the century over piecemeal work and won, then again in the mid-sixties with the introduction of numerically controlled machines around pay rates. That strike put more pay in my and everybody else's pocket because the other rates were all built off of what was won. So, I mean, fifty-plus years later, it's still paying off. All of this happened before I got there.

In the early 1970s, they tried to expand numerically controlled machinery all throughout the plant. There was growing resistance in plants all over the country. There were wildcat strikes in large towns. You had the auto-plant revolts in Detroit. So, the industrial relations people in the company started thinking about how to introduce this new technology without a lot of resistance because, you know, their goal was to take it out of our hands completely. But machinists are pretty skilled people. I mean, back in the day there's nothing you could do to these guys. The fight over pacing has gone on for 150 years, and we normally win.

The idea of the new technology committee was to educate union members on management's plans for new technology and try to figure out what we were going to do about it. The goal was primarily to keep our skills in the workforce and maintain employment. We organized a new technology conference at Breed Junior High School, with about two or three hundred people. We also used it as a way to reach out to the United Electrical (UE) workers, another union which had not had a good relationship with the IUE going back to the Red-baiting of the 1950s. We brought in people from the Erie railroad locomotive plant and others. At the conference we reestablished our ties across all unions representing GE workers.

But, after some time on the committee, it just felt to me like, what's the point of this? We could talk for days. Meanwhile we're losing members, the plants are getting smaller, and they're closing plants all over the country. We had no power. I mean, we could do certain things as a defensive measure, but nobody was asking us how we wanted to deal with numerically controlled machinery or automation. It was clear to me that we needed to organize both union and nonunion people to have the power to influence automation and new technologies.

In 1982, GE opened the Factory of the Future. They wanted to create a super-automated factory. If we didn't agree, they kept telling us they would build it "in a cornfield in Kansas" and we would become obsolete. They put $42 million into some old buildings and built a highly automated plant, which brought us into negotiations. I was appointed as a witness member of the bargaining committee. We made a proposal to them to counter this idea of super-automation, which would only create a few skilled jobs for people who ran the machines. It required twenty-four-hour operation, which meant it created shift problems.

We made a separate proposal for what was called *island production* at the time. The idea was that the workers would learn multiple skills and follow parts as opposed to deskilling their work. Management rejected this idea. It was a classic bad decision on their part. Instead, they built one of the world's most inflexible machining centers. The guys that worked there told me that the technology was pretty good, but it was built on massive orders for one or two parts. They couldn't fit everything in there. Whereas in island production, you can adjust the machines to do almost anything. This Factory of the Future was meant to make money based on massive orders of a few parts, but they didn't get them. So, the whole thing was a white elephant, and they closed it in 1992.

Of course, in large corporations like GE, nobody ever makes mistakes. There was never any public admission that this did not work. They just closed it and sold it. It's a supermarket now.

That kind of experience made me skeptical of the popular notion that technology will come, everybody will be out of work, and we're all going to starve. Automation degrades work, and if you don't have any power to integrate pay and working conditions, it is a problem. But it doesn't have to be.

Over time the company actually came around to our way of thinking. So now we have something called the special machinist, which has its own classification and pay rate. These are multiskilled people who run a bunch of different machines, and they can follow one part from machine to machine instead of making massive numbers of the same part with the highly automated technology. So, the skill goes into the worker, not the machine. Turns out workers are more flexible than machines.

Through our negotiations we were able to create this new classification. We had the power to do it. There's nothing in the technology that determines what its value is on the market or what your labor is worth. It's a question of power in terms of what kind of choices are made in technology. Even more fundamentally, it's a question of power that determines how it impacts us even on a simple thing like our hourly wage.

I do believe that power at the workplace is fundamental. And, you know, the recent teacher strikes kind of reminded people of that, including in places where they do not have the right to collective bargaining. I think for working-class people to have power, they have to have some identity. If we are to believe what we're told in the United States, there's just a big "middle class" and then there are those at the top, the supposed job creators, and those on the very bottom. There are "poor folks," which is racially coded language, and they live off the mostly white "middle class" who work. That's what many people actually think, and it's really pervasive.

Most people don't aspire to govern and certainly have no experience in it. Unions can give you that. One of the things we're trying to do here in Lynn is push ourselves to create pathways to power. Through my work at the Labor Council, we try to facilitate this. When we passed the anti–wage theft policy, we knew the city didn't have capacity, that there's no money. The city can't hire anybody to enforce it. And so we wrote ourselves into it as an advisory committee. We're going to enforce it ourselves. We have a committee that includes the Worker Center, the Labor Council, the Building Trades, the Latino Business Association, the New Lynn Coalition, and the Chamber of Commerce. It's our job to help people file complaints and to track them and all that.

Another thing we did is with the school committee. We passed a motion that union teachers should be trained in how to deal with undocumented kids and the kind of traumas that they deal with when they don't know if their folks are going to be there when they get home. We worked directly with our labor council members. A year later, after realizing this motion was not acted on, we went to the school department and offered to design the training and process. And then our members went to some of the trainings. It's still happening.

I worked at GE for thirty-three years, and I have been a union guy all my life. Now I'm talking about school foundation budgets, affordable housing policies, and all sorts of things that I didn't know anything about. Without power it doesn't matter what we think and what we know, no one's asking us. We have to build the power we need.

Data Ownership: Who Controls Information about You?

In the era of apps, gadgets, and athletic wearables, working people are confronted with individuals and companies that seek data on their behaviors, practices, and other characteristics. Once upon a time, most data were collected after people were asked if they wanted to participate in a survey or some other form of data collection. But today, new technologies often allow that data to be automatically generated and stored. In this new era, new questions arise: Who owns that data? Are working people obligated to generate the data? And how do you address the ongoing issue of privacy?

In chapter 6 we saw how the educators in West Virginia had to fight against the forced use of this type of data collection, especially insofar as such private data could be used to limit their health-care options. Without traditional collective bargaining, the teachers still face repeated attempts by the state legislature to force these practices on them. Those with access to twentieth-century collective bargaining systems have had more success.

Perhaps most widely known is the role of data and analytics in sports.[6] An entire industry has developed to measure every aspect of an athlete's behavior that might affect his or her performance—data that can then be used to move players around or even end their contracts and potentially their careers. Companies that make wearables and other products to collect data like to present these products as helpful tools for players to analyze their own performance and stay healthy. But how those data are used by the leagues or shared with the public is a source of a lot of debate, both publicly and in negotiations between players and their employers.

The unions that represent athletes have taken different approaches to ensure players have control over the data they generate. The National Football League Players Association (NFLPA) signed an agreement giving ownership of Fitbit-like data analytics to players, an agreement signed directly with the company (WHOOP) who makes the wearables. The NFLPA may have leveraged this mostly because the NFL requires players to wear Zebra tracking chips and other devices under their shoulder pads as a part of their collective bargaining agreement. The National Basketball Players Association's (NBPA) collective bargaining agreement with the NBA gives them the ability to opt out of wearables, though they do not necessarily own their data if they opt in. And there has been talk of banning all such devices until an NBA committee on data can explore the issue further. Major League Baseball (MLB) also allows players to opt in to data collection, and they prohibit the data from being used in salary arbitration discussions. However, minor league players are forced to wear data-collecting devices, and in some instances the analytics collected hurt their ability to get into the major leagues.[7]

Beyond professional sports, employers and policy-makers often use this kind of data to make broad, sweeping policy decisions that negatively impact entire communities of people. And they do it under the myth that the algorithms created are somehow objective. One of the more egregious examples of this occurred when Black residents in and around Dallas, Texas, and several other cities realized that Amazon Prime was systematically denying them free same-day delivery despite providing it for wealthier white communities—including some right down the street from them. While the company said the algorithms that led to this were not racialized, they were in fact based on data collected over many years that systemically marginalized and devalued Black and Brown communities. As Preston Gralla noted in *Computer World*, Amazon's algorithm "produced a racist outcome because the data on which it was based was the result of decades of widespread racism."[8]

Like automation and any new technology, data-collection mechanisms and uses are not inherently bad. But if the people implementing them do not have the best interests of the majority of working people at heart, their effects can be invasive and damaging. This, again, is why having those directly impacted at the table—through collective bargaining or any other democratic channel—is critical to ensure accountability in data collection with benefits for the whole of society, not just the wealthy few.

The Rise of the Gig Economy

For the past few years we have been inundated with rosy books and articles about the gig economy.[9] They feature vignettes of people working flexible hours to pick up extra cash: the graduate student who drives for Uber in her spare time, the stay-at-home parent who brings in extra spending money with EasyShift, the high school student picking up odd jobs on TaskRabbit. Whether it is being praised as the newest innovation in work-life management or as a massive new industry that will displace traditional work relationships, the gig economy is widely touted as the latest great phase of modern work.

If this were actually true, we would praise the dawn of a new era—especially one where, for once, more people could have access to equal parts work, rest, and recreation. But this trend is actually just a collection of familiar exploitative business practices repackaged as a positive twenty-first-century development. Technology is brilliant and enables scale, but too often new technologies have just scaled or amplified long-standing problems rather than disrupting them, shifting inequities entrenched offline to the new online platforms. So far, it has been optimized for efficiency and convenience for the employer, but we believe that it can be optimized for equity for everyone.

Gig-economy business models serve the interests of their investors and share-holders at the expense of their workers. What we have learned from workers who work on gig-economy platforms is that this notion defines everything: the work conditions, structures, policies, and compensation. What this means for platform workers is the following:

- They are managed by an algorithm and rarely able to talk to a live person,
- Customer ratings can determine their pay,
- They are penalized for canceling a job even if they felt unsafe,
- There is little transparency regarding the policies, protocols, data collection, and surveillance.
- They have no access to their own data, which means they cannot take their experience or reviews from one gig-economy platform elsewhere.

Under the guise of innovation, the gig companies are reinforcing the same per-nicious dynamics that working people have faced for generations—twenty-first-century Taylorism.[10] Companies lure workers by projecting their apps as the new fast way to achieve the American Dream of being your own boss. The problem is that these so-called self-employed entrepreneurs have very little autonomy. They are not setting their prices or their schedules; sometimes they cannot even choose what car they drive. The company maintains control over those decisions.

A 2020 study of gig workers commissioned by the San Francisco Local Agency Formation Commission and conducted by the Institute for Social Transforma-tion at the University of California—Santa Cruz bears this out. For example, the study found that platform companies providing services like rideshare and food delivery frequently withdraw work offers, threaten workers with deactivation, and reduce their bonuses when they decline specific job offers—something work-ers are supposed to have the freedom to do under California law.[11] In Septem-ber 2019, the California State Legislature passed Assembly Bill 5, which was aimed at including gig workers in protections designated for employees.

There is only one situation in which gig companies are willing to cede control to individual workers: when something goes wrong and someone needs to be held accountable. In those cases gig companies try to minimize their relationship with their workers. This is particularly clear in two recent lawsuits against Uber. In the first case, two women attempted to hold Uber accountable for the sexual harass-ment they experienced from a driver.[12] The company claimed the driver was an independent contractor—not an employee—and thus Uber was not liable. In the second case, workers sued the company for mileage and tip reimbursements that they currently have to cover themselves.[13] Again, the company argued that the workers are not employees—and that making them employees would undermine their business model by damaging driver flexibility and adding too many costs.

Classifying workers as independent contractors is key to many gig companies' strategies because gig workers are paid the same as or less than formal employees and receive significantly fewer benefits such as health care, paid sick leave, or workers' compensation for injuries.[14] And at the end of the day, gig companies' goals are the same as always: to keep their costs low while maximizing profits.

In 2018, the California Supreme Court took an important step toward limiting corporate executives' ability to misclassify individuals who are actually employees. In the Dynamex decision, the court implemented a basic A, B, C smell test, noting that a person is an independent contractor only if they (A) are free from the control and direction of the hiring entity in connection with the performance of work, (B) regularly perform work outside of the hiring entity's business, and (C) are engaged in an independently established trade, occupation, or business of the same nature as the work performed.[15]

Again, legislators took this even further with the passage of California Assembly Bill 5, which limited the use of classifying workers as independent contractors rather than employees by companies in the state. Employees were entitled to greater labor protections such as minimum wage laws, sick leave, and unemployment and workers' compensation benefits that do not apply to independent contractors. The law codified a stricter set of requirements than laid out in the Dynamex decision. This bill was overturned in November 2020 by Proposition 22, a ballot initiative heavily funded by gig companies.

Rideshare drivers also made gains during the COVID-19 pandemic given their status as "essential workers," ultimately winning the right to claim unemployment benefits when laid off. This victory took them one step closer in their fight against misclassification as independent contractors, thus expanding their protections under labor laws. Again, it was quickly subdued by the passage of California's Proposition 22 ballot initiative, which excluded many app-based workers from foundational labor laws.

In August 2021, the Alameda Superior Court of California ruled that Proposition 22 violated the California constitution and must be struck down in its entirety. While the decision will likely be appealed by the app-based companies, the decision represents a huge setback for companies who have been trying to rewrite U.S. labor laws and exempt themselves from labor standards that apply to all other employers. The decision also represents an important advancement in the gig-worker-led movement for employment benefits, fair wages, worker protections, and the right to exercise collective democratic power.

The gig economy is sold to workers as a type of empowerment, but the actual jobs are designed to hold them back. Flexibility for workers does not automatically gel with the on-demand needs of company executives. In fact, what working people want—and what the gig economy rarely provides—is more control of their time on the job. They want to shape decisions and redesign their jobs to meet the company and their personal needs. Both parties need room to negotiate conditions.

Unsurprisingly, gig executives militantly combat workers who attempt to form unions. Again, Uber is an illustrative example. When Seattle granted its drivers the right to unionize, the company instructed its customer service reps to call through a list of drivers to explain why unionizing was a bad idea (a spokesperson defended the practice in a statement, saying "it's not clear a traditional union can serve such a large and varied group of people.")[16] The company also has a history of deactivating—gig-speak for firing—drivers who lead unionizing efforts.[17] Uber's major competitor, Lyft, has been accused of similar tactics. (Spokespeople for both companies have denied the allegations.)[18] New York University (NYU) professor Aswath Damodaran explained that unions will ultimately hurt these companies' bottom lines, saying "they are likely to shake up the current revenue-sharing balance."[19] In other words, union workers get more of the total share, and that makes executives nervous. For them, it pays to keep gig workers from organizing.

So, while the gig economy is upon us, it is far from the worker-empowering revolution that companies are marketing and far less sizable.

However, workers at many gig companies are experimenting with different ways to negotiate over their conditions, from Seattle to New York to overseas.[20] They are proving that the only thing inevitable about the gig economy is that, as with business innovations of the past, working people will eventually figure out how to organize app-based and gig companies. These workers are designing a new generation of labor protections that will not only benefit workers at gig companies but also help to protect the interests of all part-time, temporary, or subcontracted employees.

The menacing reality just under the surface of discussions about new technology is the tension between fear and hope. When people live in fear of a thing, they immediately go into fight or flight mode, just trying to be safe. But when new technology is seen as something hopeful, something that was negotiated well with everyday people at the table, then solutions beyond our wildest imaginations may surface to address the needs of society, and most important, the humans within it. Only when workers and their allies create vehicles capable of challenging concentrated economic and political power can we hope to shape the work of the future in ways that benefit us all.

Because at the end of the day, it is all about choices. Nothing is inevitable except change—which is why we must take every step we can to ensure that we claim the power to make the big decisions that will shape the changes that impact our lives in the years to come. The Future we need.

CONCLUSION
What It Takes

In our interviews with the leaders profiled in this book, it struck us how clear they were about what needs to be done to ensure that people can achieve economic dignity. As they shared deep personal stories, including their struggles to manage the changes in work, the economy, and our politics as a nation, they were certain that this is all about choices. Choices we make as a people and as a nation. Choices that those with immense power make. Choices that we make as movements. To influence these choices and shape future changes, working people need to be able to exercise collective power and action to create a future that offers opportunities for mobility, human prosperity, and economic dignity.

Through this journey of listening, observing, and writing, and through our own histories and experiences, we learned about the needs and opportunities for our movement today. The journey also affirmed our initial goals and hypotheses. All of us want to live in a healthy democracy where our opinions and contributions really matter. Collective bargaining is fundamental to building a healthy democracy by creating pathways for elevating the decisions of workers alongside those of employers. And in an era of advanced global capitalism, where financialization, fissured employment, and entrenched white supremacy and patriarchy exist, collective bargaining must be expanded to meet the needs of modern workers, addressing all the ways that they interact with the economy.

What is more, we are not starting from scratch. Many workers—including those profiled in these pages—are already experimenting with how to expand collective bargaining to include bargaining for the common good, with the ultimate profiteer or with a corporate landlord.

Building a base of working people who desire collective bargaining power on all fronts as a fundamental right will require an aggressive assertion of the values that undergird our belief in democracy—political and economic. Only then can we ensure that our wins take root as common societal values that are codified in our laws.

This requires smart organizing, culture change strategies that shift our everyday behaviors, norms, and vision of what is possible, and the proliferation of a new school of thought that centers around our shared stories and self-interests that we are stronger when working together. We need a movement that can evolve the legal, policy, organizing, and cultural frameworks of the last century. A movement that can design a new social contract for the twenty-first century. A movement that understands the necessity of centering the fight against white supremacy and white nationalism. A movement that can engage working people as whole people and imagine a new set of supports and systems that allow people to live as their full selves. And a movement that is deeply rooted in the values of respect, dignity, agency, and collectivity.

It is a common lament that our politicians are so out of touch, but truth be told most of us are out of practice with what it means to come together and solve problems with people outside of our immediate friends and family. As essayist Yoni Applebaum has argued, Americans are going to have to get back in the habit of democracy. It is not just that people are not joining unions; they also are not joining parent-teacher associations, church associations, rotaries, and other volunteer groups with democratically elected positions within their communities. This decline in civic participation mirrors the decline in political participation. We need to remind each other of our collective power—and the pride that comes from joining together to demand an end to segregation, polluted air and water, unregulated prescription drug prices, and child labor as well as to fight for public support for parks and public education, roads and highways, and a social safety net.

Millions of people are hungry for more tools and venues for collective action. Thankfully there are stories of people banding together to make a positive change that we can take cues from and that demonstrate that people are open to and even desiring of collective models. Some of these models are embedded within this book. And there are many others. There are the neighborhoods in Flint coming together to demand clean water for their families; the students at Parkland High School who ignited a new youth movement and political will to enact commonsense gun laws; a growing number of people banning together to push for criminal justice reforms; the growth of the #MeToo movement among women across many sectors of the economy; people standing together to end family separation; the Standing Rock protest that mobilized many supporters and through which many Native American workers asserted that the choice between good jobs and clean water for their communities is a false one; and global youth mobilizations for climate change.

And this has only continued with the organizing of essential workers during the COVID-19 pandemic and the uprisings of Black activists against the state-sanctioned violence on Black bodies led by the Movement for Black Lives. The crises of this moment are deeply intertwined. Ending police violence, shifting government spending away from law enforcement to human-centered programs like job creation and education, and giving working people access to the health care, job safety, and fundamental human dignity they deserve—all of these are essential steps whose urgency has been highlighted by recent headlines, and all must be goals of the movement we seek to build.

Our movement must tend to the fundamental work of revitalizing democracy because working people cannot improve their lives without gaining an effective collective voice in shaping their world on and off the job. To do this we must be able to engage, excite, and even work on behalf of broad swaths of people outside of our institutions. Only then can we build the power we need to win the changes that will ensure that each of us can achieve economic dignity.

One of our major takeaways from the wave of teachers' strikes referenced in this book is that we must nurture and catalyze demand not just for unions but also for all forms of democratic and collective decision-making in our culture, building a movement that embodies the values of agency and the participation of the majority. This can be modeled through the work and successes of our movement, but it must also live within our broader culture.

To build the collective will and power we need to achieve our vision, we must create profound shifts in how people think and feel about collective bargaining power and the ability to govern all aspects of their lives. For far too long any discussion about bargaining and unions has been centered on the legal processes governing a small select grouping of people with official union recognition, stripping away the "why and what" we are trying to achieve through the process of collective bargaining. We must shift our culture to value respect, dignity, agency, and collectivism so that all of our wins take root as values, not just laws that can be overturned or undermined.

We need a strategy to reach the hearts and minds of everyday people in addition to engaging and learning from their views on the relationship between economic democracy, governance, and building collective bargaining power. We need a narrative environment that promotes our values of dignity, respect, and agency. We need to consistently tell our stories, however small or big, of how people can be more powerful together than alone in order to win over more people to take action with us.

We are facing many choices as a people and as a nation. We can let others imagine a future that benefits a handful of people, or we can imagine and act on a future that benefits us all for generations to come. The West African proverb "I am a citizen of a world not yet born" has inspired us to embrace this moment of change.

We have a blank canvas before us and an amazing history to build upon as a labor movement. We are witnessing the beginnings of a new movement not yet fully formed. It is up to us to keep our eyes on the prize, to push beyond the existing structures, and to imagine tomorrow by taking risks today to create a democracy worth fighting for.

Acknowledgments

SARITA

There are many people in my life who have encouraged and supported my growth as an organizer and leader. I am deeply grateful for them and the journey they have accompanied me on as I have worked at the intersections of labor unions, worker centers, and many other parts of the social justice movement. For over two decades I have been focused on this question of how we build power for working people, and I have had the good fortune of learning from and with a number of talented and brilliant people, some of whom I acknowledge here.

I thank people like Larry Cohen, the late Paul Booth, Lara Granich, Ashim Roy, Anannya Bhattacharjee, Carl Rosen, Dr. Rev. Calvin Morris, Stewart Acuff, Nik Theodore, Russ Davis, Margaret Butler, Mary Beth Maxwell, Fred Azcarate, Stephen Lerner, John Cavanagh, and Bill Fletcher Jr., who have all helped me understand the critical importance of bargaining rights and movement building in the United States and in transnational contexts. Their guidance, mentorship, sharp analysis, and the countless worker organizing and solidarity campaigns that they led have shaped my thinking over the years. They have each challenged me to stretch and inspired me to deepen my commitment to advancing workers' rights within a broader social justice framework, centering racial and gender equity.

I have been lucky to explore these questions of worker power with a brilliant cadre of peers leading important worker organizing campaigns outside of the traditional union approaches. These are organizations and leaders who have largely represented workers of color, immigrants, and women. They include member leaders and organizers of key partners to Jobs With Justice, like NDWA, ROC United, NDLON, NOWCRJ, National Guestworkers Alliance (NGA), United for Respect, Global Labor Justice, and the United Workers Congress. I want to especially thank Ai-jen Poo, Saket Soni, Saru Jayaraman, Fekkak Mamdouh, Sekou Siby, Pablo Alvarado, Jennifer Rosenbaum, Andrea Dehlendorf, Dan Schlademan, and Eddie Iny. They each invited me to think outside of the box with them and to take part in smart and innovative campaigns from which I have learned so much. I am deeply grateful for their friendship and partnership over the years.

A very special thanks to two brilliant leaders in this field, Lara Granich and Ai-jen Poo, without whom much of the work I got to do at JWJ and Caring Across

Generations as well as within broader movement spaces would not have been possible. You have both been incredible sources of inspiration and support. Thank you for modeling what it means to be bold and for being true sisters to me in this work.

Throughout my time at JWJ I worked with some of the most committed organizers, staff members, and leaders. My JWJ family is too large to name here, but I am grateful for the many local JWJ staff and leaders who have worked tirelessly to build a movement for workers' rights. And I want to especially thank the many staff members I had the privilege of working with from 1998 to 2019, spanning my time from Chicago JWJ, National JWJ, a merger with American Rights at Work, and my time at Caring Across Generations. You all know who you are. I especially want to acknowledge the late Treston Davis-Faulkner, Scarlet Jimenez, Akosua Meyers, Amy Smoucha, Liz Cattaneo, and Jessica Felix-Romero, who all encouraged, supported, and partnered with me on so much of the work that informed this book. I want to especially lift up the work of Erin Johannsson, Mackenzie Baris, Nafisah Ula, and Adam Shah, who sharpened many of the ideas and questions embedded within this book. And thank-you to Mark Leach, who has been an incredible coach and guide for me and for JWJ and who helped us create the space to envision and make meaning of our collective work with an eye toward tomorrow.

This book would not have been possible without a number of people who supported Smiley and me on this writing journey. Frances Benson, previously at Cornell University Press, whose enthusiasm inspired us to work on this manuscript. Karl Weber, who has been a phenomenal editor and thought partner. Janice Fine, who has provided us with critical guidance every step of the way and shared important feedback on our manuscript. Sheri Davis, Lane Windham, Marilyn Sneiderman, and our many friends at WILL Empower who provided a fellowship to Smiley and a platform for the both of us to talk through ideas. Joseph McCartin, who has helped me appreciate and draw from labor history, partnered with me on many writing opportunities, and provided early feedback on this book. Our friends at the North Star Network who explored early ideas and frames with us.

Thank-you to Kimberly, Allyson, Heather, Lidia, Sanchioni, Betty, Cynthia, Deloris, Rubynell, and Jeff, who all very graciously shared their personal stories and reflections with us. I learned so much through the interviews and from the actual campaigns you all talked about. I am so thrilled that we got to work with Gwenn Seemel, who created the incredible portraits that provide such rich texture to the voices of the worker leaders woven throughout this book. And thank you to the team at Cornell University Press for all of your work!

A critical member of our team is Rachel Coleman, who served as our project manager. She provided countless hours of coordination, thought partnership, feedback, and problem-solving that have made this book real. And most important, she helped Smiley and me carve out the time and space we needed to plan, write, and edit. There are not enough ways to express our gratitude to you and all that you do.

And of course, my incredible coauthor, Erica Smiley. I have had the great privilege of knowing Smiley for over twenty years and through various roles within the movement. We have a rich history of debating, developing, and collaborating on work together. Smiley has been a brilliant partner in bringing these concepts into sharp focus and leading work that has helped us build our analysis on this idea of expanded bargaining. I feel enormously grateful to have worked and learned with and from such a purposeful leader and coconspirator. She has brought not only deep intellect and smart organizing to this work but also a whole lot of joy, laughter, and creativity to my life.

I am thankful every day for having the support, love, and encouragement of my family. I am thankful to my parents, Pratap and Binita, who have always modeled what it means to live your values and provided deep love that has carried me through my life. I thank my siblings, Pronita and Prasi Gupta, Deepak Pateria, and Brenda Munoz, who not only have provided immense support and encouragement but also have taught me a great deal from their own work in the movement. And my niece and nephew, Sadhana and Julian, for inspiring me to want to make a better future possible.

My daughter has also been a real source of inspiration and grounding. Suraiya, thank you for all of your hugs, kisses, laughter, and understanding as I embarked on writing this book.

And finally, my most important acknowledgment of all: Eddie Acosta, there are no words to adequately express my deep love and appreciation for you. Your years of work in the labor movement have taught me so much. And the way you live into your values has always inspired me to be a better person. Thank you for being my brilliant grounding force, my partner in every sense of the word, and for always cheering me on. I could not do what I do without you.

SMILEY

When I think of those who made this possible, who have made *me* possible, I am overwhelmed with gratitude. From my given and chosen family to the movement mentors and colleagues who carried me, cheered me on, and agitated me to shine in ways that only I could, I am grateful.

First, I think of the patience of my given family, particularly my parents, Sharon and Bill Smiley, who managed to embrace me with unconditional love and compassion when faced with the unexpected and often radical departure from traditions and norms that I imposed on them. Thank you for putting up with *all* my interests—the fleeting and the sustained. Thank you for defending me when I challenged authority based on values and principle. And thank you for always ensuring I remained connected to our shared history—as Copelands, Harts, and Smileys as well as the shared heritage of southern Black people who always held the light of freedom from farm to factory, no matter how difficult the situation. When I feel like the work is too hard, I remember what they endured and I am regrounded. I am their victory, and this book is their receipt.

As I left home and began to make my own way in the world, I encountered people who I would only later realize were constantly holding me up and guaranteeing I did not fall through the wide cracks that society lays down for southern Black gender nonconforming women who insist on equality: the Black assistant DA who ensured my stupid decisions as a young person did not follow me throughout my life; the vice chancellor who inserted himself between me and the powers-that-be at school who felt I was shaking things up too much; the veteran movement leader who shielded me from unprincipled attacks. All of these individuals and their individual acts are the reason I am here.

Thank you to Bill Fletcher Jr., who modeled what it means to be a dogged, methodical organizer and a public intellectual constantly testing theory with practice—guiding me gently since I was eighteen years old. To Janice Fine, who also saw the potential in my ability to play a similar role and agitated me to not just be good but to be really sharp both in the arguments made in this book as well as the campaign strategies I promote in Jobs With Justice. And thanks to Frances Benson, previously at Cornell University Press, whose enthusiasm gave us the energy to lean into the manuscript. Additional thanks go to Saket Soni and Stephen Lerner, who developed some of the ideas that led to the concepts in this book, let alone helped me with strategy and campaign development. There are a series of individuals who shaped my early drive to organize, including Jon Liss, Jackie Kendall, Marvin Randolph, Eddie Acosta, Jarvis Tyner, Scott Marshall, Bryan Proffitt, the Reverend J. Herbert Nelson, and many others whose patience and kindness did not go unnoticed.

There are also a set of special union leaders who have modeled for me what it means to think outside the box and win. These include Mary Kay Henry, Nicole Berner, and John Taylor of SEIU; Elissa McBride of AFSCME; Ken Rigmaiden and Jimmie Williams Jr. of the International Union of Painters and Allied Trades; Todd Crosby and Esther Lopez of UFCW; DeMaurice Smith of NFLPA; and many others. I am also grateful to the National Labor Leadership Institute (NLLI) for holding space for these complex discussions.

A heartfelt thanks goes out to the WILL Empower Program housed across the Georgetown University Kalmanovitz Institute for Labor and the Working Poor and Rutgers University's Center for Innovation in Worker Organization.

As the first fellow of the WILL Empower Program, I received space to write, travel to engage workers, and access to important thought leaders within this field of study for feedback and guidance.

I also want to acknowledge the artist, Gwenn Seemel. She was first my friend, and she had the patience to go on an incredible journey with me to meet the workers whose stories fill these pages and paint their portraits—quite literally riding shotgun as I drove from New Jersey to West Virginia and Washington DC, from Jackson, MS to St Louis, MO, from Atlanta, GA to Tarheel, NC. Gwenn painted each of us with the treatment historically preserved solely for the wealthy and powerful. It has been a privilege to work with you. And I have much gratitude for your patience with me in this process.

I want to make a special acknowledgment of the late Treston Davis-Faulkner, former field director of Jobs With Justice. Treston saw a spark in me when I was only nineteen and always followed up despite my lack of early reciprocity. Treston ultimately recruited me to Jobs With Justice and created containers for me to grow and expand in ways that benefited those we were in solidarity with as well as my own leadership. And to his son, Na'im, and his partner Sheri Davis in their own rights who have become a part of my chosen family and keep me in the light.

I am grateful for the network leaders and staff at Jobs With Justice who stuck with me and Sarita in sharpening the ideas in this book and essentially developing the case studies by being in constant relationship with workers in motion. I want to give particular thanks to Mackenzie Baris, Erin Johannsson, Nafisah Ula, and Adam Shah, who spent a lot of time discussing strategy and tactics, applications, and open questions. And in the case of Adam Shah, I have much gratitude for some of the early research done on case studies that we eventually elaborated on. There are too many others on staff to mention here, but I will give a special thanks to the team that made up our organizing staff while I wrote this book. They put up with me transitioning to the executive director role, taking parental leave when my daughter arrived on a week's notice, and taking large chunks of time that could have been spent supporting them to write this book. So, thank you to Ada Fuentes, Natalie Patrick-Knox, Mina Itabashi, Dominique Countee, and Sam Nelson.

There are often people in the background making things happen who are not praised when all is said and done. I think about the many women who handwrote signs and prepped speakers for the March on Washington only to have Dr. Martin Luther King Jr. and the other men get all the attention. While Sarita and my names are on the cover, this book belongs just as much to Rachel Coleman, who project managed the process, having no previous experience doing it. She kept us on deadline and facilitated tasks between the artists, publisher, editor, and everyone in between. We could not have done this without you, Rachel. And to our editor, Karl Weber, you are a miracle worker.

Sarita Gupta and I have been orbiting around each other in various movement positions for well over twenty years. I love the ease with which we agitate each other and align around common strategies. And I deeply appreciate your willingness to dive into the deep end with me on this project. No, it is not the tell-all memoir that we joked about. It is much more than that, the theoretical basis for what we have struggled to build and define at Jobs With Justice and elsewhere. You are an amazing coconspirator, and I am so grateful to have proof of our collaboration documented in the pages of this book.

Last but far from least, I must acknowledge my partner of many years, Amanda Devecka-Rinear. It has not always been an easy ride. There was a period where, in short succession, you were taking care of me postsurgery only to be alerted that our newborn would arrive a week later. And then we found out we had to move out of our house so it could be lifted to adapt to increased flooding and climate change. Within all that I had the audacity to transition into the executive director role at Jobs With Justice, travel for extended periods and leave you to care for an infant alone, and take hours of time away even when at home to focus on writing this book. And yet, here we are. I will not say our love has not been tough at times. But it has been a deep love, nevertheless. And it has sustained me during some of the toughest periods of our lives, which we can now say include a global pandemic. I love you. I love our life together, watching our daughter grow into her own unique force. And I am grateful for your willingness to stick it out with me and my many projects.

Notes

ABBREVIATIONS

ACRE	Action Center on Race and the Economy
AFL	American Federation of Labor
AFL-CIO	American Federation of Labor and Congress of Industrial Organizations
AFSCME	American Federation of State, County, and Municipal Employees
AFT	American Federation of Teachers
AFWA	Asia Floor Wage Alliance
ALEC	American Legislative Exchange Council
CBA	Collective Bargaining Agreement or Community Benefits Agreement
CCA	Corrections Corporation of America
CHTU	Crown Heights Tenant Union
CIO	Congress of Industrial Organizations
CIW	Coalition of Immokalee Workers
CWA	Communications Workers of America
DWU	Domestic Workers United
FMCS	Federal Mediation and Conciliation Service
GE	General Electric
GFA	Global Framework Agreements
GM	General Motors
GUF	Global Union Federations
HPAE	Health Professionals and Allied Employees
IAM	International Association of Machinists and Aerospace Workers
IBB	Interest Based Bargaining
ICE	Immigration and Customs Enforcement
IIRON	The Illinois and Indiana Regional Organizing Network
ILGWU	International Ladies' Garment Workers' Union
ILO	International Labor Organization
ILRF	International Labor Rights Forum
IUE	International Union of Electrical Workers
IUPA	International Union of Police Associations

IWW	Industrial Workers of the World
JMA	Jobs to Move America
JWJ	Jobs With Justice
NAACP	National Association for the Advancement of Colored People
NACA	Neighborhood Assistance Corporation of America
NBAPA	National Basketball Association Players' Association
NDA	Non-Disclosure Agreements
NDLON	National Day Labor Organizing Network
NDWA	National Domestic Workers Alliance
NFLPA	National Football League Players Association
NIRA	National Industrial Recovery Act
NLLI	National Labor Leadership Institute
NLRA	National Labor Relations Act
NLRB	National Labor Relations Board
OSHA	Occupational Safety and Health Administration
OUR Walmart	Organization United for Respect at Walmart
PATCO	Professional Air Traffic Controllers Organization
PEIA	Public Employees Insurance Agency
PLA	Project Labor Agreement
PSEA	Pennsylvania State Education Association
RLA	Railway Labor Act
ROC United	Restaurant Opportunities Center United
SEIU	Service Employees International Union
SNCC	Student Non-violent Coordinating Committee
UAW	United Automobile, Aerospace, and Agricultural Implement Workers of America
UE	United Electrical, Radio and Machine Workers of America
UFCW	United Food and Commercial Workers
UNI Global	Union Network International
UNITE HERE	Union of Needletrades, Industrial, and Textile Employees (UNITE) and Hotel Employees and Restaurant Employees Union (HERE)
USAS	United Students Against Sweatshops
USDA	US Department of Agriculture
USEP	US Employment Plan
USSA	US Student Association
UTLA	United Teachers of Los Angeles
UWC	United Workers Congress
WDF	Workers Defense Project
WVEA	West Virginia Education Association

INTRODUCTION

1. Eric Foner, *The Second Founding: How the Civil War and Reconstruction Remade the Constitution* (New York: W.W. Norton, 2019).

2. Eric Foner, *A Short History of Reconstruction, 1863–1877* (New York: Harper Collins, 1990).

3. Adam Dean, Atheendar Venkataramani, and Simeon Kimmel, "Mortality Rates from COVID-19 Are Lower in Unionized Nursing Homes," *Health Affairs* 39, no. 11 (September 2020), https://doi.org/10.1377/hlthaff.2020.01011.

4. US Bureau of Labor Statistics, "Union Members Summary," Economic News Release, January 22, 2021, https://www.bls.gov/news.release/union2.nr0.htm; Drew DeSilver, "American Unions Membership Declines as Public Support Fluctuates," *Pew Research Center*, February 20, 2014, https://www.pewresearch.org/fact-tank/2014/02/20/for-american-unions-membership-trails-far-behind-public-support/.

5. David Weil, "Strategic Enforcement in the Fissured Workplace." Remarks at the John T. Dunlop Memorial Forum, Labor and Worklife Program, Harvard Law School, Cambridge, MA, February 12, 2015.

6. Lane Windham, *Knocking on Labor's Door: Union Organizing in the 1970s and the Roots of a New Economic Divide* (Chapel Hill: University of North Carolina Press, 2017).

1. COLLECTIVE BARGAINING

1. "This Week's Profile: P. J. Ciampa," Memphis Public Libraries, accessed January 12, 2021, https://www.memphislibrary.org/diversity/sanitation-strike-exhibit/sanitation-strike-exhibit-february-11-to-17-edition/this-weeks-profile-p-j-ciampa/; and Michael K. Honey, *Going Down Jericho Road: The Memphis Strike, Martin Luther King's Last Campaign* (New York: W. W. Norton, 2007).

2. "Bargaining in Good Faith with Employees' Union Representative (Section 8(d) & 8(a)(5))," About NLRB, National Labor Relations Board, accessed January 12, 2021, https://www.nlrb.gov/rights-we-protect/whats-law/employers/bargaining-good-faith-employees-union-representative-section.

3. Erin Johansson, "Collective Bargaining 101," Jobs With Justice, March 3, 2017, https://www.jwj.org/collective-bargaining-101.

4. 2021 Congressional Budget Submission, FMCS, FY 2021, 7, accessed on November 12, 2021, https://www.fmcs.gov/wp-content/uploads/2020/02/2021-Congressional-Budget.pdf

5. Paul Jacobs, *Old Before Its Time: Collective Bargaining at 28* (Santa Barbara, CA: Center for the Study of Democratic Institutions, 1963).

6. Milla Sanes and John Schmitt, *Regulation of Public Sector Collective Bargaining in the States* (Washington, DC: Center for Economic and Policy Research, 2014).

7. Ballotpedia, "Union Station: Public Sector Collective Bargaining Legal in Virginia as of May 1," April 30, 2021, https://news.ballotpedia.org/2021/04/30/union-station-public-sector-collective-bargaining-legal-in-virginia-as-of-may-1/#:~:text=In%201977%2C%20the%20Supreme%20Court,North%20Carolina%20and%20South%20Carolina.

8. Lance Compa, *Unfair Advantage: Workers' Freedom of Association in the United States under International Human Rights Standards* (New York: Human Rights Watch, 2000).

9. Minority unions, micro unions, and/or members-only unions represent the exception to this, signing up less than a majority of members but still attempting to negotiate with employers. For more information on minority unions, see Benjamin Sachs, "'Micro Unions' and Minority Unions," *Onlabor*, January 2, 2014, https://onlabor.org/micro-unions-and-minority-unions/.

10. US Bureau of Labor Statistics, "Union Members Summary."

11. The Federal Mediation and Conciliation Service (FMCS) is an independent agency created by the Taft-Hartley Act in 1947 to mediate labor disputes that substantially affect interstate commerce. For more information on the FMCS, see https://www.fmcs.gov/.

12. See Michael Wasser, "Strikes 101," Jobs With Justice, April 12, 2016, https://www.jwj.org/strikes-101.

13. See US Bureau of Labor Statistics, "Work Stoppages Summary," Economic News Release, February 11, 2020, https://www.bls.gov/news.release/wkstp.nr0.htm; and Alexia Fernández Campbell, "A Record Number of US Workers Went on Strike in 2018," Vox, February 13, 2019, https://www.vox.com/policy-and-politics/2019/2/13/18223211/worker-teacher-strikes-2018-record.

14. Daniel Thomas, "100,000 workers take action as 'Striketober' hits the US," BBC News, October 14, 2021, https://www.bbc.com/news/business-58916266.

15. See Seth Zimmerman, Labor Market Institutions and Economic Mobility (Washington, DC: Urban Institute, 2008); and Richard Freeman, Eunice Han, David Madland, and Brendan Dukle, Bargaining for the American Dream: What Unions Do for Mobility (Washington, DC: Center for American Progress, 2015).

2. WORKPLACE DEMOCRACY DOES NOT HAPPEN BY ACCIDENT

1. For a deeper dive into the story of the Atlanta washerwomen, see Tera W. Hunter, "Washing Amazons and Organized Protests," in To 'Joy My Freedom: Southern Black Women's Lives and Labor after the Civil War (Cambridge, MA: Harvard University Press, 1998); and AFL-CIO, "Atlanta's Washerwomen Strike," accessed January 12, 2021, https://aflcio.org/about/history/labor-history-events/atlanta-washerwomen-strike.

2. Erik Loomis, A History of America in Ten Strikes (New York: New Press, 2018), 29–30.

3. In this context the term organized labor refers to collections of workers who have formed unions or a federation of unions. This is in contrast to a movement of workers that may not be affiliated with a specific union, though they may be organized in other ways.

4. Leon Fink, Workingmen's Democracy: The Knights of Labor and American Politics (Champaign: University of Illinois Press, 1983), 6.

5. Clayton Sinyai, Schools of Democracy: A Political History of the American Labor Movement (Ithaca, NY: ILR Press, 2006), 74.

6. For a more detailed historical analysis of the Knights of Labor through various case studies, see Fink, Workingmen's Democracy.

7. Sinyai, Schools of Democracy, 74.

8. Woodrow Wilson, The New Freedom: A Call for the Emancipation of the Generous Energies of a People (New York: Doubleday, 1913), 64–65.

9. For a deeper dive on Woodrow Wilson and his relationship to the labor movement, see Joseph A. McCartin, Labor's Great War: The Struggle for Industrial Democracy and the Origins of Modern American Labor Relations, 1912–1921 (Chapel Hill: University of North Carolina Press, 1998).

10. To learn more about this dynamic, see Sinyai, Schools of Democracy. To learn more about the Pullman strike of 1894 in general, see David Ray Papke, The Pullman Case: The Clash of Labor and Capital in Industrial America (University Press of Kansas, 1999).

11. Ruth O'Brien, Workers' Paradox: The Republican Origins of New Deal Labor Policy, 1886–1935 (Chapel Hill: University of North Carolina Press, 1998).

12. McCartin, Labor's Great War, 12.

13. Windham, Knocking on Labor's Door.

14. Max D. Danish, The Story of the ILGWU (New York: International Ladies' Garment Workers' Union, 1951); and Cornell University ILR School, "History of the ILGWU,"

Kheel Center ILGWU Collection, accessed January 12, 2021, http://ilgwu.ilr.cornell.edu /history/.

15. See NLRA, 29 U.S.C. §158 (a)(1), (a)(3) (1935).

16. See NLRA, 29 U.S.C. § 158 (d) (1935).

17. Sinyai, *Schools of Democracy*.

18. Kate Andrias, "An American Approach to Social Democracy: The Forgotten Promise of the Fair Labor Standards Act," *Yale Law Journal* 128, no. 3 (2019): 616–709. https://www.yalelawjournal.org/pdf/Andrias_tfwmq5cj.pdf

19. Sinyai, *Schools of Democracy*, 126–127.

20. Robert Wagner, "The Ideal Industrial State—As Wagner Sees It," *New York Times Magazine*, May 9, 1937, 8.

21. Heckscher, *The New Unionism*, 7.

22. Maurice BP-Weeks, "Black Workers Give Me Hope (A Precious Commodity)," *Medium* (blog), January 9, 2017, https://medium.com/@mo87mo87/Black-workers-give -me-hope-a-precious-commodity-32b5757d605b.

23. Sophia Z. Lee, *The Workplace Constitution: From the New Deal to the New Right* (Cambridge, UK: Cambridge University Press, 2014), 13.

24. Lee, *The Workplace Constitution*.

25. For more on this dynamic, see Eric Arnesen, *Brotherhoods of Color: Black Railroad Workers and the Struggle for Equality* (Cambridge, MA: Harvard University Press, 2002).

26. Richard B. Freeman, "Spurts in Union Growth: Defining Moments and Social Processes," in *The Defining Moment: The Great Depression and the American Economy in the Twentieth Century*, ed. Michael D. Bordo, Claudia Goldin, and Eugene N. White (Chicago: University of Chicago Press, 1998), 282.

27. See NLRA, 29 U.S.C. § 158 (a)(4) (1935).

28. For a deeper dive into the series of related debates and compromises related, see Ira Katznelson, *Fear Itself: The New Deal and the Origins of Our Time* (New York: Liveright, 2014).

29. Beverly J. Silver, *Forces of Labor: Workers' Movements and Globalization since 1870* (Cambridge, UK: Cambridge University Press, 2003).

30. US Postal Service Office of Inspector General, "The Postal Strike of 1970," March 15, 2010, https://www.uspsoig.gov/blog/postal-strike-1970.

31. Juliana Kaplan, "The psychologist who coined the phrase 'Great Resignation' reveals how he saw it coming and where he sees it going. 'Who we are as an employee and as a worker is very central to who we are,'" *Business Insider*, October 2, 2021, https://www .businessinsider.com/why-everyone-is-quitting-great-resignation-psychologist -pandemic-rethink-life-2021-10.

32. For a far more detailed articulation of the pitfalls of overexaggerating the right to organize absent an analysis of the economic dynamics of global capitalism (trade, migration, etc.), see Bill Fletcher Jr. and Fernando Gapasin, *Solidarity Divided: The Crisis in Organized Labor and a New Path toward Social Justice* (Berkeley: University of California Press, 2009).

33. OurDocuments, "Transcript of National Labor Relations Act (1935),"accessed January 12, 2021, https://www.ourdocuments.gov/doc.php?flash=false&doc=67&page=tran script.

34. As Ira Katznelson wrote, "The embattled South acted to disarm unions in order to diminish the threat it believed labor posed to the economic underpinnings of the region's racial order." Ira Katznelson, *Fear Itself: The New Deal and the Origins of Our Time* (New York: Liveright, 2014), 371.

3. THE GREAT ROLLBACK

1. Nicholas Lemann, *Transaction Man: The Rise of the Deal and the Decline of the American Dream* (New York: Farrar, Straus & Giroux, 2019).

2. US Government Accountability Office, *Employment Arrangements: Improved Outreach Could Help Ensure Proper Worker Classification* (Washington, DC: US Government Accountability Office, 2006), here https://www.gao.gov/products/gao-06-656.

3. Weil, "Strategic Enforcement in the Fissured Workplace."

4. But see *Browning-Ferris Industries of California, Inc.*, 362 NLRB No. 186, 1599–1648 (2015).

5. Weil, "Strategic Enforcement in the Fissured Workplace."

6. The Labor Management Reporting and Disclosure Act (LMRDA) of 1959 was supposed to shed light on the practice of employing such antiunion hired guns by requiring companies to disclose any payments to people hired for the purpose of dissuading workers from joining a union; see LMRDA, 29 U.S.C. § 433(a)(3–5) (1959). Unfortunately, Department of Labor regulations and practice have interpreted this requirement so narrowly as to render it nearly a dead letter, and an attempt by the Obama administration to put some teeth into the regulations (see 81 *Federal Register* 15,924 *et seq.*) was blocked by a federal court (see *National Federation of Independent Business v. Perez*, No. 16-cv-066, E.D. Tex. November 16, 2016) and was in the process of being repealed by the Trump administration at the time of writing (see "Notice of Proposed Rulemaking Proposing Rescission of the Advice Exemption in the Labor-Management Reporting and Disclosure Act," June 12, 2017, available at https://www.federalregister.gov/documents/2017/06/12/2017-11983/rescission-of-rule-interpreting-advice-exemption-in-section-203c-of-the-labor-management-reporting.

7. John-Paul Ferguson, "The Eyes of the Needles: A Sequential Model of Union Organizing Drives, 1999–2004," *Industrial and Labor Relations Review* 62, no. 3 (2008).

8. Union membership density in 1935 was 16.6 percent as opposed to 10.7 percent in 2018. See US Bureau of Labor Statistics, "Union Members Summary."

9. Nancy MacLean, *Democracy in Chains: The Deep History of the Radical Right's Stealth Plan for America* (New York: Viking, 2017), 2.

10. See George C. Rogers Jr. and C. James Taylor, *A South Carolina Chronology 1497–1992*, 2nd ed. (Columbia: University of South Carolina Press, 1994); and South Carolina US Census data.

11. MacLean, *Democracy in Chains*, 9.

12. Harold Meyerson, "The Constitution's Anti-Majoritarian Bias," *American Prospect*, October 10, 2018, https://prospect.org/power/constitution-s-anti-majoritarian-bias/.

13. Thomas Piketty, *Capital in the Twenty-First Century* (Cambridge, MA: Harvard University Press, 2014).

14. For more on the prosperity gospel, see "Prosperity Gospel," *Christianity Today*, accessed January 14, 2021, https://www.christianitytoday.com/ct/topics/p/prosperity-gospel/.

15. MacLean, *Democracy in Chains*, 135.

16. The history of how the 501(c) tax code section was developed, amended, and used to limit the freedoms of people joining together collectively in a wide variety of democratic associations is well known and arguably deeply embedded in political tit for tat with its authors seeking to hurt their political opposition and/or the activities of groups they deemed "subversive." For more, see For Purpose Law Group, "The Political Ban in 501(c)(3): Its Odd History," June 23, 2016, https://forpurposelaw.com/501c3-political-ban-history/.

17. US Chamber of Commerce, *Worker Centers: Union Front Groups and the Law* (Washington, DC: US Chamber of Commerce, 2018).

18. We define *dog whistles* as coded language used to elevate fear and often discriminatory views in order to convince one section of people to impose limitations on another. For more, see Ian Haney López, *Dog Whistle Politics: How Coded Racial Appeals Have Reinvented Racism and Wrecked the Middle Class* (Oxford, UK: Oxford University Press, 2014).

19. See *Citizens United v. Federal Election Commission* case file, SCOTUS blog, accessed January 14, 2021, http://www.scotusblog.com/case-files/cases/citizens-united-v-federal-election-commission/.

20. See Brennan Center for Justice, "Debunking the Voter Fraud Myth," January 31, 2017, https://www.brennancenter.org/our-work/research-reports/debunking-voter-fraud-myth.

21. Drew DeSilver, "In Past Elections, U.S. Trailed Most Developed Countries in Voter Turnout," *Pew Research Center*, November 3, 2020, https://www.pewresearch.org/fact-tank/2020/11/03/in-past-elections-u-s-trailed-most-developed-countries-in-voter-turnout/.

22. Lane Windham, "Why Labor Law Should Stop Leaning So Hard on the Wagner Act," *American Prospect*, July 3, 2015, https://prospect.org/labor/labor-law-stop-leaning-hard-wagner-act/.

23. Windham, *Knocking on Labor's Door*.

24. See US Bureau of Labor Statistics, "Union Members Summary."

PROFILE OF THE AUTHOR: ERICA SMILEY

1. Benjamin Hensler, "Building a Coalition for Workers' Rights at Kmart," *University of Pennsylvania Journal of Labor and Employment Law* 2, no. 4 (2000).

2. Dyana Forester, "Victory! Justice for Georgia Public School Workers," Jobs With Justice, April 11, 2013, http://www.jwj.org/victory-justice-for-georgia-public-school-workers; and Natalie Patrick-Knox, *Case Study: How Community-Labor Strategies Can Bolster Immigrant Worker Organizing* (Washington, DC: Jobs With Justice, 2014).

4. WORTH FIGHTING FOR

1. US Bureau of Labor Statistics, "Work Stoppages Summary."

2. "CWA Members in Virginia/West Virginia on Strike at Frontier," Communication Workers of America, March 6, 2018, https://cwa-union.org/news/cwa-members-in-virginia-west-virginia-on-strike-frontier; and "AT&T," Communication Workers of America, accessed January 14, 2021, https://cwa-union.org/att.

3. Steven Greenhouse, "The Return of the Strike," *American Prospect*, January 3, 2019, https://prospect.org/article/return-strike.

4. Daisuke Wakabayashi, Erin Griffith, Amie Tsang, and Kate Conger, "Google Walkout: Employees Stage Protest Over Handling of Sexual Harassment," *New York Times*, November 1, 2018, https://www.nytimes.com/2018/11/01/technology/google-walkout-sexual-harassment.html.

5. Stephen Lerner, "What Is Not to Be Done," *American Prospect*, April 29, 2020, https://prospect.org/labor/what-is-not-to-be-done/.

6. Kate Taylor, "Fast-Food CEO Says He's Investing in Machines Because the Government Is Making It Difficult to Afford Employees," *Business Insider*, March 16, 2016, https://www.businessinsider.com/carls-jr-wants-open-automated-location-2016-3.

7. Sanes and Schmitt, *Regulation of Public Sector Collective Bargaining in the States*.

8. Ballotpedia, "Union Station: Public Sector Collective Bargaining Legal in Virginia as of May 1," April 30, 2021, https://news.ballotpedia.org/2021/04/30/union-station-public-sector-collective-bargaining-legal-in-virginia-as-of-may-1/#:~:text=In%201977%2C%20the%20Supreme%20Court,North%20Carolina%20and%20South%20Carolina.

9. See *Janus v. AFSCME*, Docket No. 16-466 (*cert. granted* September 28, 2017).

5. BEYOND *WORKERS*

1. Sarita Gupta, Stephen Lerner, and Joseph A. McCartin, "It's Not the 'Future of Work,' It's the Future of Workers That's in Doubt," *American Prospect*, August 31, 2018, https://prospect.org/article/its-not-future-work-its-future-workers-doubt.

2. For a detailed discussion of the idea of intersectional organizing, see Maite Tapia, Tamara L. Lee, and Mikhail Filipovitch, "Supra-Union and Intersectional Organizing: An Examination of Two Prominent Cases in the Low-Wage US Restaurant Industry," *Journal of Industrial Relations* 59, no. 4 (2017): 487–509, https://doi.org/10.1177/0022185617714817.

3. Charles C. Heckscher, *The New Unionism: Employee Involvement in the Changing Corporation* (Ithaca, NY: Cornell University Press, 1996), xiv.

4. Windham, *Knocking on Labor's Door.*

5. Put more eloquently by Martin Carnoy and Derek Shearer in their book *Economic Democracy: The Challenge of the 1980s,* "Democracy was limited to suffrage and consumer choice. The workplace was governed by the laws of private property, not the Bill of Rights. . . . Economic democracy is a crucial ingredient in political democracy and vice versa. Under the capitalist organization of production, political democracy is an imperfect concept and can be achieved in practice only through a democratization of the economy." Martin Carnoy and Derek Shearer, *Economic Democracy: The Challenge of the 1980s* (London: Routledge, 1980), 12, 131–132.

6. For a deep-dive into early advocates of organizing workers as whole people, see Robert Bussel, *Fighting for Total Person Unionism: Harold Gibbons, Ernest Calloway, and Working-Class Citizenship* (Champaign: University of Illinois Press, 2015).

6. ORGANIZING ALL PEOPLE

1. Anne Case and Sir Angus Deaton, "Mortality and Morbidity in the 21st Century," *Brookings Papers on Economic Activity* 2017, no. 1 (2017): 397–443.

2. For a deeper dive into the story of Youngstown, see Sherry Lee Linkon and John Russo, *Steeltown U.S.A.: Work and Memory in Youngstown* (Lawrence: University Press of Kansas, 2002).

3. Kirk Noden, "Why Do White Working-Class People Vote against Their Interests? They Don't," *Nation*, November 17, 2016, https://www.thenation.com/article/why-do-White-working-class-people-vote-against-their-interests-they-dont/.

4. Rev. J. C. Austin, "Don't Like Political Correctness? Then Stop Saying 'Merry Christmas,'" *Hill,* December 22, 2016, http://thehill.com/blogs/congress-blog/politics/311527-dont-like-political-correctness-then-stop-saying-merry-christmas.

5. Nicholas Carnes and Noam Lupu, "It's Time to Bust the Myth: Most Trump Voters Were Not Working Class," *Washington Post,* June 5, 2017, https://www.washingtonpost.com/news/monkey-cage/wp/2017/06/05/its-time-to-bust-the-myth-most-trump-voters-were-not-working-class/.

6. Nathalie Baptiste, "Closing the Racial Wealth Gap," *American Prospect*, August 15, 2016, http://prospect.org/article/closing-racial-wealth-gap.

7. Chris Arnade, "White Flight Followed Factory Jobs Out of Gary, Indiana. Black People Didn't Have a Choice," *Guardian*, March 28, 2017, https://www.theguardian.com/society/2017/mar/28/poverty-racism-gary-indiana-factory-jobs?CMP=share_btn_link.

8. A fairly detailed outline of the UAW's last contract with General Motors, Ford, and Fiat Chrysler can be found in Jeffrey S. Rothstein, "The New UAW Contract: A Somewhat 'Clear Path,'" *New Labor Forum*, December 2015, http://newlaborforum.cuny.edu/2015/12/11/the-new-uaw-contract-a-somewhat-clear-path/.

9. This is due to the ruling in *Hoffman Plastic Compounds, Inc v. NLRB*, 535 U.S. 137 (2002). Read the opinion at https://www.law.cornell.edu/supct/html/00-1595.ZO.html.

10. Cecilia Garza, "Meet the Crawfish-Peeling Guestworkers Who Inspired Walmart Walk-Outs," *Yes!*, October 11, 2012, http://www.yesmagazine.org/people-power/meet-the-crawfish-peeling-guestworkers-who-inspired-walmart-walkouts.

11. NBC News Exit Poll Desk, "Michigan Exit Poll Results: How Bernie Sanders Beat Hillary Clinton," *NBC News*, March 8, 2016, https://www.nbcnews.com/politics/2016-election/michigan-exit-poll-results-how-bernie-sanders-beat-hillary-clinton-n534601.

12. Summary references internal Jobs With Justice case study of organization's involvement in Justice @Smithfield campaign, drafted by Treston Davis-Faulkner in 2009; for more on the Smithfield campaign, see Matthew Barr, *Union Time: Fighting for Workers' Rights* (documentary released by Unheard Voices Project, 2016).

13. Loomis, *A History of America in Ten Strikes*, 31. See also Thomas D. Morris, *Southern Slavery and the Law, 1619–1860* (Chapel Hill: University of North Carolina Press, 2004) for further exploration of laws that validated white supremacy and patriarchy in the era of American slavery.

14. Restaurant Opportunities Center United, *Take Us Off the Menu: The Impact of Sexual Harassment in the Restaurant Industry* (New York: Restaurant Opportunities Center United, 2018).

15. PayScale, "The State of the Gender Pay Gap in 2020," accessed January 14, 2021, https://www.payscale.com/data/gender-pay-gap.

16. Amy Howe, "Opinion Analysis: Federal Employment Discrimination Law Protects Gay and Transgender Employees (Updated)," SCOTUSblog, June 15, 2020, https://www.scotusblog.com/2020/06/opinion-analysis-federal-employment-discrimination-law-protects-gay-and-transgender-employees/.

17. For a good case study on this campaign, see Chris Brooks, "Why Did Nissan Workers Vote No?" *Labor Notes*, August 11, 2017, https://www.labornotes.org/2017/08/why-did-nissan-workers-vote-no.

18. Ron Scott, "600 and Moore," *Boggs Blog*, November 6, 2009, https://conversationsthatyouwillneverfinish.wordpress.com/2009/11/06/in-memory-of-hunger-marcher-dave-moore/.

19. Nelson Lichtenstein sums up the story this way: "The modern civil rights movement arose out of the proletarianization and unionization of Black America." Nelson Lichtenstein, *Walter Reuther: The Most Dangerous Man in Detroit* (Champaign: University of Illinois Press, 1997), 207.

20. DC Jobs With Justice, "Walmart Strikers Cap Week of Action with Black Friday March," December 1, 2014, http://www.dcjwj.org/walmartstrikers-Black-friday-march/.

21. Rasheen Aldridge, testimony to the Jobs With Justice National Conference, Washington, DC, February 2016.

22. Kira Lerner, "Why Black Lives Matter and Fight for 15 Are Protesting Side-By-Side," *ThinkProgress*, April 14, 2016, https://archive.thinkprogress.org/why-black-lives-matter-and-fight-for-15-are-protesting-side-by-side-b81f562ac36d/.

23. Jpmassar, "Black Lives Matter Joins Fight for $15 Today in the Bay Area," *Daily Kos*, November 10, 2015, http://www.dailykos.com/story/2015/11/10/1448366/-Black-Lives-Matter-Joins-Fight-for-15-Today-in-the-Bay-Area.

24. In August 2015, the Greensboro City Council approved a minimum wage increase for city workers by 2020. Workers have since organized with the United Electrical, Radio, and Machine Workers of America Local 150. See "Greensboro City Council Agrees on Increasing Minimum Wage for City Workers," Fox 8 Greensboro, August 8, 2015, https://myfox8.com/news/greensboro-city-council-agrees-on-increasing-minimum-wage-for-city-workers/; and "Greensboro City Workers Unionize for Better Pay," Fox 8 Greensboro, August 8, 2015, http://myfox8.com/2017/01/17/greensboro-city-workers-unionize-for-better-pay/.

25. Movement for Black Lives, "Vision for Black Lives," accessed January 14, 2021, https://m4bl.org/policy-platforms/.

26. SEIU, "SEIU Announces Support for Movement for Black Lives," June 12, 2020, https://www.seiu.org/2020/06/seiu-announces-support-for-movement-for-black-lives; and AFT, "American Federation of Teachers Passes Resolution Expanding Its Efforts to Combat Racism, Aligning Itself with the Movement for Black Lives," June 17, 2020, https://www.aft.org/press-release/american-federation-teachers-passes-resolution-expanding-its-efforts-combat.

27. AFL-CIO, "AFL-CIO General Board Recommends Police Reform, Calls for Defense Secretary, Chairman of Joint Chiefs of Staff and President of Minneapolis Police Union to Resign," June 9, 2020, https://aflcio.org/press/releases/afl-cio-general-board-recommends-police-reform-calls-defense-secretary-chairman.

28. For more on the Asia Floor Wage Alliance, see http://asia.floorwage.org/. See chapter 6 for more.

29. As part of the annual International Labor Conference, Global Labor Justice and the Asia Floor Wage Alliance released company-specific reports on Gap, Inc., H&M, and Walmart that documenting gender-based violence within their supply chains. Part of the demands include publicly supporting a global convention that would set standards to address gender-based violence at work. Gap, Inc., and H&M have now come out in favor of one. See Global Labor Justice, "Worker Voices from the Asian Walmart Garment Supply Chain: A Report on Gender Based Violence to the 2018 International Labour Organization," May 25, 2018, https://www.globallaborjustice.org/portfolio_page/walmart-report-press-release/.

30. Anna North, "7 Positive Changes That Have Come from the #MeToo Movement," *Vox,* October 4, 2019, https://www.vox.com/identities/2019/10/4/20852639/me-too-movement-sexual-harassment-law-2019.

31. We purposefully left out the names of the union and the company as they are in active negotiations. For more information, visit the Asia Floor Wage Alliance at https://asia.floorwage.org/.

32. For a much more detailed discussion on the role of gender justice in relationship to organizing and collective bargaining among other economic policies, see Dorothy Sue Cobble, ed., *The Sex of Class: Women Transforming American Labor* (Ithaca, NY: Cornell University Press, 2007).

33. Arundhati Roy, "The Pandemic Is a Portal," *Financial Times,* April 3, 2020, https://www.ft.com/content/10d8f5e8-74eb-11ea-95fe-fcd274e920ca.

7. BEYOND THE RED AND THE BLUE

1. Interview between Erica Smiley and Jacob Staggers, January 29, 2019, Pleasant Valley, West Virginia.

2. For more on Taylorism and other company-led forms of "worker representation," see McCartin, *Labor's Great War,* chap. 2; Sinyai, *Schools of Democracy*; and chapter 11 of this book.

3. "Forced Labor on American Shores," *New York Times,* July 8, 2012, http://www.nytimes.com/2012/07/09/opinion/forced-labor-on-american-shores.html?_r=0.

4. Rachel E. Greenspan, "'It's the Legacy of Slavery': Here's the Troubling History behind Tipping Practices in the U.S.," *Time,* August 20, 2019, http://time.com/5404475/history-tipping-american-restaurants-civil-war/; Kerry Segrave, *Tipping: An American Social History of Gratuities* (Jefferson, NC: McFarland, 2009); and Saru Jayaraman, *Behind the Kitchen Door* (Ithaca, NY: Cornell University Press), 2013.

5. Abel Valenzuela Jr., "Immigrant Day Laborers: Myths and Realities," *North American Congress on Latin America,* April 10, 2008, https://nacla.org/article/immigrant-day-laborers-myths-and-realities.

6. Interview between Erica Smiley and Amelia Mullens, January 29, 2019, Pleasant Valley, West Virginia.

7. Robert Shogan, *The Battle of Blair Mountain: The Story of America's Largest Labor Uprising* (Boulder, CO: Basic, 2006).

James R. Green, *The Devil is Here in These Hills* (New York: Grove Atlantic, 2015).

8. Interview between Erica Smiley and Amelia Mullens, January 29, 2019, Pleasant Valley, West Virginia.

9. Sylvia Allegretto and Lawrence Mishel, "The Teacher Pay Penalty Has Hit a New High," *Economic Policy Institute*, September 5, 2018, https://www.epi.org/publication /teacher-pay-gap-2018/.

10. Direct conversation between Erica Smiley and a person outside of Detroit, Michigan, June 6, 2016.

11. Friedrichs v. California Teachers Association, 578. 14-915 U.S. (2016), https://www .supremecourt.gov/opinions/15pdf/14-915_1bn2.pdf; Janus v. AFSCME 16-1466. U.S. (2017), https://www.supremecourt.gov/opinions/17pdf/16-1466_2b3j.pdf.

8. BARGAINING WITH THE REAL DECISION-MAKERS

1. Weil, "Strategic Enforcement in the Fissured Workplace."

2. Windham, *Knocking on Labor's Door*, 123.

3. Windham, *Knocking on Labor's Door*, 124.

4. Silver, *Forces of Labor*, 85.

5. For specifics on how to calculate the Asia floor wage, see https://asia.floorwage.org /calculating-a-living-wage.

6. Accord on Fire and Building Safety in Bangladesh, "Safe Workplaces," accessed January 18, 2021, http://bangladeshaccord.org/.

7. Accord on Fire and Building Safety in Bangladesh, "Safe Workplaces," accessed November 4, 2021, http://bangladeshaccord.org/.

8. Erica Smiley, "One Year Later, Walmart Still Shirks Responsibility for Supply Chain Catastrophes," *Jobs With Justice*, April 23, 2014, http://www.jwj.org/one-year-later -walmart-still-shirks-responsibility-for-supply-chain-catastrophes.

9. "Precarious Work in the Walmart Global Value Chain." Report to the ILO Sponsored by the Asia Floor Wage Alliance (AFWA), Bangladesh Nari Progati Sangha (BNPS), Labor Resource Center of Indonesia (LIPS), Society for Labor and Development of India (SLD), Center for Alliance of Labor and Human Rights in Cambodia (CENTRAL), The National Centre for Development Cooperation (CNCD) of Belgium, Jobs With Justice of the United States, and the United Workers Congress of the United States, 2016).

10. For a full list of current global union federations, see https://en.wikipedia.org/wiki /Global_union_federation.

11. Jörg Sydow, Michael Fichter, Markus Helfen, Kadire Zeynep Sayim, and Dimitris Stevis, "Implementation of Global Framework Agreements: Towards a Multi-Organizational Practice Perspective," *Transfer* 20, no. 4 (2014): 489–503, https://journals.sagepub.com/doi /pdf/10.1177/1024258914546270.

12. Michael Fichter and Dimitris Stevis, "Global Framework Agreements in a Union-Hostile Environment: The Case of the USA," *Friedrich Ebert Stiftung*, December 1, 2013, https://ssrn.com/abstract=2383825.

13. The following summary is paraphrased from Stephen Lerner and Saket Soni, "Bargaining with the Top One-Tenth of the One Percent," discussion paper for the 99% Spring Leadership Team, April 2012 (used with permission from Stephen Lerner).

14. Mark Vandeveldge, "Toys R Us Workers Put Pressure on Hedge Fund," *Financial Times*, September 3, 2018, https://www.ft.com/content/17b283a8-ad6d-11e8-94bd-cba20d 67390c.

15. Kate Gibson, "$20 Million Severance Fund Started for Toys R Us Workers," *CBS News*, November 21, 2018, https://www.cbsnews.com/news/20-million-severance-fund -started-for-tens-of-thousands-of-toys-r-us-workers/; and Chavie Lieber, "Thousands of Toys R Us Workers are Getting Severance, Following Months of Protests," *Vox*, Novem- ber 21, 2018, https://www.vox.com/the-goods/2018/11/21/18106545/toys-r-us-retail-workers -severance.

16. The history of the Driscoll dispute can be found in David Bacon, "A New Farm Worker Union Is Born," *American Prospect*, June 26, 2017, https://prospect.org/labor/new -farm-worker-union-born/; and Don McIntosh, "Farmworkers at Sakuma Ratify Historic First Union Contract," *NWLaborPress*, June 16, 2017, https://nwlaborpress.org/2017/06 /farmworkers-at-sakuma-ratify-historic-first-union-contract/.

17. For more information on how undocumented workers are less protected by US labor laws, see the Hoffman Plastics court case: https://www.law.cornell.edu/supct/html /00-1595.ZO.html.

18. For more on this campaign, see Steven Greenhouse, "Wal-Mart Suspends Supplier of Seafood," *New York Times*, June 29, 2012, https://www.nytimes.com/2012/06/30/business /wal-mart-suspends-seafood-supplier-over-work-conditions.html; and "Forced Labor," https://www.nytimes.com/2012/07/09/opinion/forced-labor-on-american-shores.html.

19. Based on Walmart's own projections, accessed November 4, 2021. https://corporate .walmart.com/newsroom/company-facts#:~:text=Walmart%20employs%20more%20 than%202.3,million%20in%20the%20U.S.%20alone.

20. Used with permission from Lerner and Soni, "Bargaining with the Top One-Tenth of the One Percent."

21. Adam Bonica, Nolan McCarthy, Keith T. Poole, and Howard Rosenthal, "Why Hasn't Democracy Slowed Rising Inequality?" *Journal of Economic Perspectives* 27, no. 3 (2013): 103–124, https://doi.org/10.1257/jep.27.3.103.

9. COMMUNITY-DRIVEN BARGAINING

1. For more information on this effort, see Atlanta Jobs With Justice, "Georgia School Workers Stand Up across State," July 4, 2012, http://www.atlantajwj.org/2012/07/georgia -school-workers-stand-up-across.html; and Dyana Forester, "Victory! Justice for Geor- gia Public School Workers," Jobs With Justice, April 11, 2013, http://www.jwj.org/victory -justice-for-georgia-public-school-workers.

2. Alby Gallun, "Equity Residential to Stop Evictions, Rent Hikes," *Crain's Chicago Business*, March 24, 2020, https://www.chicagobusiness.com/commercial-real-estate /equity-residential-stop-evictions-rent-hikes.

3. Dima Williams, "May 1 Rent Strike through the Lens of Organizers, Landlords, and Industry Leaders," *Forbes*, May 1, 2020, https://www.forbes.com/sites/dimawilliams /2020/05/01/may-1-rent-strike-through-the-lens-of-organizers-landlords-and-industry -leaders/?sh=75ecbfa7b85c.

4. Bianca Agustin, Chuck Collins, Jonathan Heller, Sara Myklebust, and Omar Oc- ampo, "Billionaire Wealth vs. Community Health: Protecting Essential Workers from Pandemic Profiteers," Institute for Policy Studies, accessed December 2, 2021, https:// www.npr.org/2020/10/05/920314309/pandemic-profiteers-why-billionaires-are-getting -richer-during-an-economic-crisi.

5. Ethan Corey, "The Brooklyn Tenant Union That's Fighting Gentrification through Collective Bargaining," *In These Times*, July 22, 2015, http://inthesetimes.com/article /18226/solidarity-works-brooklyn-tenant-union-organizes-for-rent-regulation.

6. Interview between Erica Smiley and Deloris Wright, March 7, 2019, Jenkintown, PA.

7. See Crown Heights Tenant Union, "Our Demands," accessed October 17, 2021, http://www.crownheightstenantunion.org/our-demands.

8. City Life, "TAACL: Tenants Association against Corporate Landlords," accessed January 18, 2021, http://www.clvu.org/renters.

9. "Autonomous Tenants Union," Facebook, accessed January 18, 2021, https://www .facebook.com/pg/AutonomousTenantsUnion/about/?ref=page_internal.

10. The Tenants Union of Washington State's Principles of Unity declare that "we believe that all tenants have the right to organize and determine the rules and conditions of their tenancy through collective bargaining and other means." See Tenants Union of Washington State, "Principles of Unity," accessed October 17, 2021, http://www.tenan tsunion.org/en/about/principles-of-unity.

11. The Tenants Union of Washington State catalogs its victories and losses on the history page of its website. See Tenants Union of Washington State, "TU History," accessed October 17, 2021, http://www.tenantsunion.org/en/about/tu-history.

12. Strike Debt!, website, https://strikedebt.org/.

13. Lawrence B. Glickman, "The American Tradition of Consumer Politics," *Organization of American Historians*, accessed January 18, 2021, https://www.oah.org/tah /issues/2017/may/the-american-tradition-of-consumer-politics/.

14. For more info, see https://housingtrustfundproject.org/.

15. For a deeper exploration of the bad business fee, see Erica Smiley, "Fining Mc-Walmart: Charging Employers for the Social Costs of Poverty Wages," *New Labor Forum* 24, no. 3 (2015): 68–75, https://doi.org/ 10.1177/1095796015597007.

16. "Largest Employers," *Hartford Courant*, July 17, 2003, http://www.courant.com /mhc-market-employers-htmlstory.html.

17. Daniel Kennedy, Stan McMillen, and Louise Simmons, "The Economic and Fiscal Impact of Low-Wage Work in Connecticut," *Issue Brief*, April 2015, 1–6, https:// d3n8a8pro7vhmx.cloudfront.net/ctassetbuilding/pages/132/attachments/original /1476906349/issueBriefCT6.pdf?1476906349.

18. CVS Health, "Aetna Announces Changes That Will Improve Wages and Medical Benefits for Thousands of Its Employees," January 12, 2015, https://cvshealth.com /newsroom/press-releases/aetna-announces-changes-will-improve-wages-and-medical -benefits-thousands.

19. City of Seattle, "Domestic Workers Standards Board," accessed November 9, 2021, https://www.seattle.gov/domestic-workers-standards-board.

20. Erica Smiley, "Domestic Workers are Using the Gig Economy Against Itself," *The Nation*, June 25, 2021, https://www.thenation.com/article/society/domestic-workers -handy-labor/.

21. New York State Department of Labor, "Domestic Workers' Bill of Rights,", accessed January 18, 2021, https://dol.ny.gov/domestic-workers-bill-rights.

22. See, generally, Julian Gross, Greg LeRoy, and Madeline Janis-Aparicio, "Community Benefits Agreements: Making Development Projects Accountable," Good Jobs First and the California Partnership for Working Families, 2005, http://www.goodjobsfirst.org /sites/default/files/docs/pdf/cba2005final.pdf.

23. See, e.g., "HUD Office of Policy Development & Research, Community Benefits Agreement Guides Development in Milwaukee's Park East Corridor," *PD&R Edge*, accessed January 18, 2021, https://www.huduser.gov/portal/pdredge/pdr_edge_inpractice _072012.html.

24. See Kingsbridge Armory CBA (requiring an $8 million initial contribution and ongoing payments from the developer to a coalition of community organizations for community improvements, developing a small-business incubator, and other purposes), Partnership for Working Families, "Policy & Tools: Community Benefits Agreements and Policies in Effect," accessed January 18, 2021, https://www.forworkingfamilies.org /page/policy-tools-community-benefits-agreements-and-policies-effect.

25. Larissa Larson, "The Pursuit of Responsible Development: Addressing Anticipated Benefits and Unwanted Burdens through Community Benefits Agreements," Center for Local, State, and Urban Policy, 2009, https://www.researchgate.net/publication/228385987 _The_pursuit_of_responsible_development_Addressing_anticipated_benefits_and _unwanted_burdens_through_community_benefit_agreements; on requiring the developer to provide "publicly accessible park spaces," see Partnership for Working Families, "Los Angeles Sports and Entertainment District CBA: Staples Center Community Benefits Program," accessed January 18, 2021, https://www.forworkingfamilies.org/resources/staples -cba; on funding for job-training programs, see "Core Community Benefits Agreement."

26. See Matthew Raffol, "Community Benefits Agreements in the Political Economy of Urban Development," *Advocates' Forum*, University of Chicago, School of Social Service Administration, 2012, http://ssa.uchicago.edu/community-benefits-agreements -political-economy-urban-development.

27. See, e.g., Hunters Point Shipyard/Candlestick Point Integrated Development Project Core Community Benefits Agreement (2008) (listing the San Francisco Labor Council as part of the coalition of organizations that each "have the right to enforce the provisions of the [Community Benefits Agreement] against all parties incorporating this Program into contracts or other agreements) (available at https://juliangross.net/docs/CBA/Hunters _Point_Agreement.pdf.

28. See California High-Speed Rail Authority, "Community Benefits Agreement," August 7, 2013, http://www.hsr.ca.gov/docs/programs/construction/HSR13_06_Community _Benefits_Agreement_Executed.pdf.

29. For more information on the Better Builder Program, see http://www.austintexas .gov/edims/document.cfm?id=258601.

30. Janice Fine, "Enforcing Labor Standards in Partnership with Civil Society: Can Co-Enforcement Succeed Where the State Alone Has Failed?" *Politics and Society* 45, no. 3 (2017), https://doi.org/10.1177/0032329217702603.

31. Partnership for Working Families & Community Benefits Law Center, "Common Challenges in Negotiating Community Benefits Agreements and How to Avoid Them," January 2016, https://www.forworkingfamilies.org/resources/publications/common -challenges-negotiating-community-benefits-agreements-how-avoid-them.

32. Annette Bernhardt, Ruth Milkman, Nik Theodore, Douglas Heckathorn, Mirabai Auer, James DeFilippis, Ana Luz González, Victor Narro, Jason Perelshteyn, Diana Polson, and Michael Spiller, "Broken Laws, Unprotected Workers: Violations of Employment and Labor Laws in America's Cities," *UCLA: Institute for Research on Labor and Employment*, California Digital Library, University of California, 2009, https://escholarship .org/content/qt1vn389nh/qt1vn389nh.pdf; and John W. Schoen, "States in Crisis: Embroiled in the Worst Budget Battles since the Great Recession," *CNBC*, July 11, 2017, https:// www.cnbc.com/2017/07/11/states-in-crisis-the-worst-budget-battles-since-the-great -recession.html.

33. See Lewis Creekmore, Ronké Huges, Lynn Jennings, Sarah John, Janet LaBella, C. Arturo Manjarrez, Michelle Oh, Zoe Osterman, and Marta Woldu, "The Justice Gap: Measuring the Unmet Civil Legal Needs of Low-Income Americans," *Legal Services Corporation*, June 2017, https://www.lsc.gov/sites/default/files/images/TheJusticeGap-FullReport.pdf.

34. Workplace Fairness, "Non-Disclosure Agreements (NDA's)," Workplace Fairness, accessed January 18, 2021, https://www.workplacefairness.org/nondisclosure-agreements.

35. See David Cooper and Teresa Kroeger, "Employers Steal Billions from Workers' Paychecks Each Year," *Economic Policy Institute*, May 10, 2017, https://www.epi.org /publication/employers-steal-billions-from-workers-paychecks-each-year/.

36. See Janice Fine, "Co-Production: Bringing Together the Unique Capabilities of Government and Society for Stronger Labor Standards Enforcement," Labor Innovations

for the 21st Century Fund, September 2015, http://theliftfund.org/wp-content/uploads/2015/09/LIFTReportCoproductionOct_ExecSumm-rf_4.pdf.

37. See Evelyn Nieves, "Accord with Tomato Pickers Ends Boycott of Taco Bell," *Washington Post*, March 9, 2005, https://www.washingtonpost.com/wp-dyn/articles/A18187-2005Mar8.html.

38. Steven Greenhouse, "Tomato Pickers' Wages Fight Faces Obstacles," *New York Times*, December 24, 2007, https://www.nytimes.com/2007/12/24/us/24tomato.html.

39. See "Burger King Campaign Comes to an End with Historic Press Conference, Signing Ceremony at US Capital," Coalition of Immokalee Workers, May 23, 2008, http://www.ciw-online.org/blog/2008/05/burger-king-campaign-comes-to-an-end-with-historic-press-conference-signing-ceremony-at-u-s-capitol/.

40. See "2017–2019 Recipients, CEOF Past Recipients," Seattle Office of Labor Standards, accessed January 19, 2021, https://www.seattle.gov/laborstandards/funding/community-outreach-and-education-fund/coef-past-recipients

41. One of the other early fair scheduling laws was passed in Emeryville, CA.

42. Retail Workers Bill of Rights, "San Francisco's Formula Retail Economy," accessed January 19, 2021, http://retailworkerrights.com/get-the-facts/san-franciscos-formula-retail-economy/; San Francisco Office of Labor Standards Enforcement, "Formula Retail Employee Rights Ordinances," accessed October 17, 2021, https://sfgov.org/olse/formula-retail-employee-rights-ordinances. "State of the Retail Sector: Challenges and Opportunities for San Francisco's Neighborhood Commercial Districts: Final Report," San Francisco Office of Economic and Workforce Development, February 2018, https://oewd.org/sites/default/files/Invest%20In%20Neighborhoods/State%20of%20the%20Retail%20Sector%20-%20Final%20Report.pdf.

43. Eric Dirnbach, "Unions and Worker Co-Ops, Old Allies, Are Joining Forces Again," *Labor Notes*, September 5, 2017, http://www.labornotes.org/blogs/2017/09/unions-and-worker-co-ops-old-allies-are-joining-forces-again.

44. "U.S. Employment Plan," Jobs to Move to America, April 10, 2020, https://jobstomoveamerica.org/resource/u-s-employment-plan-2/.

45. See Transportation, General, and Intermodal Programs, Public Transportation, 49 U.S.C. § 5325, https://www.govinfo.gov/content/pkg/USCODE-2011-title49/html/USCODE-2011-title49-subtitleIII-chap53-sec5325.htm.

46. Avondale Industries, Inc., Petition-cross-respondent v. National Labor Relations Board, Respondent-cross-petitioner, 180 F.3d 633 (5th Circ. 1999), https://law.justia.com/cases/federal/appellate-courts/F3/180/633/486050/.

47. "Paving the High Road: Labor Standards and Procurement Policy in the Obama Era," *Berkeley Journal of Employment & Labor Law* 31, no. 2 (2010): 408–413, https://doi.org/10.15779/Z38VK8D.

48. "Paving the High Road."

10. BUILDING LONG-TERM LABOR-COMMUNITY POWER

1. The United Steelworkers have a great summary of these on their website at https://www.usw.org/workplaces/public-sector/2015-conference-material/5-Subjects-of-Bargaining.pdf.

2. NLRB, "About NLRB," accessed January 19, 2021, https://www.nlrb.gov/rights-we-protect/whats-law/unions/collective-bargaining-section-8d-8b3.

3. Lichenstein, *The Most Dangerous Man in Detroit*.

4. For more information on the General Motors strike, see David Brody, *Workers in Industrial America* (Oxford, UK: Oxford University Press, 1993), 167–174; and Lichenstein, *The Most Dangerous Man in Detroit*, 220–247.

5. Arthur Delaney and Alissa Scheller, "Who Gets Food Stamps? White People Mostly," *Huffington Post,* February 28, 2015, http://www.huffingtonpost.com/2015/02/28 /food-stamp-demographics_n_6771938.html.

6. Interview between Heather DeLuca-Nestor and Allyson Perry, January 29, 2019, Pleasant Valley, West Virginia.

7. "BCG Seven Elements," a handout/PDF of the Kalmanovitz Initiative at Georgetown, the Center for Innovation and Worker Organization at Rutgers, and the Action Center on Race and the Economy, https://www.bargainingforthecommongood.org/about/.

8. See Joseph A. McCartin, "Bargaining for the Common Good," *Dissent,* Spring 2016, https://www.dissentmagazine.org/article/bargaining-common-good-community-union -alignment.

9. See "Economic News Release."

10. See Joseph A. McCartin, "Public Sector Unionism under Assault: How to Combat the Scapegoating of Organized Labor," *New Labor Forum,* January 2016, http:// newlaborforum.cuny.edu/2016/01/19/public-sector-unionism-under-assault-how-to -combat-the-scapegoating-of-organized-labor/.

11. See Janus v. AFSCME, 16-1466 US (2018) (cert. granted September 28, 2017).

12. Heather Gillers and Jason Grotto, "How the Tribune Analyzed CPS' Bond Deals," *Chicago Tribune,* November 7, 2014, https://www.chicagotribune.com/investigations/ct -chicago-public-schools-bonds-methodology-met-20141107-story.html.

13. Mary Cathryn Ricker, "Teacher-Community Unionism: A Lesson from St. Paul," *Dissent,* Summer 2015. https://www.dissentmagazine.org/article/teacher-community -unionism-lesson-st-paul.

14. For a direct account of their experience, see Ricker, "Teacher-Community Unionism."

15. Marilyn Sneiderman and Secky Fascione, "Going on Offense during Challenging Times," *New Labor Forum,* January 2018, https://newlaborforum.cuny.edu/2018/01/18 /going-on-offense-during-challenging-times/.

16. "Concrete Examples of Bargaining for the Common Good," compiled by Rutgers School of Management and Labor Relations and the Center for Innovation in Worker Organization, Action Center on Race and the Economy (ACRE), and Georgetown University's Kalmanovitz Initiative for Labor and the Working Poor. Revised October 29, 2018.

17. This example first appeared in an article written by Erica Smiley, "Time to Tackle the Whole Squid: Confronting White Supremacy to Build Bargaining Power," *Class, Race and Corporate Power* 5, no. 2 (2017), https://doi.org/10.25148/CRCP.5.2.006505.

18. Smiley, "Time to Tackle the Whole Squid."

19. "Concrete Examples of Bargaining for the Common Good."

20. "Concrete Examples of Bargaining for the Common Good."

21. Smiley, "Time to Tackle the Whole Squid."

22. "Concrete Examples of Bargaining for the Common Good."

23. "Whistleblower: Wells Fargo Fraud 'Could Have Been Stopped,'" *CBS News,* August 3, 2018, https://www.cbsnews.com/news/whistleblower-wells-fargo-fraud-could -have-been-stopped/.

24. Renae Merle, "After Years of Apologies for Customer Abuses, Wells Fargo CEO Tim Sloan Suddenly Steps Down," *Washington Post,* March 28, 2019, https://www .washingtonpost.com/business/2019/03/28/wells-fargo-ceo-tim-sloan-step-down -immediately/?utm_term=.34e039593252.

25. Hugh Son and John Melloy, "Bank of America Is Raising Its Minimum Wage for Employees to $20 an Hour," *CNBC,* April 9, 2019, https://www.cnbc.com/2019/04/09 /bank-of-america-is-raising-its-minimum-wage-for-employees-to-20-an-hour.html.

26. For more discussion on the efforts of bank workers, see Lerner, Berlofa, McGrath, and Klemmber, "Tipping the Balance."

11. WHO BENEFITS?

1. "Black People vs. Robots: Reparations and Workers Rights in the Age of Automation," panel discussion organized by, Data for Black Lives, January 14, 2019, available on YouTube, https://youtu.be/1uOt3GriWAI; http://d4bl.org/.

2. Carnoy and Shearer, *Economic Democracy*, 195–196.

3. Carnoy and Shearer, *Economic Democracy*, 195–196.

4. Stephanie Christensen, "The Great Migration (1915–1960)," *Black Past*, December 6, 2007, http://www.Blackpast.org/aah/great-migration-1915-1960.

5. Alexis C. Madrigal, "How Automation Could Worsen Racial Inequality," *Atlantic*, January 16, 2018, https://www.theatlantic.com/technology/archive/2018/01/Black-workers-and-the-driverless-bus/550535/.

6. "What Is Sports Analytics?" Sports Management Degree Guide, accessed January 20, 2021, https://www.sports-management-degrees.com/faq/what-is-sports-analytics/.

7. For more information on the agreements of various sports leagues, see Jason Chung, "Who Owns Your Fitbit Data? Biometric Data Privacy Problems," *Healthcare Blog*, November 25, 2017, https://thehealthcareblog.com/blog/2017/11/25/who-owns-your-fitbit-data-biometric-data-privacy-problems/; and Nicholas Zych, "Collection and Ownership of Minor League Athlete Activity Biometric Data by Major League Baseball Franchises," *DePaul Journal of Sports Law* 14, no. 1 (2018), https://paperity.org/p/144523875/collection-and-ownership-of-minor-league-athlete-activity-biometric-data-by-major-league.

8. Preston Gralla, "Amazon Prime and the Racism Algorithms," *Computer World*, May 11, 2016, https://www.computerworld.com/article/3068622/amazon-prime-and-the-racist-algorithms.html.

9. This section is adapted from an original article by Erica Smiley, "The Gig Economy Is Screwing Over Workers—And It Needs to Stop," *Talk Poverty*, October 13, 2016, https://talkpoverty.org/2016/10/13/gig-economy-screwing-workers-needs-stop/, which was itself based on a presentation Smiley gave to the American Sociology Association convention in Seattle in 2016.

10. Taylorism refers to the late nineteenth-century "scientific management" practices developed by Frederick Taylor. These practices sought increased efficiency by methodically tracking the daily habits/actions of workers and attempting to streamline them. At best, workers were a part of and even in charge of tracking these adjustments. At worst, the system allowed managers to track workers as coldly as they might tweak a machine, leading to many union struggles over Taylorism. Sinyai's *Schools of Democracy* (pp. 55–71) has a strong description of Taylorism.

11. Chris Benner, Erin Johansson, Kung Feng, and Hays Witt, "On-Demand and On-the-Edge: Ride Hailing and Delivery Workers in San Francisco." A report commissioned by the Institute for Social Transformation, University of California–Santa Cruz, May 5, 2020, https://transform.ucsc.edu/on-demand-and-on-the-edge/.

12. Thomas Ahearn, "Judge Rules Women Can Sue Uber Over Alleged Sexual Assaults," *ESR News Blog*, May 10, 2016, http://www.esrcheck.com/wordpress/2016/05/10/judge-rules-women-can-sue-uber-over-alleged-sexual-assaults/.

13. Davey Alba, "Judge Rejects Uber's $100 Million Settlement with Drivers," *Wired*, August 18, 2016, https://www.wired.com/2016/08/uber-settlement-rejected/.

14. Steven Hill, "Can Workers Get a Fair Deal in the Gig Economy?" *Common Dreams*, August 24, 2016, http://www.commondreams.org/views/2016/08/24/can-workers-get-fair-deal-gig-economy.

15. Timothy Kim, "The Dynamex Decision: The California Supreme Court Restricts Use of Independent Contractors," *Labor & Employment Blog*, May 1, 2018, https://www.laboremploymentlawblog.com/2018/05/articles/class-actions/dynamex-decision-independent-contractors/.

16. Alison Griswold, "Uber Is Using Its US Customer Service Reps to Deliver Its Anti-Union Message," *Quartz*, February 20, 2016, http://qz.com/619601/uber-is-using-its-us-customer-service-reps-to-deliver-its-anti-union-message/.

17. Rebecca Smith, "Union-Busting. Now There's an App for That," *NELP*, March 7, 2016, http://www.nelp.org/commentary/union-busting-now-theres-an-app-for-that/.

18. Sydney Brownstone, "Seattle Lyft Driver Wants to Know Why She Was Deactivated after Attending a Teamsters Organizing Meeting," *Stranger*, November 19, 2015, http://www.thestranger.com/blogs/slog/2015/11/19/23163805/seattle-lyft-driver-wants-to-know-why-she-was-deactivated-after-attending-a-teamsters-organizing-meeting.

19. Cole Stangler, "Why the Uber, Lyft Driver Union Push Could Disrupt the Gig Economy," *IBTimes*, December 18, 2015, http://www.ibtimes.com/why-uber-lyft-driver-union-push-could-disrupt-gig-economy-2232778.

20. Daniel Wiessner and Dan Levine, "Uber Deal Shows Divide in Labor's Drive for Role in 'Gig Economy,'" *Reuters*, May 23, 2016, https://www.reuters.com/article/us-uber-tech-drivers-labor/uber-deal-shows-divide-in-labors-drive-for-role-in-gig-economy-idUSKCN0YE0DF.

Accord on Fire and Building Safety in Bangladesh. "Safe Workplaces." Accessed January 18, 2021. http://bangladeshaccord.org/.

AFL-CIO. "AFL-CIO General Board Recommends Police Reform, Calls for Defense Secretary, Chairman of Joint Chiefs of Staff and President of Minneapolis Police Union to Resign." June 9, 2020. https://aflcio.org/press/releases/afl-cio-general-board-recommends-police-reform-calls-defense-secretary-chairman.

AFL-CIO. "Atlanta's Washerwomen Strike." Accessed January 12, 2021. https://aflcio.org/about/history/labor-history-events/atlanta-washerwomen-strike.

AFT. "American Federation of Teachers Passes Resolution Expanding Its Efforts to Combat Racism, Aligning Itself with the Movement for Black Lives." June 17, 2020. https://www.aft.org/press-release/american-federation-teachers-passes-resolution-expanding-its-efforts-combat.

Ahearn, Thomas. "Judge Rules Women Can Sue Uber Over Alleged Sexual Assaults." *ESR News Blog*, May 10, 2016. http://www.esrcheck.com/wordpress/2016/05/10/judge-rules-women-can-sue-uber-over-alleged-sexual-assaults/.

Alba, Davey. "Judge Rejects Uber's $100 Million Settlement with Drivers." *Wired*, August 18, 2016. https://www.wired.com/2016/08/uber-settlement-rejected/.

Allegretto, Sylvia, and Lawrence Mishel. "The Teacher Pay Penalty Has Hit a New High." *Economic Policy Institute*, September 5, 2018. https://www.epi.org/publication/teacher-pay-gap-2018/.

Andrias, Kate. "An American Approach to Social Democracy: The Forgotten Promise of the Fair Labor Standards Act." *Yale Law Journal* 128, no. 3 (2019): 616–709. https://www.yalelawjournal.org/pdf/Andrias_tfwmq5cj.pdf

Arnade, Chris. "White Flight Followed Factory Jobs Out of Gary, Indiana. Black People Didn't Have a Choice." *Guardian*, March 28, 2017. https://www.theguardian.com/society/2017/mar/28/poverty-racism-gary-indiana-factory-jobs?CMP=share_btn_link.

Arnesen, Eric. *Brotherhoods of Color: Black Railroad Workers and the Struggle for Equality*. Cambridge, MA: Harvard University Press, 2002.

Atlanta Jobs With Justice. "Georgia School Workers Stand Up across State." July 4, 2012. http://www.atlantajwj.org/2012/07/georgia-school-workers-stand-up-across.html

Austin, Rev J. C. "Don't Like Political Correctness? Then Stop Saying 'Merry Christmas.'" *Hill*, December 22, 2016. http://thehill.com/blogs/congress-blog/politics/311527-dont-like-political-correctness-then-stop-saying-merry-christmas.

"Autonomous Tenants Union." Facebook. Accessed January 18, 2021. https://www.facebook.com/pg/AutonomousTenantsUnion/about/?ref=page_internal.

Bacon, David. "A New Farm Worker Union Is Born." *American Prospect*, June 26, 2017. https://prospect.org/labor/new-farm-worker-union-born/.

Baptiste, Nathalie. "Closing the Racial Wealth Gap." *American Prospect*, August 15, 2016. http://prospect.org/article/closing-racial-wealth-gap.

Barr, Matthew, dir. *Union Time: Fighting for Workers' Rights*. 2016; documentary released by Unheard Voices Project.

Benner, Chris, Erin Johansson, Kung Feng, and Hays Witt. "On-Demand and On-the-Edge: Ride Hailing and Delivery Workers in San Francisco." A report commissioned by the Institute for Social Transformation, University of California–Santa Cruz, May 5, 2020. https://transform.ucsc.edu/on-demand-and-on-the-edge/.

Bernhardt, Annette, Ruth Milkman, Nik Theodore, Douglas Heckathorn, Mirabai Auer, James DeFilippis, Ana Luz González, Victor Narro, Jason Perelshteyn, Diana Polson, and Michael Spiller. "Broken Laws, Unprotected Workers Violations of Employment and Labor Laws in America's Cities." *UCLA: Institute for Research on Labor and Employment Reports*. California Digital Library, University of California. 2009. https://escholarship.org/content/qt1vn389nh/qt1vn389nh.pdf.

Bonica, Adam, Nolan McCarthy, Keith T. Poole, and Howard Rosenthal. "Why Hasn't Democracy Slowed Rising Inequality?" *Journal of Economic Perspectives* 27, no. 3 (2013): 103–124. https://doi.org/10.1257/jep.27.3.103.

BP-Weeks, Maurice. "Black Workers Give Me Hope (A Precious Commodity)." *Medium* (blog), January 9, 2017. https://medium.com/@mo87mo87/Black-workers-give-me-hope-a-precious-commodity-32b5757d605b.

Brennan Center for Justice. "Debunking the Voter Fraud Myth." January 31, 2017. https://www.brennancenter.org/our-work/research-reports/debunking-voter-fraud-myth.

Brody, David. *Workers in Industrial America*. Oxford, UK: Oxford University Press, 1993.

Brooks, Chris. "Why Did Nissan Workers Vote No?" *Labor Notes*, August 11, 2017. https://www.labornotes.org/2017/08/why-did-nissan-workers-vote-no.

Brownstone, Sydney. "Seattle Lyft Driver Wants to Know Why She Was Deactivated after Attending a Teamsters Organizing Meeting." *Stranger*, November 19, 2015. http://www.thestranger.com/blogs/slog/2015/11/19/23163805/seattle-lyft-driver-wants-to-know-why-she-was-deactivated-after-attending-a-teamsters-organizing-meeting.

Bussel, Robert. *Fighting for Total Person Unionism: Harold Gibbons, Ernest Calloway, and Working-Class Citizenship*. Champaign: University of Illinois Press, 2015.

California High-Speed Rail Authority. "Community Benefits Agreement." August 7, 2013. http://www.hsr.ca.gov/docs/programs/construction/HSR13_06_Community_Benefits_Agreement_Executed.pdf.

Campbell, Alexia Fernández. "A Record Number of US Workers Went on Strike in 2018." *Vox*, February 13, 2019. https://www.vox.com/policy-and-politics/2019/2/13/18223211/worker-teacher-strikes-2018-record.

Carnes, Nicholas, and Noam Lupu. "It's Time to Bust the Myth: Most Trump Voters Were Not Working Class." *Washington Post*, June 5, 2017. https://www.washingtonpost.com/news/monkey-cage/wp/2017/06/05/its-time-to-bust-the-myth-most-trump-voters-were-not-working-class/.

Carnoy, Martin, and Derek Shearer. *Economic Democracy: The Challenge of the 1980s*. London: Routledge, 1980.

Case, Anne, and Sir Angus Deaton. "Mortality and Morbidity in the 21st Century." *Brookings Papers on Economic Activity* 2017, no. 1 (2017): 397–443. https://www.brookings.edu/bpea-articles/mortality-and-morbidity-in-the-21st-century/.

Christensen, Stephanie. "The Great Migration (1915–1960)." *Black Past*, December 6, 2007. http://www.Blackpast.org/aah/great-migration-1915-1960.

Christianity Today. "Prosperity Gospel." Accessed January 14, 2021. https://www.christianitytoday.com/ct/topics/p/prosperity-gospel/.

Chung, Jason. "Who Owns Your Fitbit Data? Biometric Data Privacy Problems." *Healthcare Blog*, November 25, 2017. https://thehealthcareblog.com/blog/2017/11/25/who-owns-your-fitbit-data-biometric-data-privacy-problems/.

City Life. "TAACL: Tenants Association against Corporate Landlords." Accessed January 18, 2021. http://www.clvu.org/renters.

Coalition of Immokalee Workers. "Burger King Campaign Comes to an End with Historic Press Conference, Signing Ceremony at US Capital." May 23, 2008. http://www.ciw-online.org/blog/2008/05/burger-king-campaign-comes-to-an-end-with-historic-press-conference-signing-ceremony-at-u-s-capitol/.

Cobble, Dorothy Sue, ed. *The Sex of Class: Women Transforming American Labor.* Ithaca, NY: Cornell University Press, 2007.

Communication Workers of America. "AT&T." Accessed January 14, 2021. https://cwa-union.org/att.

Communication Workers of America. "CWA Members in Virginia/West Virginia on Strike at Frontier." March 6, 2018. https://cwa-union.org/news/cwa-members-in-virginia-west-virginia-on-strike-frontier.

Compa, Lance. *Unfair Advantage: Workers' Freedom of Association in the United States under International Human Rights Standards.* New York: Human Rights Watch, 2000.

Cooper, David, and Teresa Kroeger. "Employers Steal Billions from Workers' Paychecks Each Year." *Economic Policy Institute,* May 10, 2017. https://www.epi.org/publication/employers-steal-billions-from-workers-paychecks-each-year/.

Corey, Ethan. "The Brooklyn Tenant Union That's Fighting Gentrification through Collective Bargaining." *In These Times,* July 22, 2015. http://inthesetimes.com/article/18226/solidarity-works-brooklyn-tenant-union-organizes-for-rent-regulation.

Cornell University ILR School. "History of the ILGWU." Kheel Center ILGWU Collection. Accessed January 12, 2021. http://ilgwu.ilr.cornell.edu/history/.

Creekmore, Lewis, Ronké Huges, Lynn Jennings, Sarah John, Janet LaBella, C. Arturo Manjarrez, Michelle Oh, Zoe Osterman, and Marta Woldu. "The Justice Gap: Measuring the Unmet Civil Legal Needs of Low-Income Americans." *Legal Services Corporation,* June 2017. https://www.lsc.gov/sites/default/files/images/TheJusticeGap-FullReport.pdf.

Crown Heights Tenant Union. "Our Demands." Accessed October 17, 2021. http://www.crownheightstenantunion.org/our-demands.

CVS Health. "Aetna Announces Changes That Will Improve Wages and Medical Benefits for Thousands of Its Employees." January 12, 2015. https://cvshealth.com/newsroom/press-releases/aetna-announces-changes-will-improve-wages-and-medical-benefits-thousands.

Danish, Max D. *The Story of the ILGWU.* New York: International Ladies' Garment Workers' Union, 1951.

Data for Black Lives. "Black People vs Robots: Reparations and Workers Rights in the Age of Automation." January 14, 2019. Available on YouTube, https://youtu.be/1uOt3GriWAI; http://d4bl.org/.

DC Jobs With Justice. "Walmart Strikers Cap Week of Action with Black Friday March." December 1, 2014. http://www.dcjwj.org/walmartstrikers-Black-friday-march/.

Dean, Adam, Atheendar Venkataramani, and Simeon Kimmel. "Mortality Rates from COVID-19 Are Lower in Unionized Nursing Homes." *Health Affairs* 39, no. 11 (September 2020): 1993–2001. https://doi.org/10.1377/hlthaff.2020.01011.

Delaney, Arthur, and Alissa Scheller. "Who Gets Food Stamps? White People Mostly." *Huffington Post,* February 28, 2015. http://www.huffingtonpost.com/2015/02/28/food-stamp-demographics_n_6771938.html.

DeSilver, Drew. "American Unions Membership Declines as Public Support Fluctuates." *Pew Research Center,* February 20, 2014. https://www.pewresearch.org/fact-tank

/2014/02/20/for-american-unions-membership-trails-far-behind-public
-support/.

DeSilver, Drew. "In Past Elections, U.S. Trailed Most Developed Countries in Voter Turnout," *Pew Research Center*, November 3, 2020. https://www.pewresearch.org/fact
-tank/2020/11/03/in-past-elections-u-s-trailed-most-developed-countries-in-voter
-turnout/.

Dirnbach, Eric. "Unions and Worker Co-Ops, Old Allies, Are Joining Forces Again."
Labor Notes, September 5, 2017. http://www.labornotes.org/blogs/2017/09/unions
-and-worker-co-ops-old-allies-are-joining-forces-again.

Ferguson, John-Paul. "The Eyes of the Needles: A Sequential Model of Union Organizing
Drives, 1999–2004." *Industrial and Labor Relations Review* 62, no. 3 (2008): 3–21.
https://doi.org/10.1177/001979390806200101.

Fichter, Michael, and Dimitris Stevis. "Global Framework Agreements in a Union-Hostile
Environment: The Case of the USA." *Friedrich Ebert Stiftung*, December 1, 2013.
http://dx.doi.org/10.2139/ssrn.2383825.

Fine, Janice. "Co-Production: Bringing Together the Unique Capabilities of Government
and Society for Stronger Labor Standards Enforcement." Labor Innovations for
the 21st Century Fund. September 2015. http://theliftfund.org/wp-content/uploads
/2015/09/LIFTReportCoproductionOct_ExecSumm-rf_4.pdf.

Fine, Janice. "Enforcing Labor Standards in Partnership with Civil Society: Can Co-
Enforcement Succeed where the State Alone has Failed?" *Politics and Society* 45,
no. 3 (2017): 359–388. https://doi.org/10.1177%2F0032329217702603.

Fink, Leon. *Workingmen's Democracy: The Knights of Labor and American Politics.*
Champaign: University of Illinois Press, 1983.

Fletcher, Bill, Jr., and Fernando Gapasin. *Solidarity Divided: The Crisis in Organized Labor
and a New Path toward Social Justice.* Berkeley: University of California Press, 2009.

Foner, Eric. *A Short History of Reconstruction, 1863–1877.* New York: Harper Collins, 1990.

Foner, Eric. *The Second Founding: How the Civil War and Reconstruction Remade the
Constitution.* New York: W. W. Norton, 2019.

"Forced Labor on American Shores." *New York Times,* July 8, 2012. http://www.nytimes
.com/2012/07/09/opinion/forced-labor-on-american-shores.html?_r=0.

Forester, Dyana. "Victory! Justice for Georgia Public School Workers." Jobs With Justice,
April 11, 2013. http://www.jwj.org/victory-justice-for-georgia-public-school-workers.

For Purpose Law Group. "The Political Ban in 501(c)(3): Its Odd History." June 23, 2016.
https://forpurposelaw.com/501c3-political-ban-history/.

Fox 8 Greensboro. "Greensboro City Council Agrees on Increasing Minimum Wage for
City Workers." August 8, 2015. https://myfox8.com/news/greensboro-city-council
-agrees-on-increasing-minimum-wage-for-city-workers/.

Fox 8 Greensboro. "Greensboro City Workers Unionize for Better Pay." August 8, 2015.
http://myfox8.com/2017/01/17/greensboro-city-workers-unionize-for-better-pay/.

Freeman, Richard B. "Spurts in Union Growth: Defining Moments and Social Processes."
In *The Defining Moment: The Great Depression and the American Economy in the
Twentieth Century,* ed. Michael D. Bordo, Claudia Goldin, and Eugene N. White,
265–296. Chicago: University of Chicago Press, 1998.

Freeman, Richard, Eunice Han, David Madland, and Brendan V. Duke. *Bargaining for
the American Dream: What Unions Do for Mobility.* Washington, DC: Center for
American Progress, 2015.

Gallun, Alby. "Equity Residential to Stop Evictions, Rent Hikes." *Crain's Chicago Business,* March 24, 2020. https://www.chicagobusiness.com/commercial-real-estate
/equity-residential-stop-evictions-rent-hikes.

Garza, Cecilia. "Meet the Crawfish-Peeling Guestworkers Who Inspired Walmart Walk-Outs." *Yes!*, October 11, 2012. http://www.yesmagazine.org/people-power/meet-the-crawfish-peeling-guestworkers-who-inspired-walmart-walkouts.

Gibson, Kate. "$20 Million Severance Fund Started for Toys R Us Workers." *CBS News*, November 21, 2018. https://www.cbsnews.com/news/20-million-severance-fund-started-for-tens-of-thousands-of-toys-r-us-workers/.

Gillers, Heather, and Jason Grotto. "How the Tribune Analyzed CPS' Bond Deals." *Chicago Tribune*, November 7, 2014. https://www.chicagotribune.com/investigations/ct-chicago-public-schools-bonds-methodology-met-20141107-story.html.

Glickman, Lawrence B. "The American Tradition of Consumer Politics." *Organization of American Historians*. Accessed January 18, 2021. https://www.oah.org/tah/issues/2017/may/the-american-tradition-of-consumer-politics/.

Global Labor Justice. "Worker Voices from the Asian Walmart Garment Supply Chain: A Report on Gender Based Violence to the 2018 International Labour Organization." May 25, 2018. https://www.globallaborjustice.org/portfolio_page/walmart-report-press-release/.

Gralla, Preston. "Amazon Prime and the Racism Algorithms." *Computer World*, May 11, 2016. https://www.computerworld.com/article/3068622/amazon-prime-and-the-racist-algorithms.html.

Green, James R. *The Devil Is Here in These Hills*. New York: Grove Atlantic, 2015.

Greenhouse, Steven. "Tomato Pickers' Wages Fight Faces Obstacles." *New York Times*, December 24, 2007. https://www.nytimes.com/2007/12/24/us/24tomato.html.

Greenhouse, Steven. "Wal-Mart Suspends Supplier of Seafood." *New York Times*, June 29, 2012. https://www.nytimes.com/2012/06/30/business/wal-mart-suspends-seafood-supplier-over-work-conditions.html.

Greenhouse, Steven. "The Return of the Strike." *American Prospect*, January 3, 2019. https://prospect.org/article/return-strike.

Greenspan, Rachel E. "'It's the Legacy of Slavery': Here's the Troubling History behind Tipping Practices in the U.S." *Time*, August 20, 2019. http://time.com/5404475/history-tipping-american-restaurants-civil-war/.

Griswold, Alison. "Uber Is Using Its US Customer Service Reps to Deliver Its Anti-Union Message." *Quartz*, February 20, 2016. http://qz.com/619601/uber-is-using-its-us-customer-service-reps-to-deliver-its-anti-union-message/.

Gross, Julian, Greg LeRoy, and Madeline Janis-Aparicio. "Community Benefits Agreements: Making Development Projects Accountable." Good Jobs First and California Partnership for Working Families, 2005. http://www.goodjobsfirst.org/sites/default/files/docs/pdf/cba2005final.pdf.

Gupta, Sarita, Stephen Lerner, and Joseph A. McCartin. "It's Not the 'Future of Work,' It's the Future of Workers That's in Doubt." *American Prospect*, August 31, 2018. https://prospect.org/article/its-not-future-work-its-future-workers-doubt.

Heckscher, Charles C. *The New Unionism: Employee Involvement in the Changing Corporation*. Ithaca, NY: Cornell University Press, 1996.

Hensler, Benjamin. "Building a Coalition for Workers' Rights at Kmart." *University of Pennsylvania Journal of Labor and Employment Law* 2, no. 4 (2000): 687–695. https://scholarship.law.upenn.edu/jbl/vol2/iss4/5/.

Hill, Steven. "Can Workers Get a Fair Deal in the Gig Economy?" *Common Dreams*, August 24, 2016. http://www.commondreams.org/views/2016/08/24/can-workers-get-fair-deal-gig-economy.

Honey, Michael K. *Going Down Jericho Road: The Memphis Strike, Martin Luther King's Last Campaign*. New York: W.W. Norton, 2007.

Howe, Amy. "Opinion Analysis: Federal Employment Discrimination Law Protects Gay and Transgender Employees (Updated)." SCOTUSblog, June 15, 2020. https://www.scotusblog.com/2020/06/opinion-analysis-federal-employment-discrimination-law-protects-gay-and-transgender-employees/.

"HUD Office of Policy Development & Research, Community Benefits Agreement Guides Development in Milwaukee's Park East Corridor." PD&R Edge, accessed January 18, 2021. https://www.huduser.gov/portal/pdredge/pdr_edge_inpractice_072012.html.

Hunter, Tera W. "Washing Amazons and Organized Protests." In *To 'Joy My Freedom: Southern Black Women's Lives and Labor after the Civil War*, 74–97. Cambridge, MA: Harvard University Press, 1998.

Hunters Point Shipyard/Candlestick Point Integrated Development Project Core Community Benefits Agreement (2008). https://juliangross.net/docs/CBA/Hunters_Point_Agreement.pdf.

Jacobs, Paul. *Old Before Its Time: Collective Bargaining at 28.* Santa Barbara, CA: Center for the Study of Democratic Institutions, 1963.

Jayaraman, Saru. *Behind the Kitchen Door.* Ithaca, NY: Cornell University Press, 2013.

Jobs to Move to America. "U.S. Employment Plan." April 10, 2020. https://jobstomoveamerica.org/resource/u-s-employment-plan-2/.

Johansson, Erin. "Collective Bargaining 101." Jobs With Justice. March 3, 2017. https://www.jwj.org/collective-bargaining-101.

Jpmassar. "Black Lives Matter Joins Fight for $15 Today in the Bay Area." *Daily Kos*, November 10, 2015. http://www.dailykos.com/story/2015/11/10/1448366/-Black-Lives-Matter-Joins-Fight-for-15-Today-in-the-Bay-Area.

Katznelson, Ira. *Fear Itself: The New Deal and the Origins of Our Time.* New York: Liveright, 2014.

Kennedy, Daniel, Stan McMillen, and Louise Simmons. "The Economic and Fiscal Impact of Low-Wage Work in Connecticut." *Issue Brief* (2015): 1–6. https://d3n8a8pro7vhmx.cloudfront.net/ctassetbuilding/pages/132/attachments/original/1476906349/issueBriefCT6.pdf?1476906349.

Kim, Timothy. "The Dynamex Decision: The California Supreme Court Restricts Use of Independent Contractors." *Labor & Employment Blog*, May 1, 2018. https://www.laboremploymentlawblog.com/2018/05/articles/class-actions/dynamex-decision-independent-contractors/.

"Largest Employers." *Hartford Courant.* July 17, 2003. http://www.courant.com/mhc-market-employers-htmlstory.html.

Larson, Larissa. "The Pursuit of Responsible Development: Addressing Anticipated Benefits and Unwanted Burdens through Community Benefits Agreements." Center for Local, State, and Urban Policy, 2009. https://www.researchgate.net/publication/228385987_The_pursuit_of_responsible_development_Addressing_anticipated_benefits_and_unwanted_burdens_through_community_benefit_agreements.

Lee, Sophia Z. *The Workplace Constitution: From the New Deal to the New Right.* Cambridge, UK: Cambridge University Press, 2014.

Lemann, Nicholas. *Transaction Man: The Rise of the Deal and the Decline of the American Dream.* New York: Farrar, Straus & Giroux, 2019.

Lerner, Kira. "Why Black Lives Matter and Fight for 15 Are Protesting Side-By-Side." *ThinkProgress*, April 14, 2016. https://archive.thinkprogress.org/why-black-lives-matter-and-fight-for-15-are-protesting-side-by-side-b81f562ac36d/.

Lerner, Stephen. "What Is Not to Be Done." *American Prospect*, April 29, 2020. https://prospect.org/labor/what-is-not-to-be-done/.

Lerner, Stephen, Rita Berlofa, Molly McGrath, and Corey Klemmber. "Tipping the Balance: Collective Action by Finance Workers Creates Regulation from Below." *Friedrich Ebert Stifting*, 2018. http://library.fes.de/pdf-files/iez/14711.pdf.

Lichtenstein, Nelson. *The Most Dangerous Man in Detroit: Walter Reuther and the Fate of American Labor.* New York: Basic Books, 1995.

Lichtenstein, Nelson. *Walter Reuther: The Most Dangerous Man in Detroit.* Champaign: University of Illinois Press, 1997.

Lieber, Chavie. "Thousands of Toys R Us Workers are Getting Severance, Following Months of Protests." *Vox*, November 21, 2018. https://www.vox.com/the-goods /2018/11/21/18106545/toys-r-us-retail-workers-severance.

Linkon, Sherry Lee, and John Russo. *Steeltown U.S.A.: Work and Memory in Youngstown.* Lawrence: University Press of Kansas, 2002.

Loomis, Erik. *A History of America in Ten Strikes.* New York: New Press, 2018.

López, Ian Haney. *Dog Whistle Politics: How Coded Racial Appeals Have Reinvented Racism and Wrecked the Middle Class.* Oxford, UK: Oxford University Press, 2014.

MacLean, Nancy. *Democracy in Chains: The Deep History of the Radical Right's Stealth Plan for America.* New York: Viking Press, 2017.

Madrigal, Alexis C. "How Automation Could Worsen Racial Inequality." *Atlantic*, January 16, 2018. https://www.theatlantic.com/technology/archive/2018/01/Black -workers-and-the-driverless-bus/550535/.

McCartin, Joseph A. *Labor's Great War: The Struggle for Industrial Democracy and the Origins of Modern American Labor Relations, 1912–1921.* Chapel Hill: University of North Carolina Press, 1998.

McCartin, Joseph A. "Public Sector Unionism under Assault: How to Combat the Scapegoating of Organized Labor." *New Labor Forum*, January 19, 2016. http://newlabor forum.cuny.edu/2016/01/19/public-sector-unionism-under-assault-how-to-com bat-the-scapegoating-of-organized-labor/.

McCartin, Joseph A. "Bargaining for the Common Good." *Dissent*, Spring 2016. https:// www.dissentmagazine.org/article/bargaining-common-good-community-union -alignment.

McIntosh, Don. "Farmworkers at Sakuma Ratify Historic First Union Contract." *NWLaborPress*, June 16, 2017. https://nwlaborpress.org/2017/06/farmworkers-at-sakuma-ratify -historic-first-union-contract/.

Memphis Public Libraries. "This Week's Profile: P. J. Ciampa." Accessed January 12, 2021. https://www.memphislibrary.org/diversity/sanitation-strike-exhibit/sanitation -strike-exhibit-february-11-to-17-edition/this-weeks-profile-p-j-ciampa/.

Merle, Renae. "After Years of Apologies for Customer Abuses, Wells Fargo CEO Tim Sloan Suddenly Steps Down." *Washington Post*, March 28, 2019. https://www.washin gtonpost.com/business/2019/03/28/wells-fargo-ceo-tim-sloan-step-down -immediately/?utm_term=.34e039593252.

Meyerson, Harold. "The Constitution's Anti-Majoritarian Bias." *American Prospect*, October 10, 2018. https://prospect.org/power/constitution-s-anti-majoritarian-bias/.

Movement for Black Lives. "Vision for Black Lives." Accessed January 14, 2021. https:// m4bl.org/policy-platforms/.

National Labor Relations Board. "Bargaining in Good Faith with Employees' Union Representative (Section 8(d) & 8(a)(5))." About NLRB. Accessed January 12, 2021. https://www.nlrb.gov/rights-we-protect/whats-law/employers/bargaining-good -faith-employees-union-representative-section.

National Labor Relations Board. "About NLRB." Accessed January 19, 2021. https://www .nlrb.gov/rights-we-protect/whats-law/unions/collective-bargaining-section-8d -8b3.

NBC News Exit Poll Desk. "Michigan Exit Poll Results: How Bernie Sanders Beat Hillary Clinton." *NBC News*, March 8, 2016. https://www.nbcnews.com/politics/2016-election /michigan-exit-poll-results-how-bernie-sanders-beat-hillary-clinton-n534601.

New York State Department of Labor. "Domestic Workers' Bill of Rights." Accessed January 18, 2021. https://dol.ny.gov/domestic-workers-bill-rights.

Nieves, Evelyn. "Accord with Tomato Pickers Ends Boycott of Taco Bell." *Washington Post*, March 9, 2005. https://www.washingtonpost.com/wp-dyn/articles/A18187 -2005Mar8.html.

Noden, Kirk. "Why Do White Working-Class People Vote against Their Interests? They Don't." *Nation*, November 17, 2016. https://www.thenation.com/article/why-do -White-working-class-people-vote-against-their-interests-they-dont/.

North, Anna. "7 Positive Changes That Have Come from the #MeToo Movement." *Vox*, October 4, 2019. https://www.vox.com/identities/2019/10/4/20852639/me-too -movement-sexual-harassment-law-2019.

O'Brien, Ruth. *Workers' Paradox: The Republican Origins of New Deal Labor Policy, 1886–1935*. Chapel Hill: University of North Carolina Press, 1998.

OurDocuments. "Transcript of National Labor Relations Act (1935)." Accessed January 12, 2021. https://www.ourdocuments.gov/doc.php?flash=false&doc=67&page =transcript.

Partnership for Working Families. "Los Angeles Sports and Entertainment District CBA: Staples Center Community Benefits Program." Accessed January 18, 2021. https:// www.forworkingfamilies.org/resources/staples-cba.

Partnership for Working Families. "Policy & Tools: Community Benefits Agreements and Policies in Effect." Accessed January 18, 2021. http://www.forworkingfamilies .org/sites/pwf/files/documents/Kingsbridge%20FINAL%20Exhibit%20A%20 -%20Community%20Benefits%20Program.pdf.

Partnership for Working Families & Community Benefits Law Center. "Common Challenges in Negotiating Community Benefits Agreements and How to Avoid Them." January 2016. https://www.forworkingfamilies.org/resources/publications/common -challenges-negotiating-community-benefits-agreements-how-avoid-them.

Patrick-Knox, Natalie. *Case Study: How Community-Labor Strategies Can Bolster Immigrant Worker Organizing*. Washington, DC: Jobs With Justice, 2014.

"Paving the High Road: Labor Standards and Procurement Policy in the Obama Era." *Berkeley Journal of Employment & Labor Law* 31, no. 2 (2010): 349–424. https:// lawcat.berkeley.edu/record/1123817.

PayScale. "The State of the Gender Pay Gap in 2020." Accessed January 14, 2021. https:// www.payscale.com/data/gender-pay-gap.

Piketty, Thomas. *Capital in the Twenty-First Century*. Cambridge, MA: Harvard University Press, 2014.

"Precarious Work in the Walmart Global Value Chain." Report to the ILO Sponsored by the Asia Floor Wage Alliance (AFWA), Bangladesh Nari Progati Sangha (BNPS), Labor Resource Center of Indonesia (LIPS), Society for Labor and Development of India (SLD), Center for Alliance of Labor and Human Rights in Cambodia (CENTRAL), The National Centre for Development Cooperation (CNCD) of Belgium, Jobs With Justice of the United States, and the United Workers Congress of the United States, 2016. https://www.ituc-csi.org/IMG/pdf/afwa_walmart.pdf.

Raffol, Matthew. "Community Benefits Agreements in the Political Economy of Urban Development." *Advocates Forum*. University of Chicago, School of Social Service Administration. 2012. http://ssa.uchicago.edu/community-benefits-agreements -political-economy-urban-development.

Restaurant Opportunities Center United. *Take Us Off the Menu: The Impact of Sexual Harassment in the Restaurant Industry.* New York: Restaurant Opportunities Center United, 2018.

Retail Workers Bill of Rights. "San Francisco's Formula Retail Economy." Accessed January 19, 2021. http://retailworkerrights.com/get-the-facts/san-franciscos-formula-retail-economy/.

Ricker, Mary Cathryn. "Teacher-Community Unionism: A Lesson from St. Paul." *Dissent,* Summer 2015. https://www.dissentmagazine.org/article/teacher-community-unionism-lesson-st-paul.

Rogers, George C., Jr., and C. James Taylor. *A South Carolina Chronology 1497–1992,* 2nd ed. Columbia: University of South Carolina Press, 1994.

Rothstein, Jeffrey S. "The New UAW Contract: A Somewhat 'Clear Path.'" *New Labor Forum,* December 2015. http://newlaborforum.cuny.edu/2015/12/11/the-new-uaw-contract-a-somewhat-clear-path/.

Roy, Arundhati. "The Pandemic Is a Portal." *Financial Times,* April 3, 2020. https://www.ft.com/content/10d8f5e8-74eb-11ea-95fe-fcd274e920ca.

Sachs, Benjamin. "Micro Unions and Minority Unions." *Onlabor,* January 2, 2014. https://onlabor.org/micro-unions-and-minority-unions/.

San Francisco Office of Labor Standards Enforcement. "Formula Retail Employee Rights Ordinances." Accessed October 17, 2021. https://sfgov.org/olse/formula-retail-employee-rights-ordinances.

San Francisco Office of Economic and Workforce Development. "State of the Retail Sector: Challenges and Opportunities for San Francisco's Neighborhood Commercial Districts: Final Report." February 2018. https://oewd.org/sites/default/files/Invest%20In%20Neighborhoods/State%20of%20the%20Retail%20Sector%20-%20Final%20Report.pdf.

Sanes, Milla, and John Schmitt. *Regulation of Public Sector Collective Bargaining in the States.* Washington, DC: Center for Economic and Policy Research, 2014.

Schoen, John W. "States in Crisis: Embroiled in the Worst Budget Battles since the Great Recession." *CNBC,* July 11, 2017. https://www.cnbc.com/2017/07/11/states-in-crisis-the-worst-budget-battles-since-the-great-recession.html.

Scott, Ron. "600 and Moore." *Boggs Blog,* November 6, 2009. https://conversationsthatyouwillneverfinish.wordpress.com/2009/11/06/in-memory-of-hunger-marcher-dave-moore/.

SCOTUSblog. "Citizens United v. Federal Election Commission." Accessed January 14, 2021. http://www.scotusblog.com/case-files/cases/citizens-united-v-federal-election-commission/.

Seattle Office of Labor Standards. "2017–2019 Recipients, CEOF Past Recipients." Accessed January 19, 2021. https://www.seattle.gov/laborstandards/funding/community-outreach-and-education-fund/coef-past-recipients.

Segrave, Kerry. *Tipping: An American Social History of Gratuities.* Jefferson, NC: McFarland, 2009.

SEIU. "SEIU Announces Support for Movement for Black Lives." June 12, 2020. https://www.seiu.org/2020/06/seiu-announces-support-for-movement-for-black-lives.

Shogan, Robert. *The Battle of Blair Mountain: The Story of America's Largest Labor Uprising.* Boulder, CO: Basic, 2006.

Silver, Beverly J. *Forces of Labor: Workers' Movements and Globalization since 1870.* Cambridge, UK: Cambridge University Press, 2003.

Sinyai, Clayton. *Schools of Democracy: A Political History of the American Labor Movement.* Ithaca, NY: ILR Press, 2006.

Smiley, Erica. "One Year Later, Walmart Still Shirks Responsibility for Supply Chain Ca-tastrophes." Jobs With Justice, April 23, 2014. http://www.jwj.org/one-year-later -walmart-still-shirks-responsibility-for-supply-chain-catastrophes.

Smiley, Erica. "Fining McWalmart: Charging Employers for the Social Costs of Poverty Wages." *New Labor Forum* 24, no. 3 (2015): 68–75. https://doi.org/ 10.1177/109579601 5597007.

Smiley, Erica. "The Gig Economy Is Screwing Over Workers—And It Needs to Stop." *Talk Poverty,* October 13, 2016. https://talkpoverty.org/2016/10/13/gig-economy-screwing -workers-needs-stop/.

Smiley, Erica. "Time to Tackle the Whole Squid: Confronting White Supremacy to Build Bargaining Power." *Class, Race and Corporate Power* 5, no. 2 (2017). https://doi .org/10.25148/CRCP.5.2.006505.

Smiley, Erica. "Domestic Workers are Using the Gig Economy Against Itself." *The Na-tion,* June 25, 2021. https://www.thenation.com/article/society/domestic-workers -handy-labor/.

Smith, Rebecca. "Union-Busting. Now There's an App for That." *NELP,* March 7, 2016. http://www.nelp.org/commentary/union-busting-now-theres-an-app-for-that/.

Sneiderman, Marilyn, and Secky Fascione. "Going on Offense during Challenging Times." *New Labor Forum,* January 2018. https://newlaborforum.cuny.edu/2018 /01/18/going-on-offense-during-challenging-times/.

Son, Hugh, and John Melloy. "Bank of America Is Raising Its Minimum Wage for Em-ployees to $20 an Hour." *CNBC,* April 9, 2019. https://www.cnbc.com/2019/04/09 /bank-of-america-is-raising-its-minimum-wage-for-employees-to-20-an-hour .html.

Sports Management Degree Guide. "What Is Sports Analytics?" Accessed January 20, 2021. https://www.sports-management-degrees.com/faq/what-is-sports-analytics/.

Stangler, Cole. "Why the Uber, Lyft Driver Union Push Could Disrupt the Gig Econ-omy." *IBTimes,* December 18, 2015. http://www.ibtimes.com/why-uber-lyft-driver -union-push-could-disrupt-gig-economy-2232778.

Sydow, Jörg, Michael Fichter, Markus Helfen, Kadire Zeynep Sayim, and Dimitris Stevis. "Implementation of Global Framework Agreements: Towards a Multi-Organizational Practice Perspective." *Transfer* 20, no. 4 (2014): 489–503. https://doi .org/10.1177%2F1024258914546270.

Tapia, Maite, Tamara L. Lee, and Mikhail Filipovitch. "Supra-Union and Intersectional Organizing: An Examination of Two Prominent Cases in the Low-Wage US Res-taurant Industry." *Journal of Industrial Relations* 59, no. 4 (2017): 487–509. https:// doi.org/10.1177/0022185617714817.

Taylor, Kate. "Fast-Food CEO Says He's Investing in Machines Because the Government Is Making It Difficult to Afford Employees." *Business Insider,* March 16, 2016. https:// www.businessinsider.com/carls-jr-wants-open-automated-location-2016-3.

Tenants Union of Washington State. "Principles of Unity." Accessed October 17, 2021. http://www.tenantsunion.org/en/about/principles-of-unity.

US Bureau of Labor Statistics. "Union Members Summary." Economic News Release, January 22, 2021. https://www.bls.gov/news.release/union2.nr0.htm.

US Bureau of Labor Statistics. "Work Stoppages Summary." Economic News Release, Feb-ruary 11, 2020. https://www.bls.gov/news.release/wkstp.nr0.htm.

US Chamber of Commerce. *Worker Centers: Union Front Groups and the Law.* Wash-ington, DC: US Chamber of Commerce, 2018.

US Government Accountability Office. *Employment Arrangements: Improved Outreach Could Help Ensure Proper Worker Classification.* Washington, D.C.: U.S. Govern-ment Accountability Office, July 2006.

US Postal Service Office of Inspector General. "The Postal Strike of 1970." March 15, 2010. https://www.uspsoig.gov/blog/postal-strike-1970.

Valenzuela, Abel, Jr. "Immigrant Day Laborers: Myths and Realities." *North American Congress on Latin America,* April 10, 2008. https://nacla.org/article/immigrant-day-laborers-myths-and-realities.

Vandeveldge, Mark. "Toys R Us Workers Put Pressure on Hedge Fund." *Financial Times,* September 3, 2018. https://www.ft.com/content/17b283a8-ad6d-11e8-94bd-cba20d67390c.

Wagner, Robert. "The Ideal Industrial State—As Wagner Sees It." *New York Times Magazine,* May 9, 1937.

Wakabayashi, Daisuke, Erin Griffith, Amie Tsang, and Kate Conger. "Google Walkout: Employees Stage Protest Over Handling of Sexual Harassment." *New York Times,* November 1, 2018. https://www.nytimes.com/2018/11/01/technology/google-walkout-sexual-harassment.html.

Wasser, Michael. "Strikes 101." Jobs With Justice, April 12, 2016. https://www.jwj.org/strikes-101.

"Whistleblower: Wells Fargo Fraud 'Could Have Been Stopped.'" *CBS News,* August 3, 2018. https://www.cbsnews.com/news/whistleblower-wells-fargo-fraud-could-have-been-stopped/.

Wiessner, Daniel, and Dan Levine. "Uber Deal Shows Divide in Labor's Drive for Role in 'Gig Economy.'" *Reuters,* May 23, 2016. https://www.reuters.com/article/us-uber-tech-drivers-labor/uber-deal-shows-divide-in-labors-drive-for-role-in-gig-economy-idUSKCN0YE0DF.

Williams, Dima. "May 1 Rent Strike through the Lens of Organizers, Landlords, and Industry Leaders." *Forbes,* May 1, 2020. https://www.forbes.com/sites/dimawilliams/2020/05/01/may-1-rent-strike-through-the-lens-of-organizers-landlords-and-industry-leaders/?sh=75ecbfa7b85c.

Wilson, Woodrow. *The New Freedom: A Call for the Emancipation of the Generous Energies of a People.* New York: Doubleday, 1913.

Windham, Lane. *Knocking on Labor's Door: Union Organizing in the 1970s and the Roots of a New Economic Divide.* Chapel Hill: University of North Carolina Press, 2017.

Windham, Lane. "Why Labor Law Should Stop Leaning So Hard on the Wagner Act." *American Prospect,* July 3, 2015. https://prospect.org/labor/labor-law-stop-leaning-hard-wagner-act/.

Workplace Fairness. "Non-Disclosure Agreements (NDA's)." Accessed January 18, 2012. https://www.workplacefairness.org/nondisclosure-agreements.

Zimmerman, Seth. *Labor Market Institutions and Economic Mobility.* Washington, DC: Urban Institute, 2008.

Zych, Nicholas. "Collection and Ownership of Minor League Athlete Activity Biometric Data by Major League Baseball Franchises." *DePaul Journal of Sports Law* 14, no. 1 (2018): art. 7. https://paperity.org/p/144523875/collection-and-ownership-of-minor-league-athlete-activity-biometric-data-by-major-league.

Index

Note: page numbers in *italics* refer to figures.